Microsoft

W9-BGG-402

Introducing Microsoft® SQL Server® 2012

Ross Mistry
Stacia Misner

PUBLISHED BY
Microsoft Press
A Division of Microsoft Corporation
One Microsoft Way
Redmond, Washington 98052-6399

Library of Congress Control Number: 2012933508
ISBN: 978-0-7356-6515-6

Microsoft Press books are available through booksellers and distributors worldwide. If you need support related to this book, email Microsoft Press Book Support at mspinput@microsoft.com. Please tell us what you think of this book at http://www.microsoft.com/learning/booksurvey.

Microsoft and the trademarks listed at http://www.microsoft.com/about/legal/en/us/IntellectualProperty /Trademarks/EN-US.aspx are trademarks of the Microsoft group of companies. All other marks are property of their respective owners.

The example companies, organizations, products, domain names, email addresses, logos, people, places, and events depicted herein are fictitious. No association with any real company, organization, product, domain name, email address, logo, person, place, or event is intended or should be inferred.

This book expresses the author's views and opinions. The information contained in this book is provided without any express, statutory, or implied warranties. Neither the authors, Microsoft Corporation, nor its resellers, or distributors will be held liable for any damages caused or alleged to be caused either directly or indirectly by this book.

Acquisitions Editor: Anne Hamilton
Developmental Editor: Devon Musgrave
Project Editor: Carol Dillingham
Technical Reviewer: Mitch Tulloch; Technical Review services provided by Content Master, a member of CM Group, Ltd.
Copy Editor: Roger LeBlanc
Indexer: Christina Yeager
Editorial Production: Waypoint Press
Cover: Twist Creative • Seattle

I dedicate this book to my wife, Sherry. Thank you for being one of the only people in my life who has always been there for me regardless of the situation and has never let me down. I am greatly appreciative.

—ROSS MISTRY

I dedicate this book to my husband and best friend, Gerry, who excels at keeping our dreams alive.

—STACIA MISNER

Contents at a Glance

Contents

What do you think of this book? We want to hear from you!

Microsoft is interested in hearing your feedback so we can continually improve our books and learning
resources for you. To participate in a brief online survey, please visit:

microsoft.com/learning/booksurvey

PART 2 BUSINESS INTELLIGENCE DEVELOPMENT

Chapter 6   Integration Services   93

What do you think of this book? We want to hear from you!

Microsoft is interested in hearing your feedback so we can continually improve our books and learning resources for you. To participate in a brief online survey, please visit:

microsoft.com/learning/booksurvey

Introduction

Microsoft SQL Server 2012 is Microsoft's first cloud-ready information platform. It gives organizations effective tools to protect, unlock, and scale the power of their data, and it works across a variety of devices and data sources, from desktops, phones, and tablets, to datacenters and both private and public clouds. Our purpose in *Introducing Microsoft SQL Server 2012* is to point out both the new and the improved capabilities as they apply to achieving mission-critical confidence, breakthrough insight, and using a cloud on your terms.

As you read this book, we think you will find that there are a lot of exciting enhancements and new capabilities engineered into SQL Server 2012 that allow you to greatly enhance performance and availability at a low total cost of ownership, unlock new insights with pervasive data discovery across the organization and create business solutions fast—on your terms.

Who Should Read This Book?

This book is for anyone who has an interest in SQL Server 2012 and wants to understand its capabilities. In a book of this size, we cannot cover every feature that distinguishes SQL Server from other databases or previous versions, and consequently we assume you have some familiarity with SQL Server already. You might be a database administrator (DBA), an application developer, a business intelligence solution architect, a power user, or a technical decision maker. Regardless of your role, we hope you can use this book to discover the features in SQL Server 2012 that are most beneficial to you.

Assumptions

This book expects that you have at least a minimal understanding of SQL Server from both a database administrator's perspective and business-intelligence perspective. This also includes an understanding of the components associated with the product, such as the Database Engine, Analysis Services, Reporting Services, and Integration Services.

Who Should Not Read This Book

As mentioned earlier, the purpose of this book is to provide the reader with a high-level preview of the capabilities and features associated with SQL Server 2012. This book is not intended to be a step-by-step comprehensive guide. Moreover, there have been over 250 new improvements associated with the product; therefore, the book may not cover every improvement in its entirety.

How Is This Book Organized?

SQL Server 2012, like its predecessors, is more than a database engine. It is a collection of components you can implement either separately or as a group to form a scalable, cloud-ready information platform. In broad terms, this cloud-ready information platform consists of two categories: those that help you manage data and those that help you deliver business intelligence (BI). Accordingly, we divided this book into two parts to focus on the new capabilities for each of these areas.

Part 1, "Database Administration," is written with the database administrator (DBA) in mind and introduces readers to the numerous innovations in SQL Server 2012. Chapter 1, "SQL Server 2012 Editions and Engine Enhancements," discusses the key enhancements affiliated with availability, scalability, performance, manageability, security, and programmability. It then outlines the different SQL Server 2012 editions, hardware and software requirements and installation, upgrade, and migration strategies available. In Chapter 2, "High-Availability and Disaster-Recovery Enhancements" readers learn about the new AlwaysOn features in SQL Server 2012—specifically, AlwaysOn Availability Groups and how they can be used to achieve a high level of confidence in your data and related capabilities. Chapter 3, "Performance and Scalability," introduces a new index type called *columnstore* and explains how it can be leveraged to significantly accelerate data-warehousing workloads and other queries that are similar in nature. Chapter 4, "Security Enhancements," covers the new security enhancements associated with the product, such as security manageability improvements and audit and authentication enhancements. Finally, Chapter 5, "Programmability and Beyond-Relational Enhancements," discusses the new beyond-relational enhancements positively impacting unstructured data, including refinements to existing technology features such as full-text search, spatial data, and FILESTREAM, as well as brand new capabilities like FileTables and statistical semantic search.

Part 2, "Business Intelligence Development," is written for readers who need to understand how SQL Server 2012 can help them more easily perform data integration, data quality improvements, master data management, data analysis, and reporting tasks. Chapter 6, "Integration Services," explores the comprehensive changes in this release affecting development, deployment, and administration of Integration Services packages. In Chapter 7, "Data Quality Services," readers learn about the newest BI component available in SQL Server 2012 for centralizing data-quality activities, including how to store data-quality rules in a knowledge base and how to automate the discovery of rules. Chapter 8, "Master Data Services," reviews the improved interface of this feature that simplifies the implementation, workflows, and administration of master data management. Chapter 9, "Analysis Services and PowerPivot," introduces the new tabular server mode, shows how to develop tabular models, and describes enhancements to the Analysis Services platform and PowerPivot for Excel capabilities. Last, Chapter 10, "Reporting Services," covers the improvements in SharePoint integration and details the self-service capabilities available with the new ad hoc reporting tool, Power View.

Conventions and Features in This Book

This book presents information using the following conventions, which are designed to make the information more readable and easy to follow:

- Each exercise consists of a series of tasks, presented as numbered steps (1, 2, and so on) listing each action you must take to complete the exercise.

- Boxed elements with labels such as "Note" provide additional information or alternative methods for completing a step successfully.

- Text that you type (apart from code blocks) appears in bold.

- Transact-SQL code is used to help you further understand a specific example.

Pre-Release Software

To help you get familiar with SQL Server 2012 as early as possible after its release, we wrote this book using examples that work with the Release Candidate 0 (RC0) version of the product. Consequently, the final version might include new features, and features we discuss might change or disappear. Refer to the "What's New in SQL Server 2012" topic in Books Online for SQL Server at *http://msdn.microsoft.com/en-us/library/ms130214%28v=sql.110%29.aspx* for the most up-to-date list of changes to the product. Be aware that you might also notice some minor differences between the RTM version of the product and the descriptions and screen shots that we provide.

Acknowledgments

First, I would like to thank my colleagues at Microsoft Press and O'Reilly Media for providing me with another great authorship opportunity and putting together a stellar product in such a short period of time. Special thanks goes out to Devon Musgrave, Colin Lyth, Karen Szall, Carol Dillingham, Steve Sagman, Mitch Tulloch, Roger LeBlanc, Christina Yeager, Anne Hamilton, Steve Weiss, and Ken Jones. The publishing team's support throughout this engagement is much appreciated.

Second, I would like to thank my immediate family for being very patient and understanding considering I was absent from their lives on many evenings and weekends while I worked on this book. I couldn't have done this title without their love and support.

I would also like to acknowledge Shirmattie Seenarine for assisting me on this title. Shirmattie's hard work, contributions, edits, and rewrites are much appreciated. And to my author partner, Stacia Misner, I want to thank you for once again doing an excellent job on the business intelligence part of this book.

Finally, this book would not have been possible without support from my colleagues on the SQL Server team who provided introductions, strategic technology guidance, technical reviews, and edits. I would like to thank the following people: Tiffany Wissner, Quentin Clark, Joanne Hodgins, Justin

Erickson, Santosh Balasubramanian, Gopal Ashok, Goden Yao, Jack Richins, Susan Price, Michael Rys, Srini Acharya, Darmadi Komo, and Luis Daniel Soto Maldonado.

−*Ross Mistry*

I, too, want to thank the entire team that has supported Ross and me through yet another publication. It is a pleasure to collaborate again with all of you and with Ross. I look forward to future opportunities should they arise!

Each of the product teams has been very helpful, and I am grateful for their assistance and appreciative of the products they have developed. In particular, I wish to thank Matt Masson, Akshai Mirchandani, Marius Dumitru, and Thierry D'hers for their amazing responsiveness to my questions because I know they are very busy people.

This is the first book for which my husband did not have the opportunity to demonstrate his seemingly unending supply of patience with me because he was busy in another state preparing a new home for us. Therefore, I can't really thank him for his support of this book in the typical sense, but I can thank him for ensuring that I will have a comfortable place in which to work and write later this year. He gives me great peace of mind and fuels my anticipation of things to come!

−*Stacia Misner*

Errata & Book Support

We've made every effort to ensure the accuracy of this book and its companion content. Any errors that have been reported since this book was published are listed on our Microsoft Press site at oreilly.com:

> *http://go.microsoft.com/FWLink/?Linkid=245673*

If you find an error that is not already listed, you can report it to us through the same page. If you need additional support, email Microsoft Press Book Support at *mspinput@microsoft.com*.

Please note that product support for Microsoft software is not offered through the addresses above.

We Want to Hear from You

At Microsoft Press, your satisfaction is our top priority, and your feedback our most valuable asset. Please tell us what you think of this book at:

> *http://www.microsoft.com/learning/booksurvey*

The survey is short, and we read every one of your comments and ideas. Thanks in advance for your input!

Stay in Touch

Let's keep the conversation going! We're on Twitter: *http://twitter.com/MicrosoftPress*.

Database Administration

CHAPTER 1

SQL Server 2012 Editions and Engine Enhancements

SQL Server 2012 is Microsoft's latest cloud-ready information platform. Organizations can use SQL Server 2012 to efficiently protect, unlock, and scale the power of their data across the desktop, mobile device, datacenter, and either a private or public cloud. Building on the success of the SQL Server 2008 R2 release, SQL Server 2012 has made a strong impact on organizations worldwide with its significant capabilities. It provides organizations with mission-critical performance and availability, as well as the potential to unlock breakthrough insights with pervasive data discovery across the organization. Finally, SQL Server 2012 delivers a variety of hybrid solutions you can choose from. For example, an organization can develop and deploy applications and database solutions on traditional nonvirtualized environments, on appliances, and in on-premises private clouds or off-premises public clouds. Moreover, these solutions can easily integrate with one another, offering a fully integrated hybrid solution. Figure 1-1 illustrates the Cloud Ready Information Platform ecosystem.

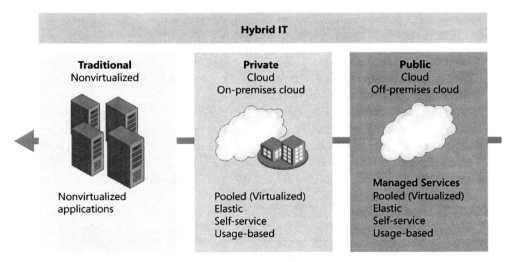

FIGURE 1-1 SQL Server 2012, cloud-ready information platform

To prepare readers for SQL Server 2012, this chapter examines the new SQL Server 2012 features, capabilities, and editions from a database administrator's perspective. It also discusses SQL Server 2012 hardware and software requirements and installation strategies.

SQL Server 2012 Enhancements for Database Administrators

Now more than ever, organizations require a trusted, cost-effective, and scalable database platform that offers mission-critical confidence, breakthrough insights, and flexible cloud-based offerings. These organizations face ever-changing business conditions in the global economy and challenges such as IT budget constraints, the need to stay competitive by obtaining business insights, and the ability to use the right information at the right time. In addition, organizations must always be adjusting because new and important trends are regularly changing the way software is developed and deployed. Some of these new trends include data explosion (enormous increases in data usage), consumerization IT, big data (large data sets), and private and public cloud deployments.

Microsoft has made major investments in the SQL Server 2012 product as a whole; however, the new features and breakthrough capabilities that should interest database administrators (DBAs) are divided in the chapter into the following categories: Availability, Manageability, Programmability, Scalability and Performance, and Security. The upcoming sections introduce some of the new features and capabilities; however, other chapters in this book conduct a deeper explanation of the major technology investments.

Availability Enhancements

A tremendous amount of high-availability enhancements were added to SQL Server 2012, which is sure to increase both the confidence organizations have in their databases and the maximum uptime for those databases. SQL Server 2012 continues to deliver database mirroring, log shipping, and replication. However, it now also offers a new brand of technologies for achieving both high availability and disaster recovery known as AlwaysOn. Let's quickly review the new high-availability enhancement AlwaysOn:

- **AlwaysOn Availability Groups** For DBAs, AlwaysOn Availability Groups is probably the most highly anticipated feature related to the Database Engine for DBAs. This new capability protects databases and allows for multiple databases to fail over as a single unit. Better data redundancy and protection is achieved because the solution supports up to four secondary replicas. Of these four secondary replicas, up to two secondaries can be configured as synchronous secondaries to ensure the copies are up to date. The secondary replicas can reside within a datacenter for achieving high availability within a site or across datacenters for disaster recovery. In addition, AlwaysOn Availability Groups provide a higher return on investment because hardware utilization is increased as the secondaries are active, readable, and can be leveraged to offload backups, reporting, and ad hoc queries from the primary replica. The solution is tightly integrated into SQL Server Management Studio, is straightforward to deploy, and supports either shared storage or local storage.

  Figure 1-2 illustrates an organization with a global presence achieving both high availability and disaster recovery for mission-critical databases using AlwaysOn Availability Groups. In addition, the secondary replicas are being used to offload reporting and backups.

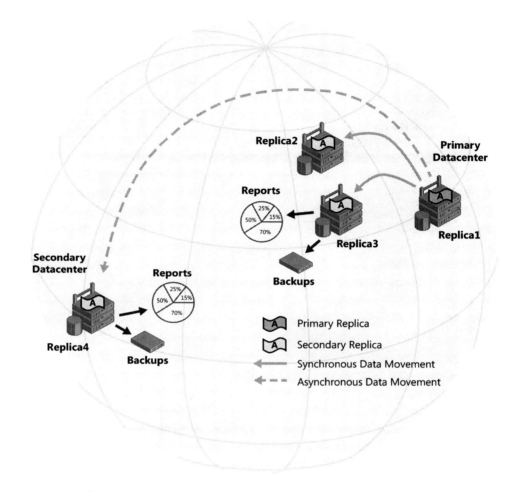

FIGURE 1-2 AlwaysOn Availability Groups for an organization with a global presence

■ **AlwaysOn Failover Cluster Instances (FCI)** AlwaysOn Failover Cluster Instances provides superior instance-level protection using Windows Server Failover Clustering and shared storage. However, with SQL Server 2012 there are a tremendous number of enhancements to improve availability and reliability. First, FCI now provides support for multi-subnet failover clusters. These subnets, where the FCI nodes reside, can be located in the same datacenter or in geographically dispersed sites. Second, local storage can be leveraged for the TempDB database. Third, faster startup and recovery times are achieved after a failover transpires. Finally, improved cluster health-detection policies can be leveraged, offering a stronger and more flexible failover.

■ **Support for Windows Server Core** Installing SQL Server 2012 on Windows Server Core is now supported. Windows Server Core is a scaled-down edition of the Windows operating system and requires approximately 50 to 60 percent fewer reboots when patching servers.

This translates to greater SQL Server uptime and increased security. Server Core deployment options using Windows Server 2008 R2 SP1 and higher are required. Chapter 2, "High-Availability and Disaster-Recovery Options," discusses deploying SQL Server 2012 on Server Core, including the features supported.

- **Recovery Advisor**   A new visual timeline has been introduced in SQL Server Management Studio to simplify the database restore process. As illustrated in Figure 1-3, the scroll bar beneath the timeline can be used to specify backups to restore a database to a point in time.

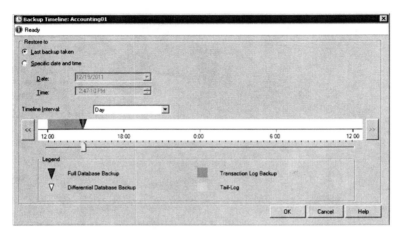

FIGURE 1-3 Recovery Advisor visual timeline

  Note For detailed information about the AlwaysOn technologies and other high-availability enhancements, be sure to read Chapter 2.

Scalability and Performance Enhancements

The SQL Server product group has made sizable investments in improving scalability and performance associated with the SQL Server Database Engine. Some of the main enhancements that allow organizations to improve their SQL Server workloads include the following:

- **Columnstore Indexes**   More and more organizations have a requirement to deliver breakthrough and predictable performance on large data sets to stay competitive. SQL Server 2012 introduces a new in-memory, columnstore index built directly in the relational engine. Together with advanced query-processing enhancements, these technologies provide blazing-fast performance and improve queries associated with data warehouse workloads by 10 to 100 times. In some cases, customers have experienced a 400 percent improvement in performance. For more information on this new capability for data warehouse workloads, review Chapter 3, "Performance and Scalability."

- **Partition Support Increased**   To dramatically boost scalability and performance associated with large tables and data warehouses, SQL Server 2012 now supports up to 15,000 partitions per table by default. This is a significant increase from the previous version of SQL Server, which was limited to 1000 partitions by default. This new expanded support also helps enable large sliding-window scenarios for data warehouse maintenance.

- **Online Index Create, Rebuild, and Drop**   Many organizations running mission-critical workloads use online indexing to ensure their business environment does not experience downtime during routine index maintenance. With SQL Server 2012, indexes containing varchar(max), nvarchar(max), and varbinary(max) columns can now be created, rebuilt, and dropped as an online operation. This is vital for organizations that require maximum uptime and concurrent user activity during index operations.

- **Achieve Maximum Scalability with Windows Server 2008 R2**   Windows Server 2008 R2 is built to achieve unprecedented workload size, dynamic scalability, and across-the-board availability and reliability. As a result, SQL Server 2012 can achieve maximum scalability when running on Windows Server 2008 R2 because it supports up to 256 logical processors and 2 terabytes of memory in a single operating system instance.

Manageability Enhancements

SQL Server deployments are growing more numerous and more common in organizations. This fact demands that all database administrators be prepared by having the appropriate tools to success- fully manage their SQL Server infrastructure. Recall that the previous releases of SQL Server included many new features tailored toward manageability. For example, database administrators could easily leverage Policy Based Management, Resource Governor, Data Collector, Data-tier applications, and Utility Control Point. Note that the product group responsible for manageability never stopped investing in manageability. With SQL Server 2012, they unveiled additional investments in SQL Server tools and monitoring features. The following list articulates the manageability enhancements in SQL Server 2012:

- **SQL Server Management Studio**   With SQL Server 2012, IntelliSense and Transact-SQL debugging have been enhanced to bolster the development experience in SQL Server Management Studio.

- **IntelliSense Enhancements**   A completion list will now suggest string matches based on partial words, whereas in the past it typically made recommendations based on the first character.

- **A new Insert Snippet menu**   This new feature is illustrated in Figure 1-4. It offers developers a categorized list of snippets to choose from to streamline code. The snippet picket tooltip can be launched by pressing CTRL+K, pressing CTRL+X, or selecting it from the Edit menu.

- **Transact-SQL Debugger**   This feature introduces the potential to debug Transact-SQL scripts on instances of SQL Server 2005 Service Pack 2 (SP2) or later and enhances breakpoint functionality.

FIGURE 1-4 Leveraging the Transact-SQL code snippet template as a starting point when writing new Transact-SQL statements in the SQL Server Database Engine Query Editor

- **Resource Governor Enhancements** Many organizations currently leverage Resource Governor to gain predictable performance and improve their management of SQL Server workloads and resources by implementing limits on resource consumption based on incoming requests. In the past few years, customers have also been requesting additional improvements to the Resource Governor feature. Customers wanted to increase the maximum number of resource pools and support large-scale, multitenant database solutions with a higher level of isolation between workloads. They also wanted predictable chargeback and vertical isolation of machine resources.

The SQL Server product group responsible for the Resource Governor feature introduced new capabilities to address the requests of its customers and the SQL Server community. To begin, support for larger scale multitenancy can now be achieved on a single instance of SQL Server because the number of resource pools Resource Governor supports increased from 20 to 64. In addition, a maximum cap for CPU usage has been introduced to enable predictable chargeback and isolation on the CPU. Finally, resource pools can be affinitized to an individual schedule or a group of schedules for vertical isolation of machine resources.

A new Dynamic Management View (DMV) called sys.dm_resource_governor_resource_pool_ affinity improves database administrators' success in tracking resource pool affinity.

Let's review an example of some of the new Resource Governor features in action. In the following example, resource pool Pool25 is altered to be affinitized to six schedulers (8, 12, 13, 14, 15, and 16), and it's guaranteed a minimum 5 percent of the CPU capacity of those schedulers. It can receive no more than 80 percent of the capacity of those schedulers. When there is contention for CPU bandwidth, the maximum average CPU bandwidth that will be allocated is 40 percent.

```
ALTER RESOURCE POOL Pool25
WITH(
     MIN_CPU_PERCENT = 5,
     MAX_CPU_PERCENT = 40,
     CAP_CPU_PERCENT = 80,
    AFFINITY SCHEDULER = (8, 12 TO 16),
     MIN_MEMORY_PERCENT = 5,
     MAX_MEMORY_PERCENT = 15,
);
```

■ **Contained Databases**   Authentication associated with database portability was a challenge in the previous versions of SQL Server. This was the result of users in a database being associated with logins on the source instance of SQL Server. If the database ever moved to another instance of SQL Server, the risk was that the login might not exist. With the introduction of contained databases in SQL Server 2012, users are authenticated directly into a user database without the dependency of logins in the Database Engine. This feature facilitates better portability of user databases among servers because contained databases have no external dependencies.

■ **Tight Integration with SQL Azure**   A new Deploy Database To SQL Azure wizard, pictured in Figure 1-5, is integrated in the SQL Server Database Engine to help organizations deploy an on-premise database to SQL Azure. Furthermore, new scenarios can be enabled with SQL Azure Data Sync, which is a cloud service that provides bidirectional data synchronization between databases across the datacenter and cloud.

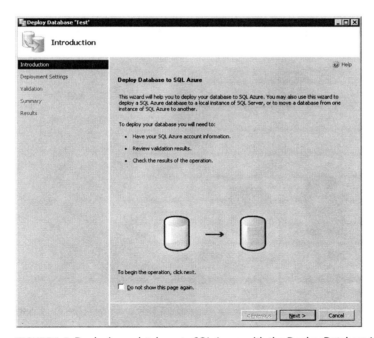

FIGURE 1-5 Deploying a database to SQL Azure with the Deploy Database Wizard

- **Startup Options Relocated**   Within SQL Server Configuration Manager, a new Startup Parameters tab was introduced for better manageability of the parameters required for startup. A DBA can now easily specify startup parameters compared to previous versions of SQL Server, which at times was a tedious task. The Startup Parameters tab can be invoked by right-clicking a SQL Server instance name in SQL Server Configuration Manager and then selecting Properties.

- **Data-Tier Application (DAC) Enhancements**   SQL Server 2008 R2 introduced the concept of data-tier applications. A data-tier application is a single unit of deployment containing all of the database's schema, dependent objects, and deployment requirements used by an application. SQL Server 2012 introduces a few enhancements to DAC. With the new SQL Server, DAC upgrades are performed in an in-place fashion compared to the previous side-by-side upgrade process we've all grown accustomed to over the years. Moreover, DACs can be deployed, imported and exported more easily across premises and public cloud environments, such as SQL Azure. Finally, data-tier applications now support many more objects compared to the previous SQL Server release.

Security Enhancements

It has been approximately 10 years since Microsoft initiated its trustworthy computing initiative. Since then, SQL Server has had the best track record with the least amount of vulnerabilities and exposures among the major database players in the industry. The graph shown in Figure 1-6 is from the National Institute of Standards and Technology (Source: *ITIC 2011: SQL Server Delivers Industry-Leading Security*). It shows common vulnerabilities and exposures reported from January 2002 to January 2010.

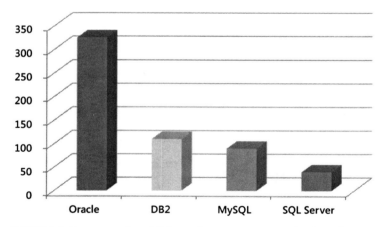

FIGURE 1-6 Common vulnerabilities and exposures reported to NIST from January 2002 to January 2010

With SQL Server 2012, the product continues to expand on this solid foundation to deliver enhanced security and compliance within the database platform. For detailed informa-tion of all the security enhancements associated with the Database Engine, review Chapter 4,

"Security Enhancements." For now, here is a snapshot of some of the new enterprise-ready security capabilities and controls that enable organizations to meet strict compliance policies and regulations:

- User-defined server roles for easier separation of duties

- Audit enhancements to improve compliance and resiliency

- Simplified security management, with a default schema for groups

- Contained Database Authentication, which provides database authentication that uses self-contained access information without the need for server logins

- SharePoint and Active Directory security models for higher data security in end-user reports

Programmability Enhancements

There has also been a tremendous investment in SQL Server 2012 regarding programmability. Specifically, there is support for "beyond *relational*" elements such as XML, Spatial, Documents, Digital Media, Scientific Records, factoids, and other unstructured data types. Why such investments?

Organizations have demanded they be given a way to reduce the costs associated with managing both structured and nonstructured data. They wanted to simplify the development of applications over all data, and they wanted the management and search capabilities for all data improved. Take a minute to review some of the SQL Server 2012 investments that positively impact programmability. For more information associated with programmability and beyond relational elements, please review Chapter 5, "Programmability and Beyond-Relational Enhancements."

- **FileTable**   Applications typically store data within a relational database engine; however, a myriad of applications also maintain the data in unstructured formats, such as documents, media files, and XML. Unstructured data usually resides on a file server and not directly in a relational database such as SQL Server. As you can imagine, it becomes challenging for organizations to not only manage their structured and unstructured data across these disparate systems, but to also keep them in sync. FileTable, a new capability in SQL Server 2012, addresses these challenges. It builds on FILESTREAM technology that was first introduced with SQL Server 2008. FileTable offers organizations Windows file namespace support and application compatibility with the file data stored in SQL Server. As an added bonus, when applications are allowed to integrate storage and data management within SQL Server, full-text and semantic search is achievable over unstructured and structured data.

- **Statistical Semantic Search**   By introducing new semantic search functionality, SQL Server 2012 allows organizations to achieve deeper insight into unstructured data stored within the Database Engine. Three new Transact-SQL rowset functions were introduced to query not only the words in a document, but also the meaning of the document.

- **Full-Text Search Enhancements**   Full-text search in SQL Server 2012 offers better query performance and scale. It also introduces property-scoped searching functionality, which allows organizations the ability to search properties such as Author and Title without the need for developers to maintain file properties in a separate database. Developers can now also benefit by customizing proximity search by using the new NEAR operator that allows them to specify the maximum number of non-search terms that separate the first and last search terms in a match.

- **Extended Events Enhancements** This new user interface was introduced to help simplify the management associated with extended events. New extended events for functional and performance troubleshooting were also introduced in SQL Server 2012.

SQL Server 2012 Editions

SQL Server 2012 is obtainable in three main editions. All three editions have tighter alignment than their predecessors and were designed to meet the needs of almost any customer with an increased investment in business intelligence. Each edition comes in a 32-bit and 64-bit version. The main editions, as shown in Figure 1-7, are the following:

- Standard edition
- Business Intelligence edition
- Enterprise edition

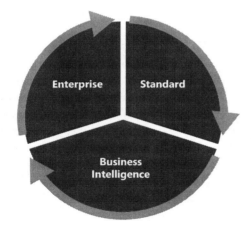

FIGURE 1-7 The main editions of SQL Server 2012

Enterprise Edition

The Enterprise edition of SQL Server 2012 is the uppermost SKU; it is meant to meet the highest demands of large-scale datacenters and data warehouse solutions by providing mission-critical performance and availability for Tier 1 applications, the ability to deploy private-cloud, highly virtualized environments, and large centralized or external-facing business-intelligence solutions.

Note The Datacenter edition included in the previous version of SQL Server is now retired. All Datacenter capabilities are included in the Enterprise edition of SQL Server 2012.

The Enterprise edition features include the following:

- Maximum number of cores is subject to the operating system being used

- Advanced high availability can be achieved with AlwaysOn

- Unlimited virtualization if the organization has software insurance

- Support for the new columnstore indexing feature

- Advanced auditing

- Transparent Data Encryption (TDE)

- Compression and partitioning

- Includes all of the Business Intelligence edition's features and capabilities:

- Reporting

- Analytics

- Multidimensional BI semantic model

- Data-quality services

- Master data services

- In-memory tabular BI semantic model

- Self-service business intelligence

Standard Edition

The Standard edition is a data-management platform tailored toward departmental databases and limited business-intelligence applications that are typically appropriate for medium-class solutions, smaller organizations, or departmental solutions. It does not include all the bells and whistles of the Enterprise and Business Intelligence editions; however, it continues to offer best-in-class manageability and ease of use. Compared to the Enterprise and Business Intelligence editions, the Standard edition supports up to 16 cores and includes the following:

- Spatial support

- FileTable

- Policy-based management

- Corporate business intelligence

- Reporting

- Analytics

- Multidimensional BI semantic model

- Basic high availability can be achieved with AlwaysOn 2-Node Failover Clustering

- Up to four processors, up to 64 GB of RAM, one virtual machine, and two failover clustering nodes

Business Intelligence Edition

For the first time in the history of SQL Server, a Business Intelligence edition is offered. The Business Intelligence edition offers organizations the full suite of powerful BI capabilities such as scalable reporting and analytics, Power View, and PowerPivot. It is tailored toward organizations trying to achieve corporate business intelligence and self-service capabilities, but that do not require the full online transactional processing (OLTP) performance and scalability found in the Enterprise edition of SQL Server 2012. Here is a high-level list of what the new Business Intelligence edition includes:

- Up to a maximum of 16 cores for the Database Engine

- Maximum number of cores for business intelligence processing

- All of the features found in the Standard edition

- Corporate business intelligence

- Reporting

- Analytics

- Multidimensional BI semantic model

- Self-service capabilities

- Alerting

- Power View

- PowerPivot for SharePoint Server

- Enterprise data management

- Data quality services

- Master data services

- In-memory tabular BI semantic model

- Basic high availability can be achieved with AlwaysOn 2-Node Failover Clustering

Specialized Editions

Above and beyond the three main editions discussed earlier, SQL Server 2012 continues to deliver specialized editions for organizations that have a unique set of requirements. Some examples include the following:

- **Developer**   The Developer edition includes all of the features and functionality found in the Enterprise edition; however, it is meant strictly for the purpose of development, testing, and demonstration. Note that you can transition a SQL Server Developer installation directly into production by upgrading it to SQL Server 2012 Enterprise without reinstallation.

- **Web**   Available at a much more affordable price than the Enterprise and Standard editions, SQL Server 2012 Web is focused on service providers hosting Internet-facing web services environments. Unlike the Express edition, this edition doesn't have database size restrictions, it supports four processors, and supports up to 64 GB of memory. SQL Server 2012 Web does not offer the same premium features found in Enterprise and Standard editions, but it still remains the ideal platform for hosting websites and web applications.

- **Express**   This free edition is the best entry-level alternative for independent software vendors, nonprofessional developers, and hobbyists building client applications. Individuals learning about databases or learning how to build client applications will find that this edition meets all their needs. This edition, in a nutshell, is limited to one processor and 1 GB of memory, and it can have a maximum database size of 10 GB. Also, Express is integrated with Microsoft Visual Studio.

Note   Review "Features Supported by the Editions of SQL Server 2012" at *http://msdn.microsoft.com/en-us/library/cc645993(v=sql.110).aspx* and *http://www.microsoft.com/sqlserver/en/us/future-editions/sql2012-editions.aspx* for a complete comparison of the key capabilities of the different editions of SQL Server 2012.

SQL Server 2012 Licensing Overview

The licensing models affiliated with SQL Server 2012 have been both simplified to better align to customer solutions and optimized for virtualization and cloud deployments. Organizations should process knowledge of the information that follows. With SQL Server 2012, the licensing for computing power is core-based and the Business Intelligence and Standard editions are available under the Server + Client Access License (CAL) model. In addition, organizations can save on cloud-based computing costs by licensing individual database virtual machines. Because each customer environment is unique, we will not have the opportunity to provide an overview of how the license changes affect your environment. For more information on the licensing changes and how they impact your organization, please contact your Microsoft representative or partner.

Review the following link for more information on SQL Server 2012 licensing: *http://www.microsoft.com/sqlserver/en/us/future-editions/sql2012-licensing.aspx.*

Hardware and Software Requirements

The recommended hardware and software requirements for SQL Server 2012 vary depending on the component being installed, the database workload, and the type of processor class that will be used. Let's turn our attention to Tables 1-1 and 1-2 to understand the hardware and software requirements for SQL Server 2012.

Because SQL Server 2012 supports many processor types and operating systems, Table 1-1 covers only the hardware requirements for a typical SQL Server 2012 installation. Typical installations include SQL Server 2012 Standard and Enterprise running on Windows Server 2008 R2 operating systems. Readers needing information for other scenarios should reference "Hardware and Software Requirements for Installing SQL Server 2012" at *http://msdn.microsoft.com/en-us/library /ms143506(v=SQL.110).aspx.*

TABLE 1-1 Hardware Requirements

Hardware Component	Requirements
Processor	Processor type: (64-bit) x64 Minimum: AMD Opteron, AMD Athlon 64, Intel Xeon with Intel EM64T support, Intel Pentium IV with EM64T support Processor speed: minimum 1.4 GHz; 2.0 GHz or faster recommended Processor type: (32-bit) Intel Pentium III-compatible processor or faster Processor speed: minimum 1.0 GHz; 2.0 GHz or faster recommended
Memory (RAM)	Minimum: 1 GB Recommended: 4 GB or more Maximum: Operating system maximum
Disk Space	Disk space requirements will vary depending on the components you install. Database Engine: 811 MB Analysis Services: 345 MB Reporting Services: 304 MB Integration Services: 591 MB Client components: 1823 MB

TABLE 1-2 Software Requirements

Software Component	Requirements
Operating system	Windows Server 2008 R2 SP1 64-bit Datacenter, Enterprise, Standard or Web edition or Windows Server 2008 SP2 64-bit Datacenter, Enterprise, Standard or Web edition
.NET Framework	Microsoft .NET Framework 3.5 SP1 and Microsoft .NET Framework 4.0

Software Component	Requirements
Windows PowerShell	Windows PowerShell 2.0
SQL Server support tools and software	SQL Server 2012 - SQL Server Native Client SQL Server 2012 - SQL Server Setup Support Files Minimum: Windows Installer 4.5
Internet Explorer	Minimum: Windows Internet Explorer 7 or later version
Virtualization	Windows Server 2008 SP2 running Hyper-V role or Windows Server 2008 R2 SP1 running Hyper-V role

Note The server hardware has supported both 32-bit and 64-bit processors for several years; however, Windows Server 2008 R2 is 64-bit only. Take this into serious consideration when planning SQL Server 2012 deployments.

Installation, Upgrade, and Migration Strategies

Like its predecessors, SQL Server 2012 is available in both 32-bit and 64-bit editions. Both can be installed with either the SQL Server Installation Wizard through a command prompt or with Sysprep for automated deployments with minimal administrator intervention. As mentioned earlier in the chapter, SQL Server 2012 can now be installed on the Server Core, which is an installation option of Windows Server 2008 R2 SP1 or later. Finally, database administrators also have the option to upgrade an existing installation of SQL Server or conduct a side-by-side migration when installing SQL Server 2012. The following sections elaborate on the different strategies.

The In-Place Upgrade

An in-place upgrade is the upgrade of an existing SQL Server installation to SQL Server 2012. When an in-place upgrade is conducted, the SQL Server 2012 setup program replaces the previous SQL Server binaries with the new SQL Server 2012 binaries on the existing machine. SQL Server data is automatically converted from the previous version to SQL Server 2012. This means data does not have to be copied or migrated. In the example in Figure 1-8, a database administrator is conducting an in-place upgrade on a SQL Server 2008 instance running on Server 1. When the upgrade is complete, Server 1 still exists, but the SQL Server 2008 instance and all of its data is upgraded to SQL Server 2012.

Note SQL Server 2005 with SP4, SQL Server 2008 with SP2, and SQL Server 2008 R2 with SP1 are all supported for an in-place upgrade to SQL Server 2012. Unfortunately, earlier versions such as SQL Server 2000, SQL Server 7.0, and SQL Server 6.5 cannot be upgraded to SQL Server 2012.

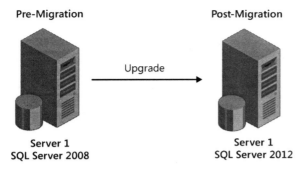

Pre-Migration   Post-Migration

Upgrade

Server 1   Server 1
SQL Server 2008   SQL Server 2012

FIGURE 1-8 An in-place upgrade from SQL Server 2008 to SQL Server 2012

Review the following link for a detailed list of upgrades supported from earlier versions of SQL Server to SQL Server 2012: *http://msdn.microsoft.com/en-us/library/ms143393(SQL.110).aspx.*

In-Place Upgrade Pros and Cons

The in-place upgrade strategy is usually easier and considered less risky than the side-by-side migration strategy. Upgrading is fairly fast, and additional hardware is not required. Because the names of the server and instances do not change during an upgrade process, applications still point to the old instances. As a result, this strategy is less time consuming because there is no need to make changes to application connection strings.

The disadvantage of an in-place upgrade is there is less granular control over the upgrade process. For example, when running multiple databases or components, a database administrator does not have the flexibility to choose individual items for upgrade. Instead, all databases and components are upgraded to SQL Server 2012 at the same time. In addition, the instance remains offline during the in-place upgrade. This means if a mission-critical database or application or an important line-of-business application is running, a planned outage is required. Furthermore, if a disaster transpires during the upgrade, the rollback strategy can be a complex and time-consuming affair. A database administrator might have to install the operating system from scratch, install SQL Server, and restore all of the SQL Server data.

SQL Server 2012 High-Level In-Place Strategy

The high-level in-place upgrade strategy for upgrading to SQL Server 2012 consists of the following steps:

1. Ensure the instance of SQL Server that will be upgraded meets the hardware and software requirements for SQL Server 2012.

2. Review the deprecated and discontinued features in SQL Server 2012. Refer to "Deprecated Database Engine Features in SQL Server 2012" at *http://technet.microsoft.com/en-us/library /ms143729(v=sql.110).aspx* for more information.

3. Ensure the version and edition of SQL Server that will be upgraded is supported. To review all the upgrade scenarios supported for SQL Server 2012, see "Supported Version and Edition Upgrades" at *http://msdn.microsoft.com/en-us/library/ms143393(SQL.110).aspx*.

4. Run the SQL Server Upgrade Advisor for SQL Server 2012. The Upgrade Advisor is a tool included with SQL Server 2012, or it can be downloaded directly from the Microsoft website. It analyzes the installed components on the SQL Server instance you plan to upgrade to ensure the system supports SQL Server 2012. The Upgrade Advisor generates a report identifying anomalies that require fixing or attention before the upgrade can begin.

5. Install the SQL Server 2012 prerequisites.

6. Begin the upgrade to SQL Server 2012 by running Setup.

Side-by-Side Migration

The term "side-by-side migration" describes the deployment of a brand-new SQL Server 2012 instance alongside a legacy SQL Server instance. When the SQL Server 2012 installation is complete, a database administrator migrates data from the legacy SQL Server database platform to the new SQL Server 2012 database platform. Side-by-side migration is depicted in Figure 1-9.

Note You can conduct a side-by-side migration to SQL Server 2012 by using the same server. The side-by-side method can also be used to upgrade to SQL Server 2012 on a single server.

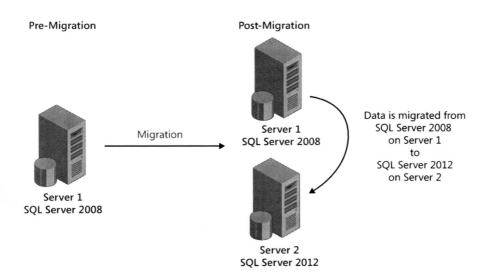

FIGURE 1-9 Side-by-side migration from SQL Server 2008 to SQL Server 2012

Side-by-Side Migration Pros and Cons

The greatest benefit of a side-by-side migration over an in-place upgrade is the opportunity to build out a new database infrastructure on SQL Server 2012 and avoid potential migration issues that can occur with an in-place upgrade. The side-by-side migration also provides more granular control over the upgrade process because you can migrate databases and components independent of one another. In addition, the legacy instance remains online during the migration process. All of these advantages result in a more powerful server. Moreover, when two instances are running in parallel, additional testing and verification can be conducted. Performing a rollback is also easy if a problem arises during the migration.

However, there are disadvantages to the side-by-side strategy. Additional hardware might need to be purchased. Applications might also need to be directed to the new SQL Server 2012 instance, and it might not be a best practice for very large databases because of the duplicate amount of storage required during the migration process.

SQL Server 2012 High-Level, Side-by-Side Strategy

The high-level, side-by-side migration strategy for upgrading to SQL Server 2012 consists of the following steps:

1. Ensure the instance of SQL Server you plan to migrate meets the hardware and software requirements for SQL Server 2012.

2. Review the deprecated and discontinued features in SQL Server 2012 by referring to "Deprecated Database Engine Features in SQL Server 2012" at *http://technet.microsoft.com/en-us/library/ms143729(v=sql.110).aspx*.

3. Although a legacy instance will not be upgraded to SQL Server 2012, it is still beneficial to run the SQL Server 2012 Upgrade Advisor to ensure the data being migrated to the new SQL Server 2012 is supported and there is no possibility of a break occurring after migration.

4. Procure the hardware, and install your operating system of choice. Windows Server 2012 is recommended.

5. Install the SQL Server 2012 prerequisites and desired components.

6. Migrate objects from the legacy SQL Server to the new SQL Server 2012 database platform.

7. Point applications to the new SQL Server 2012 database platform.

8. Decommission legacy servers after the migration is complete.

CHAPTER 2

High-Availability and Disaster-Recovery Enhancements

Microsoft SQL Server 2012 delivers significant enhancements to well-known, critical capabilities such as high availability (HA) and disaster recovery. These enhancements promise to assist organizations in achieving their highest level of confidence to date in their server environments. Server Core support, breakthrough features such as AlwaysOn Availability Groups and active secondaries, and key improvements to features such as failover clustering are improvements that provide organizations a range of accommodating options to achieve maximum application availability and data protection for SQL Server instances and databases within a datacenter and across datacenters.

This chapter's goal is to bring readers up to date with the high-availability and disaster-recovery capabilities that are fully integrated into SQL Server 2012 as a result of Microsoft's heavy investment in AlwaysOn.

SQL Server AlwaysOn: A Flexible and Integrated Solution

Every organization's success and service reputation is built on ensuring that its data is always accessible and protected. In the IT world, this means delivering a product that achieves the highest level of availability and disaster recovery while minimizing data loss and downtime. With the previous versions of SQL Server, organizations achieved high availability and disaster recovery by using technologies such as failover clustering, database mirroring, log shipping, and peer-to-peer replication. Although organizations achieved great success with these solutions, they were tasked with combining these native SQL Server technologies to achieve their business requirements related to their Recovery Point Objective (RPO) and Recovery Time Objective (RTO).

Figure 2-1 illustrates a common high-availability and disaster-recovery strategy used by organizations with the previous versions of SQL Server. This strategy includes failover clustering to protect SQL Server instances within each datacenter, combined with asynchronous database mirroring to provide disaster-recovery capabilities for mission-critical databases.

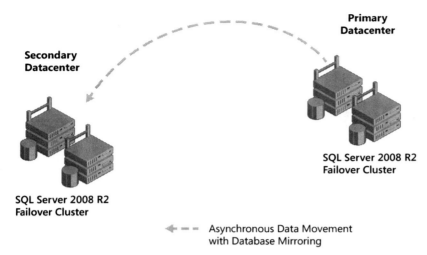

Secondary
Datacenter

Primary
Datacenter

SQL Server 2008 R2
Failover Cluster

SQL Server 2008 R2
Failover Cluster

◀ ■ ■ ■ Asynchronous Data Movement
with Database Mirroring

FIGURE 2-1 Achieving high availability and disaster recovery by combining failover clustering with database mirroring in SQL Server 2008 R2

Likewise, for organizations that either required more than one secondary datacenter or that did not have shared storage, their high-availability and disaster-recovery deployment incorporated synchronous database mirroring with a witness within the primary datacenter combined with log shipping for moving data to multiple locations. This deployment strategy is illustrated in Figure 2-2.

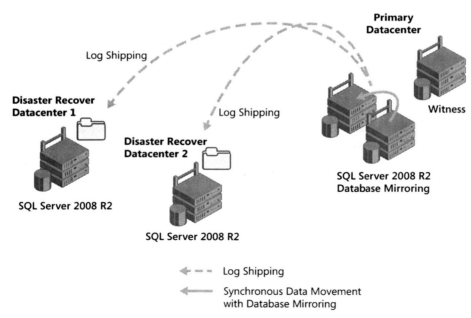

Primary
Datacenter

Log Shipping

Witness

Disaster Recover
Datacenter 1

Log Shipping

Disaster Recover
Datacenter 2

SQL Server 2008 R2
Database Mirroring

SQL Server 2008 R2

SQL Server 2008 R2

◀ ■ ■ ■ Log Shipping

◀——— Synchronous Data Movement
with Database Mirroring

FIGURE 2-2 Achieving high availability and disaster recovery with database mirroring combined with log shipping in SQL Server 2008 R2

Figures 2-1 and 2-2 both reveal successful solutions for achieving high availability and disaster recovery. However, these solutions had some limitations, which warranted making changes. In addition, with organizations constantly evolving, it was only a matter of time until they voiced their own concerns and sent out a request for more options and changes.

One concern for many organizations was regarding database mirroring. Database mirroring is a great way to protect databases; however, the solution is a one-to-one mapping, making multiple secondaries unattainable. When confronted with this situation, many organizations reverted to log shipping as a replacement for database mirroring because it supports multiple secondaries. Unfortunately, organizations encountered limitations with log shipping because it did not provide zero data loss or automatic failover capability. Concerns were also experienced by organizations working with failover clustering because they felt that their shared-storage devices, such as a storage area network (SAN), could be a single point of failure. Similarly, many organizations thought that from a cost perspective their investments were not being used to their fullest potential. For example, the passive servers in many of these solutions were idle. Finally, many organizations wanted to offload reporting and maintenance tasks from the primary database servers, which was not an easy task to achieve.

SQL Server has evolved to answer many of these concerns, and this includes an integrated solution called *AlwaysOn*. *AlwaysOn Availability Groups* and *AlwaysOn Failover Cluster Instances* are new features, introduced in SQL Server 2012, that are rich with options and promise the highest level of availability and disaster recovery to its customers. At a high level, AlwaysOn Availability Groups is used for database protection and offers multidatabase failover, multiple secondaries, active secondaries, and integrated HA management. On the other hand, AlwaysOn Failover Cluster Instances is a feature tailored to instance-level protection, multisite clustering, and consolidation, while consistently providing flexible failover polices and improved diagnostics.

AlwaysOn Availability Groups

AlwaysOn Availability Groups provides an enterprise-level alternative to database mirroring, and it gives organizations the ability to automatically or manually fail over a group of databases as a single unit, with support for up to four secondaries. The solution provides zero-data-loss protection and is flexible. It can be deployed on local storage or shared storage, and it supports both synchronous and asynchronous data movement. The application failover is very fast, it supports automatic page repair, and the secondary replicas can be leveraged to offload reporting and a number of maintenance tasks, such as backups.

Take a look at Figure 2-3, which illustrates an AlwaysOn Availability Groups deployment strategy that includes one primary replica and three secondary replicas.

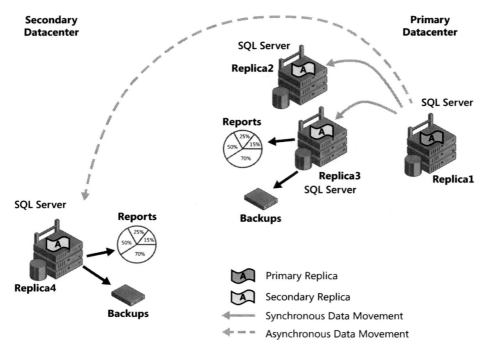

FIGURE 2-3 Achieving high availability and disaster recovery with AlwaysOn Availability Groups

In this figure, synchronous data movement is used to provide high availability within the primary datacenter and asynchronous data movement is used to provide disaster recovery. Moreover, secondary replica 3 and replica 4 are employed to offload reports and backups from the primary replica.

It is now time to take a deeper dive into AlwaysOn Availability Groups through a review of the new concepts and terminology associated with this breakthrough capability.

Understanding Concepts and Terminology

Availability groups are built on top of Windows Failover Clustering and support both shared and nonshared storage. Depending on an organization's RPO and RTO requirements, availability groups can use either an asynchronous-commit availability mode or a synchronous-commit availability mode to move data between primary and secondary replicas. Availability groups include built-in compression and encryption as well as support for file-stream replication and auto page repair. Failover between replicas is either automatic or manual.

When deploying AlwaysOn Availability Groups, your first step is to deploy a Windows Failover Cluster. This is completed by using the Failover Cluster Manager Snap-in within Windows Server 2008 R2. Once the Windows Failover Cluster is formed, the remainder of the Availability Groups configurations is completed in SQL Server Management Studio. When you use the Availability Groups wizards to configure your availability groups, SQL Server Management Studio automatically creates the appropriate services, applications, and resources in Failover Cluster Manager; hence, the deployment is much easier for database administrators who are not familiar with failover clustering.

Now that the fundamentals of the AlwaysOn Availability Groups have been laid down, the most natural question that follows is how an organization's operations are enhanced with this feature. Unlike database mirroring, which supports only one secondary, AlwaysOn Availability Groups supports one primary replica and up to four secondary replicas. Availability groups can also contain more than one availability database. Equally appealing is the fact you can host more than one availability group within an implementation. As a result, it is possible to group databases with application dependencies together within an availability group and have all the availability databases seamlessly fail over as a single cohesive unit as depicted in Figure 2-4.

FIGURE 2-4 Dedicated availability groups for Finance and HR availability databases

In addition, as shown in Figure 2-4, there is one primary replica and two secondary replicas with two availability groups. One of these availability groups is called Finance, and it includes all the Finance databases; the other availability group is called HR, and it includes all the Human Resources databases. The Finance availability group can fail over independently of the HR availability group, and unlike database mirroring, all availability databases within an availability group fail over as a single unit. Moreover, organizations can improve their IT efficiency, increase performance, and reduce total cost of ownership with better resource utilization of secondary/passive hardware because these secondary replicas can be leveraged for backups and read-only operations such as reporting and maintenance. This is covered in the "Active Secondaries" section later in this chapter.

Now that you have been introduced to some of the benefits AlwaysOn Availability Groups offers for an organization, let's take the time to get a stronger understanding of the AlwaysOn Availability Groups concepts and how this new capability operates. The concepts covered include the following:

- Availability replica roles

- Data synchronization modes

- Failover modes

- Connection mode in secondaries

- Availability group listeners

Availability Replica Roles

Each AlwaysOn availability group comprises a set of two or more failover partners that are referred to as *availability replicas*. The availability replicas can consist of either a primary role or a secondary role. Note that there can be a maximum of four secondaries, and of these four secondaries only a maximum of two secondaries can be configured to use the synchronous-commit availability mode.

The *roles* affiliated with the availability replicas in AlwaysOn Availability Groups follow the same principles as the legendary Sith rule of two doctrines in the Star Wars saga. In Star Wars, there can be only two Siths at one time, a master and an apprentice. Similarly, a SQL Server instance in an availability group can be only a primary replica or a secondary replica. At no time can it be both because the role swapping is controlled by Windows Server Failover Cluster (WSFC).

Each of the SQL Server instances in the availability group is hosted on either a SQL Server failover cluster instance (FCI) or a stand-alone instance of SQL Server 2012. Each of these instances resides on different nodes of a WSFC. WSFC is typically used for providing high availability and disaster recovery for well-known Microsoft products. As such, availability groups use WSFC as the underlying mechanism to provide internode health detection, failover coordination, primary health detection, and distributed change notifications for the solution.

Each availability replica hosts a copy of the availability databases in the availability group. Because there are multiple copies of the databases being hosted on each availability replica, there isn't a prerequisite for using shared storage like there was in the past when deploying traditional SQL Server failover clusters. On the flip side, when using nonshared storage, an organization must realize that storage requirements increase as the number of replicas it plans on hosting increases.

Data Synchronization Modes

To move data from the primary replica to the secondary replica, each mode uses either synchronous-commit availability mode or asynchronous-commit availability mode. Give consideration to the following items when selecting either option:

- When you use the *synchronous-commit mode*, a transaction is committed on both replicas to guarantee transactional consistency. This, however, means increased latency. As such, this option might not be appropriate for partners who don't share a high-speed network or who reside in different geographical locations.

- The *asynchronous-commit mode* commits transactions between partners without waiting for the partner to write the log to disk. This maximizes performance between the application and the primary replica and is well suited for disaster-recovery solutions.

Availability Groups Failover Modes

When configuring AlwaysOn availability groups, database administrators can choose from two failover modes when swapping roles from the primary to the secondary replicas. For administrators who are familiar with database mirroring, you'll see that to obtain high availability and disaster recovery the failover modes are very similar to the modes in database mirroring. These are the two AlwaysOn failover modes available when using the New Availability Group Wizard:

- **Automatic Failover**   This replica uses synchronous-commit availability mode, and it supports both automatic failover and manual failover between the replica partners. A maximum of two failover replica partners are supported when choosing automatic failover.

- **Manual Failover**   This replica uses synchronous or asynchronous commit availability mode and supports only manual failovers between the replica partners.

Connection Mode in Secondaries

As indicated earlier, each of the secondaries can be configured to support read-only access for reporting or other maintenance tasks, such as backups. During the final configuration stage of AlwaysOn availability groups, database administrators decide on the connection mode for the secondary replicas. There are three connection modes available:

- **Disallow connections**   In the secondary role, this availability replica does not allow any connections.

- **Allow only read-intent connections**   In the secondary role, this availability replica allows only read-intent connections.

- **Allow all connections**   In the secondary role, this availability replica allows all connections for read access, including connections running with older clients.

Availability Group Listeners

The availability group listener provides a way of connecting to databases within an availability group via a virtual network name that is bound to the primary replica. Applications can specify the network name affiliated with the availability group listener in connection strings. After the availability group fails over from the primary replica to a secondary replica, the network name directs connections to the new primary replica. The availability group listener concept is similar to a Virtual SQL Server Name when using failover clustering; however, with an availability group listener, there is a virtual network name for each availability group, whereas with SQL Server failover clustering, there is one virtual network name for the instance.

You can specify your availability group listener preferences when using the Create A New Availability Group Wizard in SQL Server Management Studio, or you can manually create or modify an availability group listener after the availability group is created. Alternatively, you can use Transact-SQL to create or modify the listener too. Notice in Figure 2-5 that each availability group listener requires a DNS name, an IP address, and a port such as 1433. Once the availability group listener is created, a server name and an IP address cluster resource are automatically created within Failover Cluster Manager. This is certainly a testimony to the availability group's flexibility and tight integration with SQL Server, because the majority of the configurations are done within SQL Server.

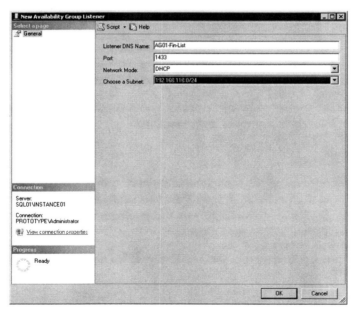

FIGURE 2-5 Specifying availability group listener properties

Be aware that there is a one-to-one mapping between availability group listeners and availability groups. This means you can create one availability group listener for each availability group. However, if more than one availability group exists within a replica, you can have more than one availability group listener. For example, there are two availability groups shown in Figure 2-6: one is for the Finance availability databases, and the other is for the Accounting availability databases. Each availability group has its own availability group listener that clients and applications connect to.

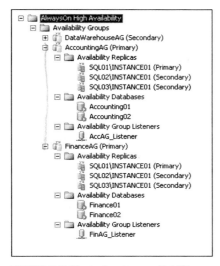

FIGURE 2-6 Illustrating two availability group listeners within a replica

Configuring Availability Groups

When creating a new availability group, a database administrator needs to specify an availability group name, such as AvailablityGroupFinance, and then select one or more databases to be part of in the availability group. The next step involves first specifying one or more instances of SQL Server to host secondary availability replicas, and then specifying your availability group listener preference. The final step is selecting the data-synchronization preference and connection mode for the secondary replicas. These configurations are conducted with the New Availability Group Wizard or with Transact-SQL PowerShell scripts.

Prerequisites

To deploy AlwaysOn Availability Groups, the following prerequisites must be met:

- All computers running SQL Server, including the servers that will reside in the disaster-recovery site, must reside in the same Windows-based domain.

- All SQL Server computers must participate in a single Windows Server failover cluster even if the servers reside in multiple sites.

- All servers must partake in a Windows Server failover cluster.

- AlwaysOn Availability Groups must be enabled on each server.

- All the databases must be in full recovery mode.

- A full backup must be conducted on all databases before deployment.

- The server cannot host the Active Directory Domain Services role.

Deployment Examples

Figure 2-7 shows the Specify Replicas page you see when using the New Availability Group Wizard. In this example, there are three SQL Server instances in the availability group called Finance: SQL01\Instance01, SQL02\Instance01, and SQL03\Instance01. SQL01\Instance01 is configured as the Primary replica, whereas SQL02\Instance01 and SQL03\Instance01 are configured as secondaries. SQL01\Instance01 and SQL02\Instance01 support automatic failover with synchronous data movement, whereas SQL-03\Instance01 uses asynchronous-commit availability mode and supports only a forced failover. Finally, SQL01\Instance01 does not allow read-only connections to the secondary, whereas SQL02\Instance01 and SQL03\Instance01 allow read-intent connections to the secondary. In addition, for this example, SQL01\Instance01 and SQL02\Instance01 reside in a primary datacenter for high availability within a site, and SQL03\Instance01 resides in the disaster recovery datacenter and will be brought online manually in the event the primary datacenter becomes unavailable.

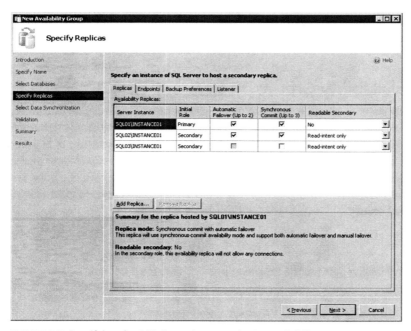

FIGURE 2-7 Specifying the SQL Server instances in the availability group

One thing becomes vividly clear from Figure 2-7 and the preceding example: there are many different deployment configurations available to satisfy any organization's high-availability and disaster-recovery requirements. See Figure 2-8 for the following additional deployment alternatives:

- Nonshared storage, local, regional, and geo target

- Multisite cluster with another cluster as the disaster recovery (DR) target

- Three-node cluster with similar DR target

- Secondary targets for backup, reporting, and DR

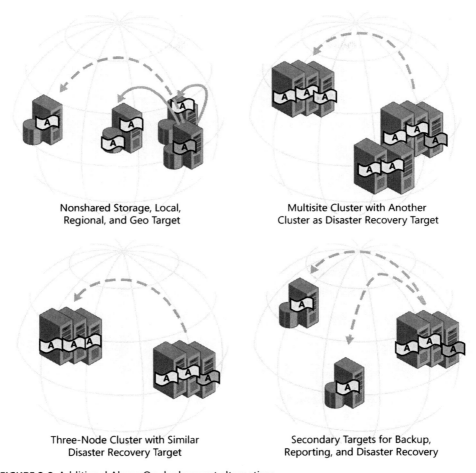

Nonshared Storage, Local,
Regional, and Geo Target

Multisite Cluster with Another
Cluster as Disaster Recovery Target

Three-Node Cluster with Similar
Disaster Recovery Target

Secondary Targets for Backup,
Reporting, and Disaster Recovery

FIGURE 2-8 Additional AlwaysOn deployment alternatives

Monitoring Availability Groups with the Dashboard

Administrators have an opportunity to leverage a new and remarkably intuitive manageability
dashboard in in SQL Server 2012 to monitor availability groups. The dashboard, shown in Figure 2-9,
reports the health and status associated with each instance and availability database in the availability
group. Moreover, the dashboard displays the specific replica role of each instance and provides synchronization status. If there is an issue or if more information on a specific event is required, a database administrator can click the availability group state, server instance name, or health status hyperlinks for additional information. The dashboard is launched by right-clicking the Availability Groups
folder in the Object Explorer in SQL Server Management Studio and selecting Show Dashboard.

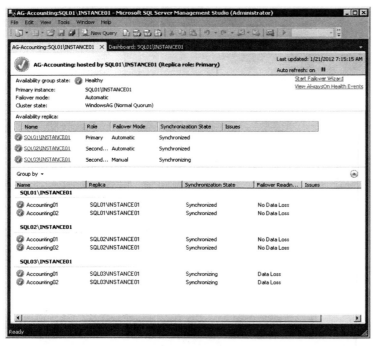

FIGURE 2-9 Monitoring availability groups with the new Availability Group dashboard

Active Secondaries

As indicated earlier, many organizations communicated to the SQL Server team their need to improve IT efficiency by optimizing their existing hardware investments. Specifically, organizations hoped their production systems for passive workloads could be used in some other capacity instead of remaining in an idle state. These same organizations also wanted reporting and maintenance tasks offloaded from production servers because these tasks negatively affected production workloads. With SQL Server 2012, organizations can leverage the AlwaysOn Availability Group capability to configure secondary replicas, also referred to as *active secondaries*, to provide read-only access to databases affiliated with an availability group.

All read-only operations on the secondary replicas are supported by row versioning and are automatically mapped to snapshot isolation transaction level, which eliminates reader/writer contention. In addition, the data in the secondary replicas is near real time. In many circumstances, data latency between the primary and secondary databases should be within seconds. Note that the latency of log synchronization affects data freshness.

For organizations, active secondaries are synonymous with performance optimization on a primary replica and increases to overall IT efficiency and hardware utilization.

Read-Only Access to Secondary Replicas

Recall that when configuring the connection mode for secondary replicas, you can choose Disallow Connections, Allow Only Read-Intent Connections, and Allow All Connections. The Allow Only Read-Intent Connections and Allow All Connections options both provide read-only access to secondary replicas. The Disallow Connections alternative does not allow read-only access as implied by its name.

Now let's look at the major differences between Allow Only Read-Intent Connections and Allow All Connections. The Allow Only Read-Intent Connections option allows connections to the databases in the secondary replica when the Application Intent Connection property is set to Read-only in the SQL Server native client. When using the Allow All Connections settings, all client connections are allowed independent of the Application Intent property. What is the Application Intent property in the connection string? The Application Intent property declares the application workload type when connecting to a server. The possible values are Read-only and Read Write. Commands that try to create or modify data on the secondary replica will fail.

Backups on Secondary

Backups of availability databases participating in availability groups can be conducted on any of the replicas. Although backups are still supported on the primary replica, log backups can be conducted on any of the secondaries. Note that this is independent of the replication commit mode being used—synchronous-commit or asynchronous-commit. Log backups completed on all replicas form a single log chain, as shown in Figure 2-10.

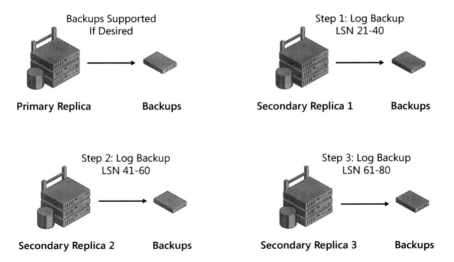

FIGURE 2-10 Forming a single log chain by backing up the transaction logs on multiple secondary replicas

As a result, the transaction log backups do not all have to be performed on the same replica. This in no way means that serious thought should not be given to the location of your backups. It is recommended that you store all backups in a central location because all transaction log backups are required to perform a restore in the event of a disaster. Therefore, if a server is no longer available and it contained the backups, you will be negatively affected. In the event of a failure, use the new Database Recovery Advisor Wizard; it provides many benefits when conducting restores. For example, if you are performing backups on different secondaries, the wizard generates a visual image of a chronological timeline by stitching together all of the log files based on the Log Sequence Number (LSN).

AlwaysOn Failover Cluster Instances

You've seen the results of the development efforts in engineering the new AlwaysOn Availability Groups capability for high availability and disaster recovery, and the creation of active secondaries. Now you'll explore the significant enhancements to traditional capabilities such as SQL Server failover clustering that leverage shared storage. The following list itemizes some of the improvements that will appeal to database administrators looking to gain high availability for their SQL Server instances. Specifically, this section discusses the following features:

- **Multisubnet Clustering**   This feature provides a disaster-recovery solution in addition to high availability with new support for multisubnet failover clustering.

- **Support for TempDB on Local Disk**   Another storage-level enhancement with failover clustering is associated with TempDB. TempDB no longer has to reside on shared storage as it did in previous versions of SQL Server. It is now supported on local disks, which results in many practical benefits for organizations. For example, you can now offload TempDB I/O from shared-storage devices (SSD) like a SAN and leverage fast SSD storage locally within the server nodes to optimize TempDB workloads, which are typically random I/O.

- **Flexible Failover Policy**   SQL Server 2012 introduces improved failure detection for the SQL Server failover cluster instance by adding failure condition-level properties that allow you to configure a more flexible failover policy.

 Note AlwaysOn failover cluster instances can be combined with availability groups to offer maximum SQL Server instance and database protection.

With the release of Windows Server 2008, new functionality enabled cluster nodes to be connected over different subnets without the need for a stretch virtual local area network (VLAN) across networks. The nodes could reside on different subnets within a datacenter or in another geographical location, such as a disaster recovery site. This concept is commonly referred to as *multisite clustering*, *multisubnet clustering*, or *stretch clustering*. Unfortunately, the previous versions of SQL Server could not take advantage of this Windows failover clustering feature. Organizations that wanted to create either a multisite or multisubnet SQL Server failover cluster still had to create a stretch VLAN to expose a single IP address for failover across sites. This was a complex and challenging task for many organizations. This is no longer the case because SQL Server 2012 supports multisubnet and multisite clustering out of the box; therefore, the need for implementing stretch VLAN technology no longer exists.

Figure 2-11 illustrates an example of a SQL Server multisubnet failover cluster between two subnets spanning two sites. Notice how each node affiliated with the multisubnet failover cluster resides on a different subnet. Node 1 is located in Site 1 and resides on the 192.168.115.0/24 subnet, whereas Node 2 is located in Site 2 and resides on the 192.168.116.0/24 subnet. The DNS IP address associated with the virtual network name of the SQL Server cluster is automatically updated when a failover from one subnet to another subnet occurs.

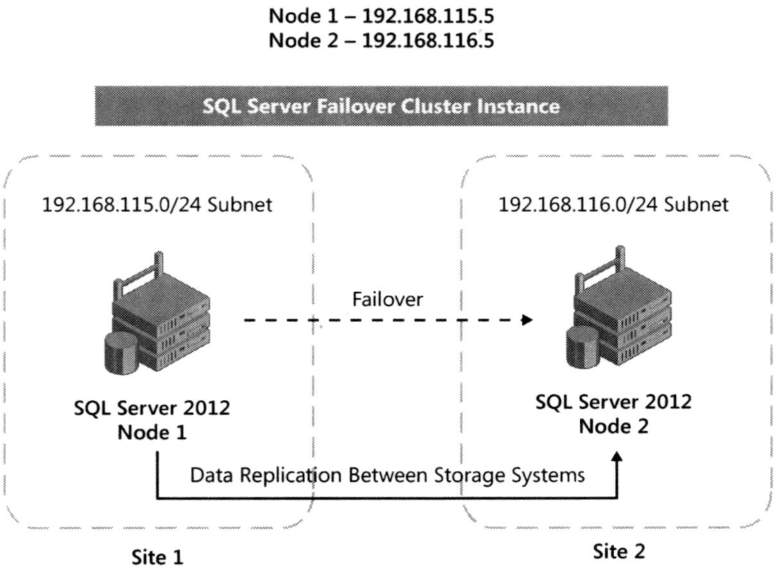

FIGURE 2-11 A multisubnet failover cluster instance example

For clients and applications to connect to the SQL Server failover cluster, they need two IP addresses registered to the SQL Server failover cluster resource name in WSFC. For example, imagine your server name is SQLFCI01 and the IP addresses are 192.168.115.5 and 192.168.116.5. WSFC automatically controls the failover and brings the appropriate IP address online depending on the node that currently owns the SQL Server resource. Again, if Node 1 is affiliated with the 192.168.115.0/24 subnet and owns the SQL Server failover cluster, the IP address resource 192.168.115.6 is brought online as shown in Figure 2-12. Similarly, if a failover occurs and Node 2 owns the SQL Server resource, IP address resource 192.168.115.6 is taken offline and the IP address resource 192.168.116.6 is brought online.

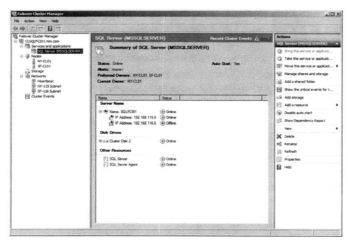

FIGURE 2-12 Multiple IP addresses affiliated with a multisubnet failover cluster instance

Because there are multiple IP addresses affiliated with the SQL Server failover cluster instance virtual name, the online address changes automatically when there is a failover. In addition, Windows failover cluster issues a DNS update immediately after the network name resource name comes online. The IP address change in DNS might not take effect on clients because of cache settings; therefore, it is recommended that you minimize the client downtime by configuring the HostRecordTTL in DNS to 60 seconds. Consult with your DNS administrator before making any DNS changes, because additional load requests could occur when tuning the TTL time with a host record.

Support for Deploying SQL Server 2012 on Windows Server Core

Windows Server Core was originally introduced with Windows Server 2008 and saw significant enhancements with the release of Windows Server 2008 R2. For those who are unfamiliar with Server Core, it is an installation option for the Windows Server 2008 and Windows Server 2008 R2 operating systems. Because Server Core is a minimal deployment of Windows, it is much more secure because its attack surface is greatly reduced. Server Core does not include a traditional Windows graphical interface and, therefore, is managed via a command prompt or by remote administration tools.

Unfortunately, previous versions of SQL Server did not support the Server Core operating system, but that has all changed. For the first time, Microsoft SQL Server 2012 supports Server Core installations for organizations running Server Core based on Windows Server 2008 R2 with Service Pack 1 or later.

Why is Server Core so important to SQL Server, and how does it positively affect availability? When you are running SQL Server 2012 on Server Core, operating-system patching is drastically reduced—by up to 60 percent. This translates to higher availability and a reduction in planned downtime for any organization's mission-critical databases and workloads. In addition, surface-area attacks are greatly reduced and overall security of the database platform is strengthened, which again translates to maximum availability and data protection.

When first introduced, Server Core required the use and knowledge of command-line syntax to manage it. Most IT professionals at this time were accustomed to using a graphical user interface (GUI) to manage and configure Windows, so they had a difficult time embracing Server Core. This affected its popularity and, ultimately, its implementation. To ease these challenges, Microsoft created SCONFIG, which is an out-of-the-box utility that was introduced with the release of Windows Server 2008 R2 to dramatically ease server configurations. To navigate through the SCONFIG options, you only need to type one or more numbers to configure server properties, as displayed in Figure 2-13.

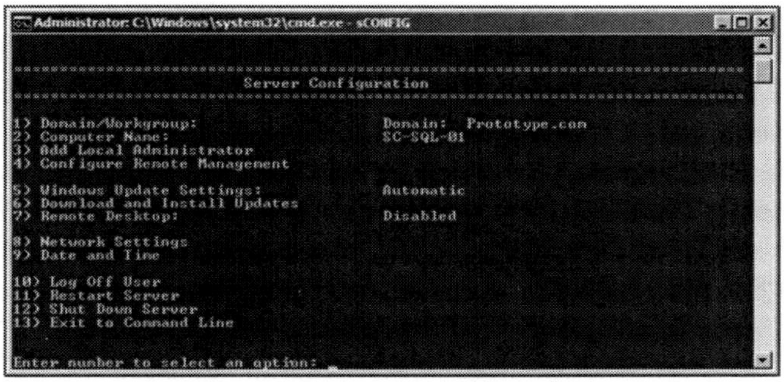

FIGURE 2-13 SCONFIG utility for configuring server properties in Server Core

The following sections articulate the SQL Server 2012 prerequisites for Server Core, SQL Server features supported on Server Core, and the installation alternatives.

SQL Server 2012 Prerequisites for Server Core

Organizations installing SQL Server 2012 on Windows Server 2008 R2 Server Core must meet the following operating system, features, and components prerequisites.

The operating system requirements are as follows:

- Windows Server 2008 R2 SP1 64-bit x64 Data Center Server Core

- Windows Server 2008 R2 SP1 64-bit x64 Enterprise Server Core

- Windows Server 2008 R2 SP1 64-bit x64 Standard Server Core

- Windows Server 2008 R2 SP1 64-bit x64 Web Server Core

Here is the list of features and components:

- .NET Framework 2.0 SP2

- .NET Framework 3.5 SP1 Full Profile

- .NET Framework 4 Server Core Profile

- Windows Installer 4.5

- Windows PowerShell 2.0

Once you have all the prerequisites, it important to become familiar with the SQL Server components supported on Server Core.

SQL Server Features Supported on Server Core

There are numerous SQL Server features that are fully supported on Server Core. They include Database Engine Services, SQL Server Replication, Full Text Search, Analysis Services, Client Tools Connectivity, and Integration Services. Likewise, Sever Core does not support many other features, including Reporting Services, Business Intelligence Development Studio, Client Tools Backward Compatibility, Client Tools SDK, SQL Server Books Online, Distributed Replay Controller, SQL Client Connectivity SDK, Master Data Services, and Data Quality Services. Some features such as Management Tools – Basic, Management Tools – Complete, Distributed Replay Client, and Microsoft Sync Framework are supported only remotely. Therefore, these features can be installed on editions of the Windows operating system that are not Server Core, and then used to remotely connect to a SQL Server instance running on Server Core. For a full list of supported and unsupported features review the information at this link: *http://msdn.microsoft.com/en-us/library/hh231669(SQL.110).aspx*.

> **Note** To leverage Server Core, you need to plan your SQL Server installation ahead of time. Give yourself the opportunity to fully understand which SQL Server features are required to support your mission-critical workloads.

SQL Server on Server Core Installation Alternatives

The typical SQL Server Installation Setup Wizard is not supported when installing SQL Server 2012 on Server Core. As a result, you need to automate the installation process by either using a command-line installation, using a configuration file, or leveraging the DefaultSetup.ini methodology. Details and examples for each of these methods can be found in Books Online: *http://technet.microsoft.com /en-us/library/ms144259(SQL.110).aspx*.

> **Note** When installing SQL Server 2012 on Server Core, ensure that you use Full Quiet mode by using the */Q* parameter or Quiet Simple mode by using the */QS* parameter.

Additional High-Availability and Disaster-Recovery Enhancements

This section summarizes some of the additional high-availability and disaster recovery enhancements found in SQL Server 2012.

Support for Server Message Block

A common trend for organizations in recent years has been the movement toward consolidating databases and applications onto fewer servers—specifically, hosting many instances of SQL Server running on a failover cluster. When using failover clustering for consolidation, the previous versions of SQL Server required a single drive letter for each SQL Server failover cluster instance. Because there are only 23 drive letters available, without taking into account reservations, the maximum amount of SQL Server instances supported on a single failover cluster was 23. Twenty-three instances sounds like an ample amount; however, the drive letter limitation negatively affects organizations running power-ful servers that have the compute and memory resources to host more than 23 instances on a single server. Going forward, SQL Server 2012 and failover clustering introduces support for Server Message Block (SMB).

> **Note** You might be thinking you can use mount points to alleviate the drive-letter pain point. When working with previous versions of SQL Server, even with mount points, you need at least one drive letter for each SQL Server failover cluster instance.

Some of the SQL Server 2012 benefits brought about by SMB are, of course, database-storage consolidation and the potential to support more than 23 clustering instances in a single WSFC. To take advantage of these features, the file servers must be running Windows Server 2008 or later versions of the operating system.

Database Recovery Advisor

The Database Recovery Advisor is a new feature aimed at optimizing the restore experience for database administrators conducting database recovery tasks. This tool includes a new timeline feature that provides a visualization of the backup history, as shown in Figure 2-14.

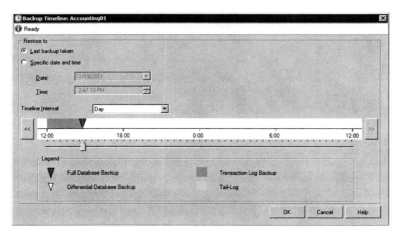

FIGURE 2-14 Database Recovery Advisor backup and restore visual timeline

Online Operations

SQL Server 2012 also includes a few enhancements for online operation that reduce downtime during planned maintenance operations. Line-of-business (LOB) re-indexing and adding columns with defaults are now supported.

Rolling Upgrade and Patch Management

All of the new AlwaysOn capabilities reduce application downtime to only a single manual failover by supporting rolling upgrades and patching of SQL Server. This means a database administrator can apply a service pack or critical fix to the passive node or nodes if using a failover cluster or to secondary replicas if using availability groups. Once the installation is complete on all passive nodes or secondaries, a database administrator can conduct a manual failover and then apply the service pack or critical fix to the node in an FCI or replica. This rolling strategy also applies when upgrading the database platform.

CHAPTER 3

Performance and Scalability

M icrosoft SQL Server 2012 introduces a new index type called *columnstore*. The columnstore index feature was originally referred to as project *Apollo* during the development phases of SQL Server 2012 and during the distribution of the Community Technology Preview (CTP) releases of the product. This new index combined with the advanced query-processing enhancements offer blazing-fast performance optimizations for data-warehousing workloads and other similar queries. In many cases, data-warehouse query performance has improved by tens to hundreds of times.

This chapter aims to teach, enlighten, and even dispel flawed beliefs about the columnstore index so that database administrators can greatly increase query performance for their data warehouse workloads. The questions this chapter focuses are the following:

- What is a columnstore index?

- How does a columnstore index drastically increase the speed of data warehouse queries?

- When should a database administrator build a columnstore index?

- Are there any well-established best practices for a columnstore index deployment?

Let's look under the hood to see how organizations will benefit from significant data-warehouse performance gains with the new, in-memory, columnstore index technology, which also helps with managing increasing data volumes.

Columnstore Index Overview

Because of a proliferation of data being captured across devices, applications, and services, organizations today are tasked with storing massive amounts of data to successfully operate their businesses. Using traditional tools to capture, manage, and process data within an acceptable time is becoming increasingly challenging as the data users want to capture continues to grow. For example, the volume of data is overwhelming the ability of data warehouses to execute queries in a timely manner, and considerable time is spent tuning queries and designing and maintaining indexes to try to get acceptable query performance. In many cases, so much time might have elapsed between the time the query is launched and the time the result sets are returned that organizations have difficulty recalling what the original request was about. Equally unproductive are the cases where the delay causes the business opportunity to be lost.

With the many issues organizations are facing as one of their primary concerns, the Query Processing and Storage teams from the SQL Server product group set to work on new technologies that would allow very large data sets to be read quickly and accurately while transforming the data into useful information and knowledge for organizations in a timely manner. The Query Processing team reviewed academic research in columnstore data representations and analyzed improved query-execution capabilities for data warehousing. In addition, they collaborated with the SQL Server product group Analysis Services team to gain a stronger understanding about the other team's work with their columnstore implementation known as *PowerPivot* for SQL Server 2008 R2. Their research and analysis led the Query Processing team to create the new columnstore index and query optimizations based on vector-based execution capability, which significantly improves data-warehouse query performance.

When developing the new columnstore index, the Query Processing team committed to a number of goals. They aimed to ensure that end users who consume data had an interactive and positive experience with all data sets, whether large or small, which meant the response time on data must be swift. These strategies also apply to ad hoc and reporting queries. Moreover, database administrators might even be able to reduce their needs for manually tuning queries, summary tables, indexed views, and in some cases OLAP cubes. All these goals naturally impact total cost of ownership (TCO) because hardware costs are lowered and fewer people are required to get a task accomplished.

Columnstore Index Fundamentals and Architecture

Before designing, implementing, or managing a columnstore index, it is beneficial to understand how they work, how data is stored in a columnstore index, and what type of queries can benefit from a columnstore index.

How Is Data Stored When Using a Columnstore Index?

With traditional tables (heaps) and indexes (B-trees), SQL Server stores data in pages in a row-based fashion. This storage model is typically referred to as a *row store*. Using column stores is like turning the traditional storage model 90 degrees, where all the values from a single column are stored contiguously in a compressed form. The columnstore index stores each column in a separate set of disk pages rather than storing multiple rows per page, which has been the traditional storage format. The following examples illustrate the differences.

Let's use a common table populated with employee data, as illustrated in Table 3-1, and then evaluate the different ways data can be stored. This employee table includes typical data such as an employee ID number, employee name, and the city and state the employee is located in.

TABLE 3-1 Traditional Table Containing Employee Data

EmployeeID	Name	City	State
1	Ross	San Francisco	CA
2	Sherry	New York	NY
3	Gus	Seattle	WA
4	Stan	San Jose	CA
5	Lijon	Sacramento	CA

Depending on the type of index chosen—traditional or columnstore—database administrators can organize their data by row (as shown in Table 3-2) or by column (as shown in Table 3-3).

TABLE 3-2 Employee Data Stored in a Traditional "Row Store" Format

Row Store
1 Ross San Francisco CA
2 Sherry New York NY
3 Gus Seattle WA
4 Stan San Jose CA
5 Lijon Sacramento CA

TABLE 3-3 Employee Data Stored in the New Columnstore Format

Columnstore
1 2 3 4 5
Ross Sherry Gus Stan Lijon
San Francisco New York Seattle San Jose Sacramento
CA NY WA CA CA

As you can see, the major difference between the columnstore format in Table 3-3 and the row store method in Table 3-2 is that a columnstore index groups and stores data for each column and then joins all the columns to complete the whole index, whereas a traditional index groups and stores data for each row and then joins all the rows to complete the whole index.

Now that you understand how data is stored when using columnstore indexes compared to traditional B-tree indexes, let's take a look at how this new storage model and advanced query optimizations significantly speed up the retrieval of data. The next section describes three ways that SQL Server columnstore indexes significantly improve the speed of queries.

How Do Columnstore Indexes Significantly Improve the Speed of Queries?

The new columnstore storage model significantly improves data warehouse query speeds for many reasons. First, data organized in a column shares many more similar characteristics than data organized across rows. As a result, a much higher level of compression can be achieved compared to data organized across rows. Moreover, the columnstore index within SQL Server uses the VertiPaq compression algorithm technology, which in SQL Server 2008 R2 was found only in Analysis Server for PowerPivot. VertiPaq compression is far superior to the traditional row and page compression used in the Database Engine, with compression rates of up to 15 to 1 having been achieved with VertiPag. When data is compressed, queries require less IO because the amount of data transferred from disk to memory is significantly reduced. Reducing IO when processing queries equates to faster performance-response times. The advantages of columnstore do not come to an end here. With less data transferred to memory, less space is required in memory to hold the working set affiliated with the query.

Second, when a user runs a query using the columnstore index, SQL Server fetches data only for the columns that are required for the query, as illustrated in Figure 3-1. In this example, there are 15 columns in the table; however, because the data required for the query resides in Column 7, Column 8, and Column 9, only these columns are retrieved.

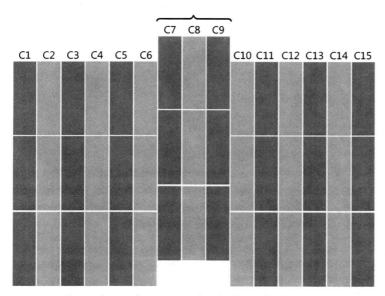

FIGURE 3-1 Improving performance and reducing IO by fetching only columns required for the query

Because data-warehouse queries typically touch only 10 to 15 percent of the columns in large fact tables, fetching only selected columns translates into savings of approximately 85 to 90 percent of an organization's IO, which again increases performance speeds.

Batch-Mode Processing

Finally, an advanced technology for processing queries that use columnstore indexes speeds up queries yet another way. Speaking about processes, it is a good time to dig a little deeper into how queries are processed.

First, the data in the columns are processed in batches using a new, highly-efficient vector technology that works with columnstore indexes. Database administrators should take a moment to review the query plan and notice the groups of operators that execute in batch mode. Note that not all operators execute in batch mode; however, the most important ones affiliated with data warehousing do, such as *Hash Join* and *Hash Aggregation*. All of the algorithms have been significantly optimized to take advantage of modern hardware architecture, such as increased core counts and additional RAM, thereby improving parallelism. All of these improvements affiliated with the columnstore index contribute to better batch-mode processing than traditional row-mode processing.

Columnstore Index Storage Organization

Let's examine how the storage associated with a columnstore index is organized. First I'll define the new storage concepts affiliated with columnstore indexes, such as a *segment* and a *row group*, and then I'll elucidate how these concepts relate to one another.

As illustrated in Figure 3-2, data in the columnstore index is broken up into segments. A segment contains data from one column for a set of up to about 1 million rows. Segments for the same set of rows comprise a row group. Instead of storing the data page by page, SQL Server stores the row group as a unit. Each segment is internally stored in a separate Large Object (LOB). Therefore, when SQL Server reads the data, the unit reading from disk consists of a segment and the segment is a unit of transfer between the disk and memory.

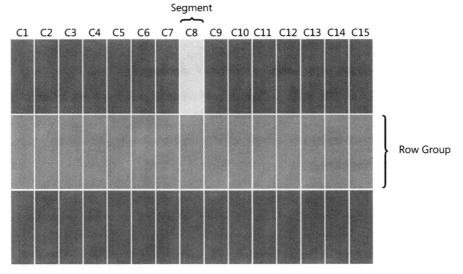

FIGURE 3-2 How a columnstore index stores data

Columnstore Index Support and SQL Server 2012

Columnstore indexes and batch-query execution mode are deeply integrated in SQL Server 2012, and they work in conjunction with many of the Database Engine features found in SQL Server 2012. For example, database administrators can implement a columnstore index on a table and still successfully use AlwaysOn Availability Groups (AG), AlwaysOn failover cluster instances (FCI), database mirroring, log shipping, and SQL Server Management Studio administration tools. Here are the common business data types supported by columnstore indexes:

- *char* and *varchar*
- All Integer types (*int*, *bigint*, *smallint*, and *tinyint*)
- *real* and *float*
- *string*
- *money* and *small money*
- All date, time, and *DateTime* types, with one exception (*datetimeoffset* with precision greater than 2)
- Decimal and numeric with precision less than or equal to 18 (that is, with less than or exactly 18 digits)
- Only one columnstore index can be created per table.

Columnstore Index Restrictions

Although columnstore indexes work with the majority of the data types, components, and features found in SQL Server 2012, columnstore indexes have the following restrictions and cannot be leveraged in the following situations:

- You can enable PAGE or ROW compression on the base table, but you cannot enable PAGE or ROW compression on the columnstore index.
- Tables and columns cannot participate in a replication topology.
- Tables and columns using Change Data Capture are unable to participate in a columnstore index.
- Create Index: You cannot create a columnstore index on the following data types:
  - decimal greater than 18 digits
  - binary and varbinary
  - BLOB
  - CLR
  - *(n)varchar(max)*

- *uniqueidentifier*

- *datetimeoffset* with precision greater than 2

- Table Maintenance: If a columnstore index exists, you can read the table but you cannot directly update it. This is because columnstore indexes are designed for data-warehouse workloads that are typically read based. Rest assured that there is no need to agonize. The upcoming "Columnstore Index Design Considerations and Loading Data" section articulates strategies on how to load new data when using columnstore indexes.

- Process Queries: You can process all read-only T-SQL queries using the columnstore index, but because batch processing works only with certain operators, you will see that some queries are accelerated more than others.

- A column that contains filestream data cannot participate in a columnstore index.

- INSERT, UPDATE, DELETE, and MERGE statements are not allowed on tables using columnstore indexes.

- More than 1024 columns are not supported when creating a columnstore index.

- Only nonclustered columnstore indexes are allowed. Filtered columnstore indexes are not allowed.

- Computed and sparse columns cannot be part of a columnstore index.

- A columnstore index cannot be created on an indexed view.

Columnstore Index Design Considerations and Loading Data

When working with columnstore indexes, some queries are accelerated much more than others. Therefore, to optimize query performance, it is important to understand when to build a columnstore index and when not to build a columnstore index. The next sections cover when to build columnstore indexes, design considerations, and how to load data when using a columnstore index.

When to Build a Columnstore Index

The following list describes when database administrators should use a columnstore index to optimize query performance:

- When workloads are mostly read based—specifically, data warehouse workloads.

- Your workflow permits partitioning (or a drop-rebuild index strategy) to handle new data. Most commonly, this is associated with periodic maintenance windows when indexes can be rebuilt or when staging tables are switching into empty partitions of existing tables.

- If most queries fit a star join pattern or entail scanning and aggregating large amounts of data.

- If updates occur and most updates append new data, which can be loaded using staging tables and partition switching.

You should use columnstore indexes when building the following types of tables:

- Large fact tables

- Large (millions of rows) dimension tables

When Not to Build a Columnstore Index

Database administrators might encounter situations when the performance benefits achieved by using traditional B-tree indexes on their tables are greater than the benefits of using a columnstore index. The following list describes some of these situations:

- Data in your table constantly requires updating.

- Partition switching or rebuilding an index does not meet the workflow requirements of your business.

- You encounter frequent small look-up queries. Note, however, that a columnstore index might still benefit you in this situation. As such, you can implement a columnstore index without any repercussions because the query optimizer should be able to determine when to use the traditional B-tree index instead of the columnstore index. This strategy assumes you have updated statistics.

- You test columnstore indexes on your workload and do not see any benefit.

Loading New Data

As mentioned in earlier sections, tables with a columnstore index cannot be updated directly. However, there are three alternatives for loading data into a table with a columnstore index:

- **Disable the Columnstore Index**   This procedure consists of the following three steps:

  1. First disable the columnstore index.

  2. Update the data.

  3. Rebuild the index when the updates are complete.

  Database administrators should ensure a maintenance window exists when leveraging this strategy. The time affiliated with the maintenance window will vary per customers workload. Therefore test within a prototype environment to determine time required.

- **Leverage Partitioning and Partition Switching**   Partitioning data enables database administrators to manage and access subsets of their data quickly and efficiently while maintaining the integrity of the entire data collection. Partition switching also allows database administrators to quickly and efficiently transfer subsets of their data by assigning a table as a partition to an already existing partitioned table, switching a partition from one partitioned table to another, or reassigning a partition to form a single table. Partition switching is fully supported with a columnstore index and is a practical way for updating data.

To use partitioning to load data, follow these steps:

1. Ensure you have an empty partition to accept the new data.

2. Load data into an empty staging table.

3. Switch the staging table (containing the newly loaded data) into the empty partition.

To use partitioning to update existing data, use the following steps:

1. Determine which partition contains the data to be modified.

2. Switch the partition into an empty staging table.

3. Disable the columnstore index on the staging table.

4. Update the data.

5. Rebuild the columnstore index on the staging table.

6. Switch the staging table back into the original partition (which was left empty when the partition was switched into the staging table).

■ **Union All** Database administrators can load data by storing their main data in a fact table that has a columnstore. Next, create a secondary table to add or update data. Finally, leverage a UNION ALL query so that it returns all of the data between the large fact table with the columnstore index and smaller updateable tables. Periodically load the table from the secondary table into the main table by using partition switching or by disabling and rebuilding the columnstore index. Note that some queries using the UNION ALL strategy might not be as fast as when all the data is in a single table.

Creating a Columnstore Index

Creating a columnstore index is very similar to creating any other traditional SQL Server indexes. You can use the graphical user interface in SQL Server Management Studio or Transact-SQL. Many individuals prefer to use the graphical user interface because they want to avoid typing all of the column names, which is what they have to do when creating the index with Transact-SQL.

A few questions arise frequently when creating a columnstore index. Database administrators often want to know the following:

■ Which columns should be included in the columnstore index?

■ Is it possible to create a clustered columnstore index?

When creating a columnstore index, a database administrator should typically include all of the supported columnstore index columns associated with the table. Note that you don't need to include all of the columns. The answer to the second question is "No." All columnstore indexes must be nonclustered; therefore, a clustered columnstore index is not allowed.

The next sections explain the steps for creating a columnstore index using either of the two methods mentioned: SQL Server Management Studio and Transact-SQL.

Creating a Columnstore Index by Using SQL Server Management Studio

Here are the steps for creating a columnstore index using SQL Server Management Studio (SSMS):

1. In SQL Server Management Studio, use Object Explorer to connect to an instance of the SQL Server Database Engine.

2. In Object Explorer, expand the instance of SQL Server, expand Databases, expand a database, and expand a table in which you would like to create a new columnstore index.

3. Expand the table, right-click the Index folder, choose New Index, and then click Non-Clustered Columnstore Index.

4. On the General tab, in the Index name box, type a name for the new index, and then click Add.

5. In the Select Columns dialog box, select the columns to participate in the columnstore index and then click OK.

6. If desired, configure the settings on the Options, Storage, and Extended Properties pages. If you want to maintain the defaults, click OK to create the index, as illustrated in Figure 3-3.

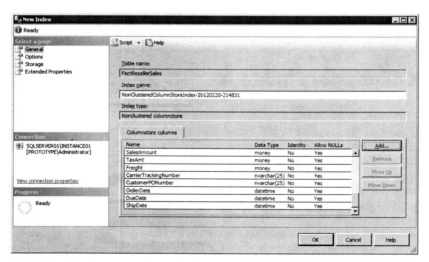

FIGURE 3-3 Creating a nonclustered columnstore index with SSMS

Creating a Columnstore Index Using Transact-SQL

As mentioned earlier, you can use Transact-SQL to create a columnstore index instead of using the graphical user interface in SQL Server Management Studio. The following example illustrates the syntax for creating a columnstore index with Transact-SQL:

```
CREATE [ NONCLUSTERED ] COLUMNSTORE INDEX index_name
    ON <object> ( column  [ ,...n ] )
    [ WITH ( <column_index_option> [ ,...n ] ) ]
    [ ON {
            { partition_scheme_name ( column_name ) }
            | filegroup_name
            | "default"
        }
    ]
[ ; ]
<object> ::=
{
    [database_name. [schema_name ] . | schema_name . ]
     table_name
{

<column_index_option> ::=
{
      DROP_EXISTING = { ON | OFF }
    | MAXDOP = max_degree_of_parallelism
 }
```

The following bullets explain the arguments affiliated with the Transact-SQL syntax to create the nonclustered columnstore index:

- NONCLUSTERED   This argument indicates that this index is a secondary representation of the data.

- COLUMNSTORE   This argument indicates that the index that will be created is a columnstore index.

- *index_name*   This is where you specify the name of the columnstore index to be created. Index names must be unique within a table or view but do not have to be unique within a database.

- *column*   This refers to the column or columns to be added to the index. As a reminder, a columnstore index is limited to 1024 columns.

- ON *partition_scheme_name(column_name)*   Specifies the partition scheme that defines the file groups on which the partitions of a partitioned index are mapped. The *column_name* specifies the column against which a partitioned index will be partitioned. This column must match the data type, length, and precision of the argument of the partition function that the *partition_scheme_name* is using: *partition_scheme_name* or *filegroup*.. If these are not specified and the table is partitioned, the index is placed in the same partition scheme using the same partitioning column as the underlying table.

- ON *filegroup_name* The file group name represents the name of the file group to create the specified index.

- ON "default" Use this argument when you want to create the specified index on the default file group.

- DROP_EXISTING If the parameter ON is used, this option specifies that the pre-existing index should be dropped if it exists. On the flip side, if OFF is used, an error will be displayed if the index already exists.

- MAXDOP = max_degree_of_parallelism You can use the max degree of parallelism option to limit the number of processors to use in parallel plan execution. The purpose of this setting is to override max degree of parallelism configuration option for the duration of the index operation. The value of *1* suppresses parallel plan generation, a value of *greater than 1* restricts the maximum number of processors used, and *0* represents the actual number of processors.

Using Columnstore Indexes

Now that you have created a new columnstore index to speed up your queries, you need to understand how to determine if the columnstore index is actually being used to accelerate your query. The first step is to examine the execution plan associated with query being fired. In the results window of the graphical execution show plan, there is a new Columnstore Index Scan Operator icon, as illustrated in Figure 3-4. The Columnstore Index Scan Operator icon indicates that a columnstore index is being used for index scans.

FIGURE 3-4 New Columnstore Index Scan Operator icon

You can obtain additional columnstore indicators and performance cost details if you highlight the icon. For example, in Figure 3-5, the Physical Operation element indicates Columnstore Index Scan was used and the Storage element is shown as Columnstore.

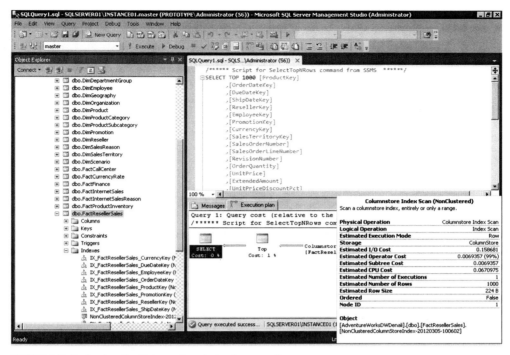

FIGURE 3-5 Reviewing the Columnstore Index Scan results

Using Hints with a Columnstore Index

Finally, if you believe the query can benefit from a columnstore index and the query execution plan is not leveraging it, you can force the query to use a columnstore index. You do this by using the WITH (INDEX(*<indexname>*)) hint where the *<indexname>* argument is the name of the columnstore index you want to force.

The following example illustrates a query with an index hint forcing the use of a columnstore index:

```
SELECT DISTINCT (SalesTerritoryKey)
FROM dbo.FactResellerSales WITH (INDEX (Non-ClusteredColumnStoreIndexSalesTerritory)
GO
```

The next example illustrates a query with an index hint forcing the use of a different index, such as a traditional clustered B-tree index over a columnstore index. For example, let's say there are two indexes on this table called *SalesTerritoryKey*, a clustered index called *ClusteredIndexSalesTerritory*, and a nonclustered columnstore index called *Non-ClusteredColumnStoreIndexSalesTerritory*. Instead of using the columnstore index, the hint forces the query to use the clustered index known as *ClusteredIndexSalesTerritory*:

```
SELECT DISTINCT (SalesTerritoryKey)
FROM dbo.FactResellerSales with (index (ClusteredIndexSalesTerritory)
GO
```

The final example illustrates a query with an index hint option forcing the query to ignore the columnstore index:

```
SELECT DISTINCT (SalesTerritoryKey)
FROM dbo.FactResellerSales
Option (ignore_nonclustered_columnstore_index)
GO
```

Columnstore Index Observations and Best Practices

Without a doubt, the SQL Server product group made major investments in the creation of columnstore indexes to optimize query-processing times affiliated with data-warehouse workloads. The Query Optimization, Query Execution, and Storage Engine teams, in collaboration with the SQL Server Performance Team, SQL Server Customer Advisory Team (SQLCAT), and Microsoft Technology Centers (MTCs) have been testing columnstore indexes with numerous customers since the new technology came into existence. Based on results from these tests, customers have indicated their queries are currently, "Ridiculously fast," and the results are "Mind boggling."

To help you achieve similar results, here are some columnstore index best practices that are based on initial testing results:

- Try to write your queries to match the "sweet spot" for columnstore indexes. Star join queries, for example, are especially fast.

- Whenever possible, avoid constructs that might reduce the benefit of columnstore indexes, such as Outer Joins, Unions, and Union All.

- Include all columns in the columnstore index whenever possible.

- If possible convert decimal/numeric to precision less than or equal to 18.

- Creating indexes requires a considerable amount of memory; therefore, size the memory on the SQL Server system accordingly. A rule of thumb for estimating the memory grant that will be requested for creating a columnstore index is the following:

  Memory grant request in MB = [(4.2 *Number of columns in the CS index) + 68]*DOP + (Number of string cols * 34)

- Ensure your query leverages batch-mode processing whenever possible. It is very important and provides considerable benefits to speed up queries.

- Use integer types whenever possible because they provide more compact representation and more opportunity for early filtering.

- Consider table partitioning to facilitate updates.

- Even when your query cannot use batch mode, you can still experience performance benefits using columnstore indexes by reducing I/O.

Chapter 4

Security Enhancements

The general consensus on the previous version of Microsoft SQL Server was that it delivered exceptional data protection, access control, and compliance. SQL Server 2008 R2 came equipped with numerous capabilities for organizations to leverage including, but not limited to, Transparent Data Encryption (TDE) to protect data at rest, Extensible Key Management (EKM) to fulfill data and key separation, Kerberos Authentication to achieve the strongest authentication, and SQL Server Audit, Policy-Based Management, and change data capture for fulfilling compliance requirements. SQL Server 2008 R2 was unquestionably robust from a security perspective and a fervent leader in the database-platform industry, with the least amount of vulnerabilities and least amount of security patches required to maintain the system. SQL Server 2012 increases SQL Server's popularity as it delivers several security enhancements to help organizations improve their control of data access while maintaining the highest level of data protection and compliance.

Security Enhancements in SQL Server 2012

The following list shows a few of the improvements that will appeal to organizations looking to gain maximum security and control of their database platform:

- Security manageability improvements
    - Default schema for groups
    - User-defined server roles
- Audit enhancements
    - Audit supported on all SKUs
    - Improved resilience
    - User-defined audit event
    - Record filtering
    - T-SQL stack information
- Database authentication enhancement: contained databases authentication

- Crypto changes

  - Hashing algorithms

  - Certificate key length

  - Service master key and database master key encryption changes from 3DES to AES

- Miscellaneous security enhancements

  - Tight Integration with SharePoint and Active Directory

  - Provisioning enhancements

  - New permissions

This chapter describes each of these new security enhancements introduced in SQL Server 2012, starting with security manageability improvements.

Security Manageability Improvements

Two small but very significant changes are introduced to improve security manageability in SQL Server 2012. The first improvement is the default schema for groups, and the second improvement is user-defined server roles.

> **Note** The default schema for groups is the number one security feature request from the SQL Server community on the Microsoft Connect site.

Default Schema for Groups

In the previous versions of SQL Server, it was possible to define a default schema for SQL Server users. This action improved security and simplified administration. The default schema was the first schema searched when resolving the names of objects it referenced. When a default schema for an account did not exist, SQL Server assumed *dbo* was the default schema. One not so minor setback was the inability to define default schemas for Windows groups. As you might have guessed, this caused administrative challenges. If a user was authenticated by SQL Server as a member of a Windows group, a default schema was not associated with the user. If a user created an object such as a table, a new schema was generated and the default name of the schema was the same as the user. As you can imagine, this was a managerial nightmare for database administrators. Just think, if there are 500 users associated with a Windows group and all of the users within the Windows group created objects, a database administrator would need to manage 500 different schemas.

Fortunately, with SQL Server 2012, the security management associated with schemas for groups is not only simplified, but now default schemas can be created for Windows groups. By assigning default schemas to Windows groups, organizations can simplify database schema administration and database schema management. Equally important, the possibility of delegating a schema to the wrong users is thwarted when users change groups. On the flip side, if an incorrect schema is used, query errors are prevented with the new default schema for groups. Finally, unnecessary implicit schema creation is prevented.

A frequent question is raised when discussing schemas. What happens if users are affiliated with more than one Windows group? If no default schema is defined for a user account, SQL Server reviews the sys.principal table and chooses the group with the lowest principal ID as the default schema.

> **Note** With SQL Server 2012, the default schema for a group can be defined by using the DEFAULT_SCHEMA option of CREATE USER or ALTER USER. If no default schema is defined for a group, SQL Server assumes *dbo* is the default schema.

The following Transact-SQL script demonstrates the creation of a default schema for a new Windows group local group:

```
-- Create User based on Local Group [SQL01\CDBUsers]
CREATE USER [SQL01\CDBUsers]
GO
--Allocate Database Role Membership
ALTER ROLE DB_DATAREADER ADD MEMBER [SQL01\CDBUsers]
ALTER ROLE DB_DATAWRITER ADD MEMBER [SQL01\CDBUsers];
GO
--Create Default Schema for Group
CREATE SCHEMA Users AUTHORIZATION [SQL01\CDBUsers];
GO
-- Set the default schema for Group
ALTER USER [SQL01\CDBUsers] WITH DEFAULT_SCHEMA = Users
GO
--Create Table with Group and Default Schema
CREATE TABLE Users.t1(c1 int)
GO
--Insert Value
INSERT INTO Users.t1 VALUES (1)
```

The example creates the local group called [SQL01\CDBUsers], allocates the appropriate database role membership, and creates and then allocates the default schema for the group. The final piece creates a table with the default schema for the group and then inserts one record.

User-Defined Server Roles

Role-based security and separation of duties are strategies that organizations must adhere to in order to achieve compliance with their systems. The main goal of these strategies is to limit system access to authorized users to reduce security threats, compromised security, and operational mistakes while improving the manageability of users and their privileges. These strategies are typically achieved by creating a role, applying permissions to the role, and then assigning members to the roles instead of just applying the same level of permissions to every user or administrator who requires access or administrative rights.

In previous versions of SQL Server, the user-defined role ensured role-based security in order to achieve separation of duties. However, the user-defined role provided separation of duties at the database level, not at the server level. This is because at the server level, administrators had access to fixed roles. As the name implies, unlike the user-defined role, server roles were fixed and database administrators could not customize the securable from a granular perspective. This typically led to database administrators providing members with elevated access, such as the *sysadmin* role, because they couldn't find a fixed role that closely met the business and security requirements. With SQL Server 2012, user-defined roles have been introduced at the server level to increase flexibility, increase manageability, and facilitate compliance with better separation of duties when administering the server.

Creating and Managing Server Roles

When it's time to create server roles use SQL Server Management Studio (SSMS) by expanding the Security folder in Object Explorer and then right-clicking Server Roles and choosing New Server Role. Alternatively, create and manage server roles with the following Transact-SQL statements: CREATE SERVER ROLE, ALTER SERVER ROLE, and DROP SERVER ROLE.

Creating Server Roles with SQL Server Management Studio

The following example demonstrates how to create a server role with SSMS:

1. In SQL Server Management Studio, use Object Explorer to connect to an instance of the SQL Server Database Engine.

2. In Object Explorer, expand the instance of SQL Server, and expand the Security folder.

3. Right-click the Server Roles folder, and select New Server Role.

4. On the General page of the New Server Role Wizard, do the following:

    a. Specify the name of the new server role.

    b. Select the owner for the new server role.

    c. Choose the appropriate securables as they pertain to the new server role.

    d. When a securable is selected, apply explicit permission by selecting the checkbox for one of the following permissions: Grant, With Grant, or Deny. (See Figure 4-1.)

5. On the Members page, add logins that represent individuals or groups to be added to one or more server roles.

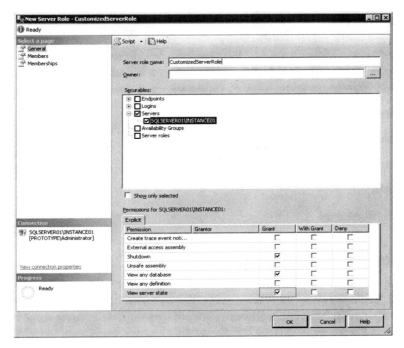

FIGURE 4-1 Applying securables for a new server role tailored toward availability groups

6. Finally, on the Memberships page, because a user-defined server role can be a member of another server role, specify the appropriate server roles that the new server Role will be a member of.

Creating Server Roles with Transact-SQL

Alternatively, use Transact-SQL to create a server role and apply the appropriate permissions, members, and server-role membership. The following Transact-SQL statement creates a new server role called DBAControlServer, adds the Windows Finance group membership, and allows the group to create databases and availability groups. However, this group cannot alter logins or server audits.

```
USE [master]
CREATE SERVER ROLE [DBAControlServer] AUTHORIZATION [sysadmin]
ALTER SERVER ROLE [DBAControlServer] ADD
 MEMBER [PROTOTYPE\Finance]
GRANT CONTROL SERVER TO [DBAControlServer]
GO
GRANT CREATE ANY DATABASE TO [DBAControlServer]
GRANT CREATE AVAILABILITY GROUP TO [DBAControlServer]
DENY ALTER ANY LOGIN TO [DBAControlServer]
DENY ALTER ANY SERVER AUDIT TO [DBAControlServer]
GO
```

Audit Enhancements

With more and more organizations governed by some form of regulatory compliance, the SQL Server product group responsible for security, decided to invest in and enhance the existing audit capabilities affiliated with servers and databases. Enhancements are seen in the following areas:

- Audit supported on all SKUs

- Improved resilience

- User-defined audit event

- Record filtering

- T-SQL stack information

Audit Supported on All SKUs

The Server Audit Specification and Database Audit Specification objects, found in SQL Server 2008 and SQL Server 2008 R2 were common features embraced by many organizations to achieve their audit and compliance needs. However, customers were not very satisfied because these features were available only in the premium SKUs of SQL Server. As such, customers were forced to revert to using SQL Trace to capture auditing information when using the Standard edition of SQL Server. As you can imagine, this brought about many challenges because SQL Trace has limited audit functionality compared to Server and Database Audit Specifications. At times, this could negatively impact performance, and it left organizations without a single, holistic audit solution to achieve their business goals—specifically, goals related to collecting audit data from trace and security logs. Now SQL Trace will eventually be retired, and basic audit functionality will be available on all SQL Server 2012 SKUs.

Improved Resilience

One of the challenges organizations faced with previous versions of SQL Server was the possibility of losing audit data in the event of a failure. For example, if audit logs are being written to a network share and it suddenly becomes unavailable, audit information would no longer be captured. This would negatively affect an organization during a forensic investigation because audit data would be missing. Moreover, if the setting is configured to shut down the server if a failure takes place (ON_FAILURE = SHUTDOWN), a SQL Server systemwide outage can take place. This would not only affect audit data, but also system availability until the problem was resolved.

With SQL Server 2012, the product group responsible for security addressed these concerns by improving resilience associated with audit log failures by introducing new alternatives for Audit Log Failure. These enhancements include the following:

- **On Audit Shut Down Server**   This is a common feature found in the previous versions of SQL Server. If data could not be written to the audit log, the system running SQL Server would automatically shut down. This feature was typically used for organizations looking to achieve the highest form of auditing and security compliance. Note that the login issuing the shutdown must have the Shutdown permission; otherwise, this function will fail and an error message will be raised.

- **On Audit Log Failure: Continue** This new option allows SQL Server to continue operations if data cannot be written to the audit log. During the failure the system continues to attempt to write events to the audit logs; however, note that audit records are not retained during the failure. Use this option only if it is more important to ensure that SQL Server is operational during an audit failure and the organization's corporate policy is not in violation.

- **On Audit Log Failure: Fail Operation** When this option is selected, SQL Server will fail transactions if it cannot write audit events to the audit log. However, transactions that are not governed by audits will continue to process. For example, if you have two tables, such as Customer and Sales, and you audit only the Customer table because it contains sensitive data. A failure will occur to transactions associated with the Customer table; however, because auditing is not enabled on the Sales table, sales data will continue to work during a Log failure.

There are additional auditing enhancements that improve resilience. These enhancements are above and beyond the improvements associated with handling audit log failures, which was discussed in the previous section. These additional audit improvements include the following:

- A new option, Maximum Files (or Max_Files), has been introduced when using a file as the audit destination. Compared to the previous version of SQL Server, which allowed an indeterminate number of log files to be retained, this option caps the amount of audit files to be used without rolling them over.

- With the previous version of the SQL Server, it was challenging to determine whether a query was issued through a stored procedure or an application. The audit log now provides additional Transact-SQL stack frame information; therefore, auditors can differentiate between the methods used.

- The new *sp_audit_write* (Transact-SQL) procedure allows applications to write customized information to the audit log because the SQL Server audit specifications now support a user-defined audit group. A common request was to be able to capture additional information, such as the application user who in many cases connected with a common login.

- To better track user-defined audit events, additional columns are added to *sys.server_file_audits*, *sys.server_audits*, and *sys.fn_get_audit_file*. The potential to filter unwanted audit events has been introduced in SQL Server 2012. For more information, see the WHERE clause in CREATE SERVER AUDIT and ALTER SERVER AUDIT.

- Users affiliated with contained databases can be audited.

Create a New Audit with SSMS

The following steps illustrate some of the new audit functionality, such as the Audit Log Failure and Audit File Maximum Files options, when creating an audit with SQL Server Management Studio.

1. In SQL Server Management Studio, use Object Explorer to connect to an instance of the SQL Server Database Engine.

2. In Object Explorer, expand the instance of SQL Server, and expand the Security folder.

3. Right-click the Audits folder, and select New Audit.

4. On the General page of the Create Audit Wizard, specify the name of the new audit. Then specify the queue delay in milliseconds, and choose the appropriate Audit Log Failure option. Finally, choose one of the Audit Destination options.

5. If you select File as your Audit Log Failure option, specify the following additional items: File Path, Audit File Maximum Limit, Maximum File Size, or Enable Reserve Disk Space (if you want to pre-allocate space on the disk to accommodate for the size of the audit files).

6. Alternatively, use the Audit Properties Filter page to add a predicate (Where clause) to a server audit.

7. Click OK, as illustrated in Figure 4-2, to finalize the creation of the new audit.

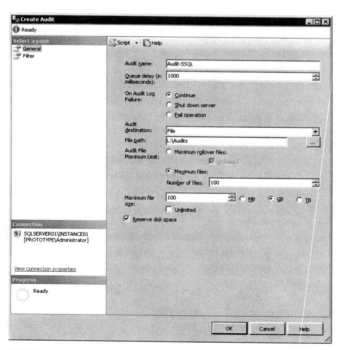

FIGURE 4-2 Creating a new SQL Server Audit with SSMS

As you can see from the illustration, a new audit was created with the option to Fail Operations in cases where SQL Server Audit cannot write to the audit log. In addition, when the maximum number of files is reached, such as 10, any action that causes additional audit events to be generated will fail with an error.

The same example used to create an audit can be generated with Transact-SQL:

```
USE [master]

GO
CREATE SERVER AUDIT [Audit-SQL01]
TO FILE
(   FILEPATH = N'D:\Audits'
    ,MAXSIZE = 10 GB
    ,MAX_FILES = 100
    ,RESERVE_DISK_SPACE = OFF
)
WITH
(   QUEUE_DELAY = 1000
    ,ON_FAILURE = FAIL_OPERATION
)
GO
```

User-Defined Audit Event

The new user-defined audit event allows applications to write custom events into the audit log to allow more flexibility in storing audit information. The following Transact-SQL example illustrates a user-defined audit event in action:

```
CREATE DATABASE app1
GO
USE app1
GO
CREATE SCHEMA app
GO
CREATE TABLE app.accounts
(name nvarchar(128), passwordHash varbinary(128))
INSERT INTO app.accounts (name, passwordHash) values (N'jackr', 0x1234)
INSERT INTO app.accounts (name, passwordHash) values (N'rob', 0x12345)
CREATE PROCEDURE app.sp_establishId
(@name nvarchar(128),
@passwordHash varbinary(128))
AS
BEGIN
    DECLARE @hashMatches bit
    DECLARE @hash varbinary(128)
    DECLARE @additionalInfo nvarchar(512)

    SELECT @hash = passwordHash FROM app.accounts WHERE name = @name;
    IF (@hash = @passwordHash)
```

```
        BEGIN
            SET @hashMatches = 1;
        END
        ELSE
        BEGIN
            SET @hashMatches = 0;
        END
        SELECT @additionalInfo = NTech webuser=' + @name;
        EXEC sys.sp_audit_write 1, @hashMatches, @additionalInfo
        RETURN @hashMatches
END
-- configure audit of logins and user defined events
DECLARE @authOK bit
EXEC @authOK = app.sp_establishId N'jackr', 0x1234
SELECT @authOK
DECLARE @authOK bit
EXEC @authOK = app.sp_establishId N'rob', 0x1234
SELECT @authOK
SELECT * from sys.fn_get_audit_file('c:\auditlogs\*', NULL, NULL)
// cleanup
use master
go
drop database app1
go
```

In this sample code, there are tables of accounts that store middle-tier user names, passwords and a stored procedure called *sp_establishId*, which validates the password. During middle-tier authentication, the middle tier takes a user name and password and hashes the password. It then calls *sp_establishId* to validate the password to authenticate the user. At the end of *sp_establishId*, an audit event is fired, recording the name of the user and whether the password matched or not. By examining these login events and subsequent events on the same session, auditors will be able to determine what events were performed on behalf of middle-tier users even though the middle-tier application server or web server might be authenticating to SQL Server using a service account. After creating the procedure, the script demonstrates the audit by calling *sp_establishId* with different values to show the success and failure cases. With an audit collecting the user-defined audit group and recording to a file in c:\auditlogs, the final select returns the audit records that result from these calls to *sp_establishId*.

Record Filtering

Note that SQL Server auditing is built on top of SQL Server Extended Events (Extended Events). For those who are not familiar with this feature, Extended Events is a general event-handling system for server systems. The Extended Events infrastructure supports the correlation of data from SQL Server and, under certain conditions, the correlation of data from the operating system and database applications. Extended Events provides SQL Server Audit the framework for fast performance and throughput. SQL Server 2012 leverages the Extended Event filtering capability; therefore, it is possible to filter unwanted events before they are written into an audit log. For example, let's say you have an application that accesses a table by using an application account. You might not want to audit this type of activity if the table is accessed by the application account; however, if a user accesses the same table from outside the application, you would want to audit this event. In such a case, you set up a filter to exclude the application account from being audited when accessing the table.

The following example creates a database, a schema, and two tables. The table named DataSchema.SensitiveData will contain confidential data, and access to the table must be recorded in the audit. The table named DataSchema.GeneralData does not contain confidential data. The database audit specification audits access to all objects in the DataSchema schema. The server audit is created with a WHERE clause that limits the server audit to only the SensitiveData table. The server audit presumes an audit folder exists at C:\SQLAudit.

```
CREATE DATABASE TestDB;
GO
USE TestDB;
GO
CREATE SCHEMA DataSchema;
GO
CREATE TABLE DataSchema.GeneralData (ID int PRIMARY KEY, DataField varchar(50) NOT NULL);
GO CREATE TABLE DataSchema.SensitiveData (ID int PRIMARY KEY, DataField varchar(50) NOT NULL);
GO
-- Create the server audit in the master database USE master;
GO
CREATE SERVER AUDIT AuditDataAccess TO FILE ( FILEPATH ='C:\SQLAudit\' ) WHERE object_name =
'SensitiveData' ;
GO
ALTER SERVER AUDIT AuditDataAccess WITH (STATE = ON);
GO
-- Create the database audit specification in the TestDB database USE TestDB;
GO
CREATE DATABASE AUDIT SPECIFICATION [FilterForSensitiveData]
FOR SERVER AUDIT [AuditDataAccess]
ADD (SELECT ON SCHEMA::[DataSchema]
BY [public]) WITH (STATE = ON);
GO
-- Trigger the audit event by selecting from tables
SELECT ID, DataField FROM DataSchema.GeneralData;
SELECT ID, DataField FROM DataSchema.SensitiveData;
GO
-- Check the audit for the filtered content
SELECT * FROM fn_get_audit_file
('C:\SQLAudit\AuditDataAccess_*.sqlaudit',default,default);
GO
```

Database Authentication Enhancements

When working with previous versions of SQL Server, a user needed to log in within the Database Engine to authenticate to a database. The login could be a Windows User account, Windows group account, or a SQL Server account. At times, this dependency caused authentication issues—especially with database portability. For example, if a database was migrated or failed over from one SQL Server instance (source) to another SQL Server instance (target), a database administrator had to ensure that all logins on the source SQL Server instance existed on the target SQL Server instance. If the login did not exist on the target instance, a user, group, or application would no longer be able to authenticate to the database, causing a systemwide outage. Organizations often experienced this challenge during failover when using database mirroring.

SQL Server 2012 addresses these authentication and login dependency challenges by introducing Contained Database Authentication to enhance compliance, authorization, and portability of user databases. Contained Database Authentication allows users to be authenticated directly into a user database without logins that reside in the Database Engine. This feature facilitates better portability of user databases among servers because contained database have no external dependencies.

So how do you authenticate against a user database without a login that resides in the SQL Server Database Engine? When using Contained Database Authentication, user information affiliated with a login, such as a username and password, is stored directly in the user database and not in the master database. Authentication is robust because authenticated users cannot perform database instance-level operations and can perform only data manipulation language (DML) operations inside the user databases. Another benefit of Contained Database Authentication is that it eliminates orphaned or unused logins in the database instance, which was a management challenge many database administrators encountered with the previous versions of SQL Server.

Note Contained Database Authentication allows authentication without logins for both SQL users with passwords and Windows authentication without login. It is a great feature to leverage when implementing AlwaysOn Availability Groups.

Enabling Contained Databases

Contained Database Authentication is a serverwide property and is very straightforward to enable. It can be enabled and disabled via the Advanced Server Properties page in SQL Server Management Studio or with Transact-SQL.

Enable Contained Database Authentication with SQL Server Management Studio

Follow these steps to enable Contained Database Authentication with SQL Server Management Studio:

1. In Object Explorer, right-click a SQL Server instance, and then click Properties.

2. Select the Advanced page, and in the Containment section, set the Enable Contained Databases to *True*, and then click OK.

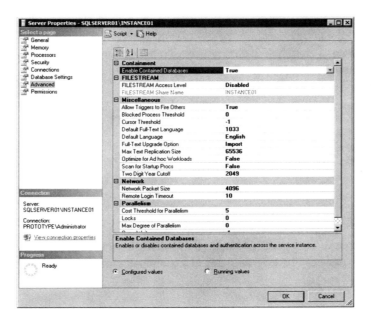

Enable Contained Database Authentication with Transact-SQL

The following Transact-SQL example illustrates how to use the *sp_configure* option to enable Contained Database Authentication for a SQL Server instance:

```
sp_configure 'show advanced options' 1,
GO
sp_configure 'contained database authentication', 1;
GO
RECONFIGURE;
GO
```

When using Transact-SQL, the Contained Database Authentication option is enabled when the option is set to (1) and it allows contained databases to be created or attached to the Database Engine. On the other hand, when the option is set to (0), contained databases are not supported and cannot be created or attached to the Database Engine.

Creating Users

As mentioned earlier, a contained database is an excellent way to decouple the user and database from the SQL Server Database Engine; therefore, an organization can achieve database portability by moving databases between instances of SQL Server. Note there are some special considerations for contained databases. For example, when connecting to a contained database, if the user does not have a login in the master database, the connection string must include the contained database name as the initial catalog. The initial catalog parameter is always required for a contained database user with a password.

Creating a Contained Database User with a Password

The following example creates a contained database user with a password. This example can be executed only in a contained database:

```
USE AdventureWorks2012;
GO
CREATE USER SherryS
WITH PASSWORD='3e4w3cREs$mE_uk'
    , DEFAULT_LANGUAGE=[English]
    , DEFAULT_SCHEMA=[dbo]
GO
```

Creating a Contained Database User for a Domain Login

The following example creates a contained database user for a login named Kyanna in a domain named Prototype. This example can be executed only in a contained database.

```
USE AdventureWorks2012;
GO
CREATE USER [Prototype\Kyanna] ;
GO
```

In many cases, you might want to change a database user who already exists within the Database Engine from a SQL Server authentication login to a contained database user with a password. The following Transact-SQL *sp_migrate_user_to_contained* procedure accomplishes this capability and is illustrated in this example:

```
sp_migrate_user_to_contained
@username = N'<User Name>',
@rename = N'keep_name',
@disablelogin = N'do_not_disable_login' ;
Go
```

> **Note** When migrating users, be careful not to disable or delete all the administrator logins from the instance of SQL Server.

Contained Database Authentication Security Concerns

Although Contained Database Authentication is a great way to achieve database portability, a database administrator must understand that contained databases have some security threats that need to be carefully managed. First, a user can grant and create contained database users within her database without the knowledge of the administrators if she has the ALTER ANY USER permission. Second, if a user gains access to a database via Contained Database Authentication, he has the potential to access other databases within the database engine if these databases have the guest account enabled. It is possible to experience a denial-of-service attack if you create duplicate logins. For example, if a contained database user with a password is created, using the same name as a SQL Server login, and if the SQL Server login connects specifying the contained database as the initial catalog, then the SQL Server login will be unable to connect. Finally, it is beneficial to leverage Windows Authentication whenever possible because Windows Authentication can take advantage Kerberos Authentication and the Windows password policies are far superior and much more robust.

Additional Security Enhancements

As you can see, there have been a tremendous amount of enhancements for security with SQL Server 2012. The following sections outline additional security enhancements that are above and beyond what has already been discussed in this chapter.

Cryptography Changes

More and more organizations are demanding the highest forms of security when it comes to using encryption to protect their data. With SQL Server 2012, the product group responsible for security has greatly enhanced SQL Server cryptography; therefore, organizations can deploy SQL Server with the highest level of confidence when achieving compliance. The major cryptography enhancements include the following:

- **Advanced Encryption Standard (AES)**   AES is a specification for encryption that supersedes DES as the industry standard. SQL Server 2012 uses the AES encryption algorithm to protect the service master key (SMK) and the database master key (DMK).

- **Certificate Key Length**   When creating certificates, the maximum length of private keys imported from an external source is expanded from 3456 bits to 4096 bits.

- **Hashing Algorithms**   In cryptography, SHA-2 is a set of cryptographic hash functions developed by the National Security Agency (NSA). With regard to SQL Server 2012, the HASHBYTES function now supports the SHA2_256 and SHA2_512 algorithms.

- **Binary Support**   You can create certificates from bytes when using the Transact-SQL CREATE CERTIFICATE procedure. The FROM BINARY option allows you to specify the binary description of an ASN-encoded certificate.

Tight Integration with SharePoint and Active Directory

SharePoint and SQL Server are two tightly-coupled technologies to deliver business productivity, business intelligence, and reports to organizations. New SharePoint and Active Directory security modules have been introduced to better secure end-user reports shared and published in SharePoint.

Enhanced security models provide control at row and column levels and allow organizations the ability to better achieve the following:

- Enforce password policies

- Use roles and proxy accounts

- Provide security-enhanced metadata access

- Enhance security features with execution context

Provisioning Enhancements

There are three modifications to further bolster security and role separation during the provisioning process of the SQL Server Database Engine during installation:

- The BUILTIN\administrators and Local System (NT AUTHORITY\SYSTEM) are no longer automatically added in the sysadmin fixed server role. However, local administrators can still access the Database Engine when in single-user mode.

- SQL Server now supports managed service accounts and virtual accounts when installed on Windows 7 or Windows Server 2008 R2.

- The protection of operating services under a per-service SID is now extended to all operating systems.

New Permissions

New permissions are available for securing and managing authorization to elements within the database. These new permissions include the following:

- New GRANT, REVOKE, and DENY permissions to a SEARCH PROPERTY LIST are available.

- New GRANT, REVOKE, and DENY permissions to CREATE SERVER ROLE and ALTER ANY SERVER ROLE.

Chapter 5

Programmability and Beyond-Relational Enhancements

A tremendous number of enhancements have been made to bolster the programmability and beyond-relational paradigm with Microsoft SQL Server 2012. For readers who are unfamiliar with the concept of *beyond relational*, it refers to data and services that go above and beyond the traditional table paradigms found in SQL Server. Some of the beyond-relational enhancements in SQL Server 2012 positively affecting the ability to build applications managing all data include refinements to existing technology features such as full-text search, spatial data, and FILESTREAM. SQL Server 2012 also introduces brand new capabilities, such as FileTables and statistical semantic searches.

Before delivering a high-level overview of these enhancements, this chapter will first review some beyond-relational pain points, some goals of SQL Server 2012 with regard to beyond-relational functionality, and the data and services ecosystem of SQL Server 2012, which is also branded as the *beyond-relational paradigm* in SQL Server.

Pain Points of Using the Beyond Relational Paradigm

Building and maintaining applications with both relational and nonrelational data is an extremely complex task that organizations face today for a variety of reasons. For one thing, it is challenging to integrate structured and nonstructured data because the data is altogether different. Second, structured data usually resides in a relational database whereas unstructured data is stored in file folders or shares on a server. In this situation, there aren't a lot of integration points you can use to correlate the data or stitch it together. This creates management issues for organizations. For example, a database administrator will need to manage two different sets of storage spaces: a relational database that stores structured data, and files shares that host unstructured data. Moreover, each strategy requires a different approach to achieve both high availability and disaster recovery, and there isn't an easy way to keep the structured and unstructured synchronized data. Finally, it's challenging to obtain a single search experience to obtain relevant data across structured and nonstructured formats.

SQL Server 2012 Beyond-Relational Goals

The pain points discussed in the previous section led to the SQL Server development team establishing several goals to enhance the beyond-relational strategy and capabilities in SQL Server 2012. These goals included reducing the cost of managing disparate data, simplifying the development process of applications over all data types, providing management and programming services for all data regardless of whether it is structured or nonstructured, and finally, providing a rich search experience across all data, thereby allowing organizations to unlock rich business insights and build meaningful relationships between the various data being stored.

Additional reasons for investing in the beyond-relational paradigm in SQL Server 2012 can be seen in industry trends. Eighty percent of all data in organizations is not structured, is not stored in databases, is not managed, and cannot scale. SQL Server can give organizations a way to manage unstructured data while providing a rich application experience and the opportunity to gain valuable insight from the data. In addition, this solution can scale to support several hundred million documents.

Before we introduce the new SQL Server 2012 beyond-relational capabilities, let's review SQL Server 2012's unstructured data and services ecosystem.

Rich Unstructured Data and Services Ecosystem

Figure 5-1 provides an overview of the unstructured data and services ecosystem you'll find in SQL Server 2012, including the improvements Microsoft has made over the past few releases of SQL Server. The focus on beyond-relational capabilities started to mature with the release of SQL Server 2008. In the past, you had to use binary large objects (BLOBs) such as varbinary max columns to store unstructured data in tables within a database. This approach provided integration; however, the solution lacked the same streaming speed organizations typically received when documents were stored directly in the Windows file system.

To address these concerns, FILESTREAM was introduced with SQL Server 2008. FILESTREAM enabled SQL Server–based applications to store unstructured data, such as documents and images, on the file system. Applications could leverage the rich streaming APIs and performance of the file system while maintaining transactional consistency between the unstructured data and corresponding structured data. However, FILESTREAM still left a gap for some Windows applications that required the Windows 32 Directory Hierarchy file system to function, because you needed to provide a transactional context to the *FileOpen* command that you could achieve only with the FileStream APIs. Those applications still could not leverage the FILESTREAM feature.

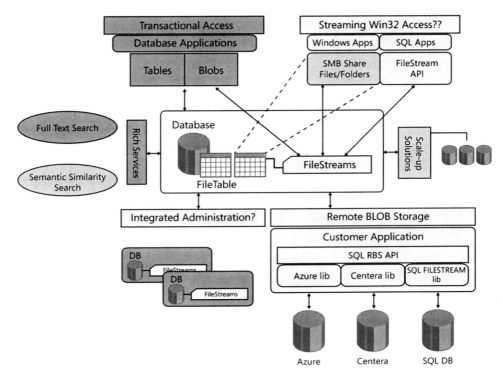

FIGURE 5-1 SQL Server's data and services ecosystem

Another new capability introduced in SQL Server 2008 to address unstructured data was Remote BLOB Store (RBS). The RBS standardized API set allowed for a binary large object (BLOB), such as an office document or video, to be stored within a vendor-independent API. RBS provides a vendor-independent API to store BLOB IDs of documents stored in remote BLOB storage inside the database and to manage the link consistency. The actual size and location of the files and documents were stored in the database instead of by its structure. RBS allowed database administrators to tie the relational data with the RBS data in a loosely coupled manner. RBS does not integrate with full-text search, nor does it provide full transactional integration between the two stores, but it does allow database administrators to build applications in a standardized way, allowing a store to pass data back and forth.

In SQL Server 2012, the beyond-relational paradigm has been enhanced with FileTable, FILESTREAM, some full-text search features, and the ability to conduct semantic searches across unstructured data.

Beyond-Relational Example

An excellent example of a popular beyond-relational database and application is Microsoft Outlook with Microsoft Exchange. The applications store both structured data and unstructured data, and they provide traditional search capabilities that are similar to semantic search by finding related documents across all of the elements in the application. For example, each email message received, including its date and priority, is stored in a structured database, whereas the actual content of the message—including attachments such as pictures and Microsoft PowerPoint presentations—is considered to be unstructured data. By using the search inbox tool, you have the ability to achieve both structured and unstructured search capability across your messages with specific keywords. In addition, semantic search can be achieved by using tools to find related messages in a conversation or related messages from a particular sender. Again, this is an excellent way to illustrate using beyond-relational capabilities with semantic search.

So let's turn our attention to the context of SQL Server 2012 to understand the beyond-relational and semantic-search investments in the Database Engine.

FILESTREAM Enhancements

As mentioned earlier, FILESTREAM enables SQL Server–based applications to store unstructured data, such as documents and images, on the file system. With regard to FILESTREAM in SQL Server 2008 R2, only one storage container per FILESTREAM file group is supported. This limits storage capacity scaling and I/O scaling.

SQL Server 2012 has made investments in FILESTREAM by adding support for multiple storage containers, to achieve maximum scale-up functionality. In addition, the following list articulates other new features associated with FILESTREAM:

- Support for multiple storage containers and file groups:

  - Data Definition Language (DDL) changes to *Create/Alter Database* statements

  - Ability to set *max_size* for the containers

  - Database Console Commands (DBCC) *Shrinkfile Emptyfile* support

- Scaling flexibility

  - Storage scaling by adding additional storage drives

  - I/O scaling with multiple disks

Based on customer testing, the use of multiple disks improved FILESTREAM I/O scalability and performance. Figure 5-2 illustrates the improvements according to tests that compared SQL Server 2012 to SQL Server 2008 R2. This graph shows the stability and throughput improvement with multiple containers (the upward-trending line near the top) vs. using a single container (the rather flat line near the bottom). Improvement using multiple containers (the previously mentioned upward-trending line) also outperforms complicated application-level workarounds using two separate tables for distributing data across two containers (represented by the erratic line showing multiple dips and peaks). The dips in the line representing the more complicated workaround are due to application-code complexity and some testing anomalies. You can ignore those dips.

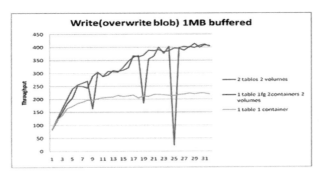

FIGURE 5-2 Graph representing FILESTREAM performance improvements

Performance improvements also can be seen when reading FILESTREAM data with multiple containers. In several cases, when reading a 1-MB file, read throughput performance was five times better.

FileTable

FileTable is a new user table that gets created within a database in the Database Engine. FileTable has a fixed schema and contains FILESTREAM and file attributes. Users can define indexes, constraints, and triggers; however, columns and system-defined constraints cannot be altered or dropped. However, note that a database administrator (DBA) can temporarily disable constraints for bulk-load and debugging scenarios. Each row within the table represents a file or a directory, and the tree integrity is maintained by system-defined constraints. This is because there is a need to enforce the Windows semantics to ensure the solution works the way NTFS expects.

In summary, FileTable provides a specialized table that makes use of the FILESTREAM feature. An organization can now store files and documents in special tables in SQL Server and access them from Windows applications as if they were stored in the file system, without making any changes to the Windows applications, while providing a Server Message Block (SMB) share view and full Win32 application compatibility.

FileTables are a great way for organizations to remove barriers to using SQL Server to store unstructured data that is currently residing as files on file servers.

FileTable Prerequisites

To leverage the FileTable feature, the following prerequisites are required. FILESTREAM must be enabled at the SQL Server Database Engine instance level, Nontransactional Access must be enabled at the database level and a directory must be specified for FileTables at the database level. The following tasks articulate how to ensure the prerequisites are successfully configured.

Enabling FILESTREAM on a SQL Server Instance

As previously mentioned, the first prerequisite step you must complete to leverage FileTable is to enable FILESTREAM on a SQL Server instance. Follow these steps by using SQL Server Configuration Manager:

1. Click Start, All Programs, Microsoft SQL Server 2012, and then click SQL Server Configuration Manager.

2. In the left pane, highlight SQL Server Services.

3. Now in the SQL Server Configuration Manager snap-in, right-click the SQL Server instances in which you want to enable FILESTREAM and click Properties.

4. On the FILESTREAM tab, enable FILESTREAM For Transact-SQL Access.

5. Next, click Enable FILESTREAM For File I/O Access so that you can read and write FILESTREAM data from Windows. In addition, type the name of the Windows share in the Windows Share Name box.

6. Click Allow Remote Clients Access To FILESTREAM Data if there is a need for remote clients to access FILESTREAM data from the share.

7. Click Apply and then click OK to close the SQL Server Properties box.

Next, conduct these steps in SQL Server Management Studio:

1. In SQL Server Management Studio, click New Query to display the Query Editor.

2. In Query Editor, type the following Transact-SQL code:

```
EXEC sp_configure filestream_access_level, 2
RECONFIGURE
```

3. Click Execute.

4. Restart the SQL Server service.

Enabling Directory Name and Nontransactional Access at the Database Level

Conduct these steps in SQL Server Management Studio to enable nontransactional access at the database level:

1. In Object Explorer, connect to the instance of SQL Server you plan on using to create a FileTable.

2. Expand the Database Folder. Then right-click a database in which you would like to enable the Nontransactional Access database option, and Select Properties. For this example, the database used is called FileTableExampleDB.

3. Select the Option Page in the Database Properties dialog box.

4. Specify a Directory Name in the FILESTREAM Directory Name text box, such as FileTableExampleDir.

5. In the FILESTREAM Non-Transacted Access section, specify either the Full or ReadOnly option.

6. Click OK to close the Database Properties dialog box.

As an alternative to using SQL Server Management Studio (SSMS), the following Transact-SQL statement can be used to enable the directory name and nontransactional access at the database level:

```
USE [master]
GO
ALTER DATABASE [FileTableExampleDB] SET FILESTREAM( NON_TRANSACTED_ACCESS = FULL, DIRECTORY_NAME
 = N'FileTableExampleDir' ) WITH NO_WAIT
GO
```

Configuring FILESTREAM File Groups and Database Files, and Specifying a Directory for FileTables

This is an optional step, if you haven't already configured the FILESTREAM file group and database file. In this Transact-SQL example, the FILESTREAM name used is *FileTableExampleDBFileStreamFG* and the database file name used for the FILESTREAM data file type is *FileTableExample_FilestreamFile*, which will reside in the c:\temp folder:

```
USE [master]
GO
ALTER DATABASE [FileTableExampleDB]
ADD FILEGROUP [FileTableExampleDBFilestreamFG] CONTAINS FILESTREAM
GO
ALTER DATABASE [FileTableExampleDB]
ADD FILE ( NAME = N'FileTableExampleDB_FilestreamFile',
 FILENAME = N'C:\Temp\FileTableExampleDB_FilestreamFile' ) TO FILEGROUP
 [FileTableExampleDBFilestreamFG]
GO
USE [FileTableExampleDB]
GO
IF NOT EXISTS (SELECT name FROM sys.filegroups WHERE is_default=1
AND name = N'FileTableExampleDBFilestreamFG')
ALTER DATABASE [FileTableExampleDB]
MODIFY FILEGROUP [FileTableExampleDBFilestreamFG] DEFAULT
GO
USE [FileTableExampleDB]
GO
ALTER DATABASE [FileTableExampleDB]  REMOVE FILE [FIleTableExampleDBFilestreamFile]
GO
```

Creating a FileTable

Now that the prerequisites have been met, it is time to create a FileTable:

1. In Object Explorer, select a database in which you would like to create a FileTable.

2. Expand the objects under the selected database, right-click on the Tables folder, and then select New FileTable.

3. This option opens a new script window that contains a Transact-SQL script template you can customize and run to create a FileTable.

4. Use the Specify Values For Template Parameters option on the Query menu to customize the script easily.

   Alternatively, use this Transact-SQL statement to generate a FileTable called FileTable01:

```
Use FileTableExampleDB
GO
CREATE TABLE FileTable01 AS FILETABLE
GO
```

Copying Documents and Files to the FileTable

The next step is to copy documents and files to the newly created FileTable in Windows Explorer. The can be done with a traditional cut and paste operation, by dragging files to the folder, or with Transact-SQL. In this example, two paint files and two Microsoft Word documents have been copied to the FileTable, as illustrated in Figure 5-3.

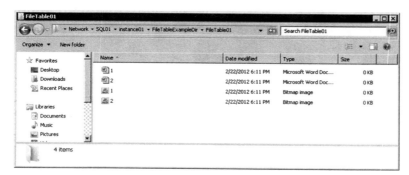

FIGURE 5-3 SMB share illustrating documents exposed by FileTable

Viewing Documents via FileTable in SSMS

The final step is to conduct a *Select* * query on the FileTable that you created in the earlier steps. As illustrated in Figure 5-4, the results window displays the four documents that were copied to the SMB share.

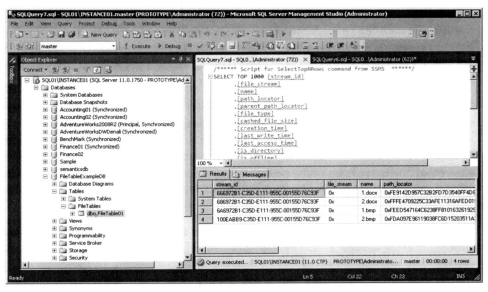

FIGURE 5-4 Viewing documents in a FileTable in SSMS

Managing FileTable

Managing and securing FileTable is similar to a traditional table stored within the SQL Server Database Engine. FileTable data supports backup and restore operations and SQL Server 2012 AlwaysOn Availability Groups for both high availability and disaster recovery.

Full-Text Search

A great deal of time has been invested to improve the full-text search feature in SQL Server 2012. The improved full-text search boasts improvements in performance and scale, new functionality, including a new semantic-similarity search capability. From a performance and scale perspective, full-text search in SQL Server 2012 now scales over 100 million documents; some test cases have even reached 350 million documents. Another significant improvement can be seen in the traditional full-text query performance. It is approximately seven to ten times faster than in the previous versions of SQL Server. In fact, the worse query-response time noted for a large corpus, such as 350 million documents, was less than three seconds, which is very impressive. Additional architecture developments positively affecting scale include improved internal implementation, improved query plans, and preventing queries from blocking index updates.

The new functionality associated with full-text search is divided into three areas:

- **Property Search** Any time a search was initiated in past versions of SQL Server, the entire document was subjected to the search. It was impossible to conduct a keyword search within a title or on other properties. With the ability to create a full-text index in SQL Server 2012, users are now able to conduct property-scoped searches. A property such as the author's name or the title of a work can be made searchable by creating a search property list and then choosing the property or properties you will make searchable. Note, however, that some properties are searchable only in specific types of documents types, such as varbinary, varbinary(max), or image binary data column.

- **Customizable Near**   The Custom Proximity Operator—or *Customizable Near* as it is more commonly referred to—makes it possible for users to specify how close a search term must appear to others before it is considered a successful match. For example, you might want to find documents where the words "cognition" and "psychology" appear within three words of each other. The order in which the keywords must appear can also be indicated. For example, you can specify that "Ross" must appear before "Mistry." Following are other examples that use Customizable Near.

  This first example can be used to specify the distance between the keywords. The parameter *5* specifies that the keywords must be five tokens apart if they are to be considered a successful match:

  ```
  select * from FullTextTable
  where contains(*, 'near((test, Space), 5,false)')
  ```

  Next, if your initial search is unsuccessful, you might want to reduce the distance between the keywords by changing the maximum distance parameter from *5* to another number such as *7*. Here is how to make this change:

  ```
  select * from FullTextTable
  where contains(*, 'near((test, Space), 7,false)')
  ```

  In the final example, not only is the distance between the keywords important, but so is the order in which the words appear. To satisfy both requirements, it is necessary to change the final match order parameter from *false* to *true*:

  ```
  select * from FullTextTable
  where contains(*, 'near((test, Space), 5,true)')
  ```

- **New Wordbreaks**   In SQL Server 2012, the word breakers and stemmers commonly applied by full-text search and semantic search are fully updated. Once your upgrade is complete, repopulate your existing full-text indexes to ensure consistency is maintained between the contents of the indexes and the results of the queries

Statistical Semantic Search

Statistical semantic search extends the full-text search capability by providing semantic insight into textual content. While full-text search lets organizations query specific words in a document, statistical semantic search extracts pertinent key phrases using statistics to identify the meaning of documents and similarities between them. This improvement is achieved by providing deep insight into unstructured documents stored within one or many databases that reside in the Database Engine and by using three Transact-SQL rowset functions to extract results.

You can now include automatic tag extraction, related content discovery, and hierarchical navigation across similar content. For example, you can query the key phrases index to build the taxonomy for an organization or a corpus of documents. Similarly, you might want to query the document similarity index to identify resumes that match a job description.

Before an organization can index documents with semantic search and return relevant results, the documents must be stored in a SQL Server database. The FileTable and FILESTREAM feature in Microsoft SQL Server 2012 is a prerequisite.

Configuring Semantic Search

To leverage the full-text semantic search capability within SQL Server, a database administrator must ensure the Full-Text And Semantic Extractions For Search feature was installed. If you cannot recall whether or not this feature was installed during the initial installation, use the following Transact-SQL statement to determine if the Full-Text and Semantic Extractions for Search feature is installed:

```
Select SERVERPROPERTY('IsFullTextInstalled');
GO
```

If a value of *1* is returned, the Full-Text And Semantic Extractions For Search feature is installed. A return value of *0*, on the other hand, indicates the feature is not installed. If the feature is not installed, you have the option to run setup and add features to an existing instance of SQL Server. Select the Full-Text And Semantic Extractions For Search option on the Feature Selection page as illustrated in Figure 5-5.

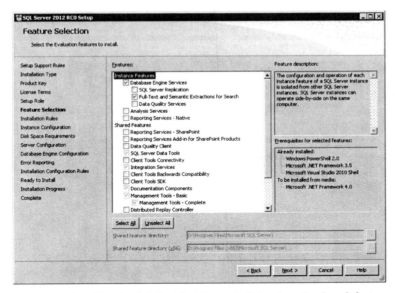

FIGURE 5-5 Installing the Full-Text And Semantic Extractions For Search feature

The next step is to install the semantic language statistics database, which is an external dependency that does not get configured when the Full-Text And Semantic Extractions For Search feature is installed. Most likely, the database does not exist if you just installed the Full-Text And Semantic Extractions For Search feature. To be certain, however, you can check by using the following Transact-SQL statement:

```
SELECT * FROM sys.fulltext_semantic_language_statistics_database;
GO
```

The following steps outline the process to install the semantic language statistics database:

1. Insert the SQL Server 2012 media, and locate the SemanticLanguageDatabase.msi. There are two versions. Choose either the 32-bit or 64-bit version, depending on the SQL Server version being used.

> **Note** The SemanticLanguageDatabase.msi can also be downloaded directly from MSDN.

2. Double-click the SemanticLanguageDatabase.msi to initiate the installation.

3. On the License Agreement page, read and accept the terms in the license agreement and then click Next.

4. On the Feature Selection page, configure the installation path and then click Next.

5. Click Install to commence the installation.

6. Click Finish once the installation is complete.

7. Next, attach the semantic language database data and log files to the SQL Server instance you installed the Full-Text And Semantic Extractions For Search feature. The database is known as semeticsdb and resides in the folder specified in step 4. The default location is c:\Program Files\Microsoft Semantic Language Database.

8. The final step is registering the sematic language statistics database. This can be achieved by leveraging the *sp_fulltext_semantic_register_language_statistics_db* stored procedure and providing the name of the database you attached in the previous step. Here is an example of the Transact-SQL statement that can be used:

```
EXEC sp_fulltext_semantic_register_language_statistics_db @dbname = N'semanticsdb';
GO
```

9. It is now time to start leveraging the statistical semantic search functionality.

Semantic Search Examples

A typical semantic search use-case scenario includes finding key phrases in a document, finding similar documents, or finding related documents. Let's review a few samples.

Find the Key Phrases in a Document

This query is referred to as the *semantickeyphrasetable* (Transact-SQL) function. In the following example, the query locates and retrieves the key phrases in the sample document. A score is assigned to each key phrase based on its statistical significance. This score determines the order in which each key phrase is reported.

```
SET @Title = 'Sample Document.docx'
SELECT @DocID = DocumentID
    FROM Documents
    WHERE DocumentTitle = @Title
SELECT @Title AS Title, keyphrase, score
    FROM SEMANTICKEYPHRASETABLE(Documents, *, @DocID)
    ORDER BY score DESC
```

Find Similar or Related Documents

The next query shown is known as the *semanticsimilaritytable* (Transact-SQL) function and is responsible for locating and retrieving documents that are similar or related to the sample document. The results are scored based on their similarity to the sample document and then displayed in ranked order.

```
SET @Title = 'Sample Document.docx'
SELECT @DocID = DocumentID
    FROM Documents
    WHERE DocumentTitle = @Title
SELECT @Title AS SourceTitle, DocumentTitle AS MatchedTitle,
        DocumentID, score
    FROM SEMANTICSIMILARITYTABLE(Documents, *, @DocID)
    INNER JOIN Documents ON DocumentID = matched_document_key
    ORDER BY score DESC
```

Find the Key Phrases That Make Documents Similar or Related

The following query gets the key phrases that make the two sample documents similar or related to one another. It presents the results in descending order by the score that ranks the weight of each key phrase. This query calls the *semanticsimilaritydetailstable* (Transact-SQL) function.

```
SET @SourceTitle = 'first.docx'
SET @MatchedTitle = 'second.docx'
SELECT @SourceDocID = DocumentID FROM Documents WHERE DocumentTitle = @SourceTitle
SELECT @MatchedDocID = DocumentID FROM Documents WHERE DocumentTitle = @MatchedTitle
SELECT @SourceTitle AS SourceTitle, @MatchedTitle AS MatchedTitle, keyphrase, score
    FROM semanticsimilaritydetailstable(Documents, DocumentContent,
        @SourceDocID, DocumentContent, @MatchedDocID)
    ORDER BY score DESC
```

Spatial Enhancements

Spatial data typically refers to the geographic location of features and boundaries in relation to the Earth, including but not limited to land masses, oceans, and natural or constructed features. Spatial data is stored as coordinates and topology in either a raster or vector data format that can be mapped.

SQL Server 2008 supports geometry and geography data types so that organizations can store spatial vector data. These geometry and geography data types support methods and properties allowed for the creation, comparison, analysis, and retrieval of spatial data. Improvements in spatial support continue with SQL Server 2012, especially with regard to spatial type and performance.

Before discussing the enhancements, it is useful to review the types of spatial-data scenarios commonly used in the industry and the spatial-data vector types supported in the previous version of SQL Server.

Spatial Data Scenarios

Many organizations don't quite understand how to leverage spatial data to increase their competitive advantage. Therefore, this section summarizes typical spatial-data scenarios businesses encounter. These scenarios include real-estate development and analysis, customer-base management and development, environmental-related data-impact analysis and planning, financial and economic analyses in communities, government-based planning and development analysis, market segmentation and analysis, and scientific-research study design and analysis.

Spatial Data Features Supported in SQL Server

Table 5-1 shows the vector data and spatial types supported in SQL Server 2008. These included point, multipoint, linestring, multilinestring, polygon, multipolygon, and collections of these shapes. Each of these vector data types is ISO 19125 compliant and also compliant with the open-geospatial consortium simple features for open SQL.

TABLE 5-1 Spatial Data Features Supported in SQL Server

Spatial Data Features	Visual Representation of Spatial Data Features	Possible Use Cases
POINT		Can be used to draw a tree, pole, hydrant, value
MULTIPOINT		Can be used to draw a tree, pole, hydrant, value
LINESTRING		Can be used to draw a road, river, railway, pipeline

Spatial Data Features	Visual Representation of Spatial Data Features	Possible Use Cases
MULTILINESTRING		Can be used to draw a road, river, railway, pipeline
POLYGON		Can be used to draw a cadastre, park, administrative boundary
MULTIPOLYGON		Can be used to draw a Ccadastre, park, administrative boundary
COLLECTION		A collection of all spatial data features can be used to draw graphics and markups

Raster data such as satellite imagery and digitized aerial photos, on the other hand, are supported in SQL Server 2008 as unstructured data. The images could be stored in SQL Server as BLOBs. Unfortunately, semantics cannot be directly obtained from this data.

Spatial Type Improvements

With the launch of SQL Server 2012, new spatial type features are introduced. Specifically, there are new subtypes for geometry and geography data types that support circular arc segments such as circular strings, compound curves, and curve polygons. All of the methods support circular arcs, including circular-arc support on an ellipsoid. Table 5-2 illustrates the new spatial data features in SQL Server 2012.

Note SQL Server 2012 is the first commercial database system to support spherical circular arcs.

TABLE 5-2 New Spatial Data Features in SQL Server 2012

Circular strings	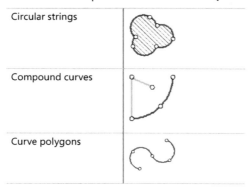
Compound curves	
Curve polygons	

Here are descriptions of the elements shown in the preceding table:

- **Circular strings**   Circular data support includes circular strings. Circular strings are defined by at least three points. The first and third points denote the start and end of the line, respectively, while the second coordinate, which appears in between the first and third points, signifies the arc of the line. The third point of a circular string can be used to link another circular string and, in so doing, transforms the third coordinate of the first circular string into the first point of the linked circular string. Your linked circular Strings are likely valid if they have an odd number of points. The following is an example:

```
DECLARE @g GEOGRAPHY;
SET @g = GEOGRAPHY::STGeomFromText('
  CIRCULARSTRING(0 -23.43778, 0 0, 0 23.43778)
',4326);

DECLARE @g GEOGRAPHY;
SET @g = GEOGRAPHY::STGeomFromText('
  COMPOUNDCURVE(
    CIRCULARSTRING(0 -23.43778, 0 0, 0 23.43778),
    CIRCULARSTRING(0 23.43778, -45 23.43778, -90 23.43778),
    CIRCULARSTRING(-90 23.43778, -90 0, -90 -23.43778),
    CIRCULARSTRING(-90 -23.43778, -45 -23.43778, 0 -23.43778))
',4326);
```

- **Compound curves**   A compound curve is a collection of either circular strings or a combination of circular and linear strings. The end point of each string in the collection must be reflected in the starting point of the next string. Here is an example of a compound curve made up of circular strings and linear strings. Note that linear strings do not contain a keyword.:

```
DECLARE @g GEOGRAPHY;
SET @g = GEOGRAPHY::STGeomFromText('
  COMPOUNDCURVE(
    (0 -23.43778, 0 23.43778),     --Linear Segment*
    CIRCULARSTRING(0 23.43778, -45 23.43778, -90 23.43778),
    (-90 23.43778, -90 -23.43778), --Linear Segment*
```

```
    CIRCULARSTRING(-90 -23.43778, -45 -23.43778, 0 -23.43778))
  ',4326);
```

- **Curve polygons**   A curved polygon is made up of at least one ring representing a closed shape and can consist of holes in the shape representing inner rings. Unlike ordinary polygons, the ring of curve polygons can include circular strings, compound curves or both. In a given ring, the end point of each string in the collection must be reflected in the starting point of the next string. The following example provides a clear illustration:

```
DECLARE @g GEOGRAPHY;
SET @g = GEOGRAPHY::STGeomFromText('
  CURVEPOLYGON(
    COMPOUNDCURVE(
      (0 -23.43778, 0 23.43778),
      CIRCULARSTRING(0 23.43778, -45 23.43778, -90 23.43778),
      (-90 23.43778, -90 -23.43778),
      CIRCULARSTRING(-90 -23.43778, -45 -23.43778, 0 -23.43778)
    )
  )
  ',4326);
```

Additional Spatial Improvements

This chapter focused on a high-level overview of the most important features in the discussion of spatial enhancements. However, a great number of other spatial improvements have been made in SQL Server 2012—enough to keep readers immersed in the topic for hours. If you are interested in learning more, you can read a 30-page whitepaper titled "New Spatial Features in SQL Server 2012." This whitepaper goes into detail on all the new spatial improvements. Some other spatial improvements you should consider reading more about include the following:

- Spatial index improvements

  - Autogrid spatial index

  - New spatial index hint

  - Spatial index compression

  - Improved "Create Spatial Index" time for point data

- Spatial types improvements

  - New circular arcs feature

  - New and updated methods and aggregates for all types

  - Improved precision

  - Geography type-specific modifications

- Performance improvements

  - New nearest-neighbor query plan

  - Other performance improvements, including optimized relations for point operators, STBuffer optimization, new spatial helper stored procedures, general engine improvements related to spatial types, and changes to the client-side library.

Extended Events

SQL Server Extended Events is a general event-handling system for server systems. The following new Extended Events have been introduced with SQL Server 2012 to further support the correlation of data from SQL Server and, under certain conditions, the correlation of data from the operating system and database applications:

- **page_allocated**   The fields include *worker_address, number_pages, page_size, page_location, allocator_type, page_allocator_type*, and *pool_id*.

- **page_freed**   The fields include *worker_address, number_pages, page_size, page_location, allocator_type, page_allocator_type*, and *pool_id*.

- **allocation_failure**   The fields include *worker_address, failure_type, allocation_failure_type, resource_size, pool_id*, and *factor*.

Unlike the items included in the preceding list, the following Extended Events have been modified to provide better functionality in SQL Server 2012:

- *resource_monitor_ring_buffer_record*:

  - Fields removed include *single_pages_kb* and *multiple_pages_kb*.

  - Fields added include *target_kb* and *pages_kb*.

- *memory_node_oom_ring_buffer_recorded*:

  - Fields removed include *single_pages_kb* and *multiple_pages_kb*.

  - Fields added include *target_kb* and *pages_kb*.

Business Intelligence Development

CHAPTER 6

Integration Services

Since its initial release in Microsoft SQL Server 2005, Integration Services has had incremental changes in each subsequent version of the product. However, those changes were trivial in comparison to the number of enhancements, performance improvements, and new features introduced in SQL Server 2012 Integration Services. This product overhaul affects every aspect of Integration Services, from development to deployment to administration.

Developer Experience

The first change that you notice as you create a new Integration Services project is that Business Intelligence Development Studio (BIDS) is now a Microsoft Visual Studio 2010 shell called SQL Server Data Tools (SSDT). The Visual Studio environment alone introduces some slight user-interface changes from the previous version of BIDS. However, several more significant interface changes of note are specific to SQL Server Integration Services (SSIS). These enhancements to the interface help you to learn about the package-development process if you are new to Integration Services, and they enable you to develop packages more easily if you already have experience with Integration Services. If you are already an Integration Services veteran, you will also notice the enhanced appearance of tasks and data flow components with rounded edges and new icons.

Add New Project Dialog Box

To start working with Integration Services in SSDT, you create a new project by following the same steps you use to perform the same task in earlier releases of Integration Services. From the File menu, point to New, and then select Project. The Add New Project dialog box displays. In the Installed Templates list, you can select the type of Business Intelligence template you want to use and then view only the templates related to your selection, as shown in Figure 6-1. When you select a template, a description of the template displays on the right side of the dialog box.

FIGURE 6-1 New Project dialog box displaying installed templates

There are two templates available for Integration Services projects:

- **Integration Services Project**   You use this template to start development with a blank package to which you add tasks and arrange those tasks into workflows. This template type was available in previous versions of Integration Services.

- **Integration Services Import Project Wizard**   You use this wizard to import a project from the Integration Services catalog or from a project deployment file. (You learn more about project deployment files in the "Deployment Models" section of this chapter.) This option is useful when you want to use an existing project as a starting point for a new project, or when you need to make changes to an existing project.

Note The Integration Services Connections Project template from previous versions is no longer available.

General Interface Changes

After creating a new package, several changes are visible in the package-designer interface, as you can see in Figure 6-2:

- **SSIS Toolbox**   You now work with the SSIS Toolbox to add tasks and data flow components to a package, rather than with the Visual Studio toolbox that you used in earlier versions of Integration Services. You learn more about this new toolbox in the "SSIS Toolbox" section of this chapter.

- **Parameters**   The package designer includes a new tab to open the Parameters window for a package. Parameters allow you to specify run-time values for package, container, and task properties or for variables, as you learn in the "Parameters" section of this chapter.

- **Variables button**   This new button on the package designer toolbar provides quick access to the Variables window. You can also continue to open the window from the SSIS menu or by right-clicking the package designer and selecting the Variables command.

- **SSIS Toolbox button**   This button is also new in the package-designer interface and allows you to open the SSIS Toolbox when it is not visible. As an alternative, you can open the SSIS Toolbox from the SSIS menu or by right-clicking the package designer and selecting the SSIS Toolbox command.

- **Getting Started**   This new window displays below the Solution Explorer window and provides access to links to videos and samples you can use to learn how to work with Integration Services. This window includes the Always Show In New Project check box, which you can clear if you prefer not to view the window after creating a new project. You learn more about using this window in the next section, "Getting Started Window."

- **Zoom control**   Both the control flow and data flow design surface now include a zoom control in the lower-right corner of the workspace. You can zoom in or out to a maximum size of 500 percent of the normal view or to a minimum size of 10 percent, respectively. As part of the zoom control, a button allows you to resize the view of the design surface to fit the window.

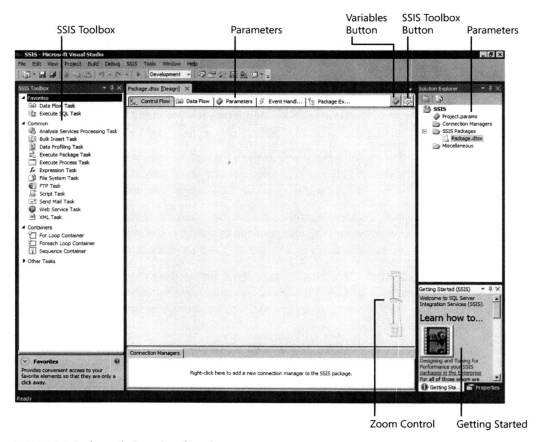

FIGURE 6-2 Package-designer interface changes

Getting Started Window

As explained in the previous section, the Getting Started window is new to the latest version of Integration Services. Its purpose is to provide resources to new developers. It will display automatically when you create a new project unless you clear the check box at the bottom of the window. You must use the Close button in the upper-right corner of the window to remove it from view. Should you want to access the window later, you can choose Getting Started on the SSIS menu or right-click the design surface and select Getting Started.

In the Getting Started window, you find several links to videos and Integration Services samples. To use the links in this window, you must have Internet access. By default, the following topics are available:

■ **Designing and Tuning for Performance Your SSIS Packages in the Enterprise** This link provides access to a series of videos created by the SQL Server Customer Advisory Team

(SQLCAT) that explain how to monitor package performance and techniques to apply during package development to improve performance.

- **Parameterizing the Execute SQL Task in SSIS**   This link opens a page from which you can access a brief video explaining how to work with parameterized SQL statements in Integration Services.

- **SQL Server Integration Services Product Samples**   You can use this link to access the product samples available on Codeplex, Microsoft's open-source project-hosting site. By studying the package samples available for download, you can learn how to work with various control flow tasks or data flow components.

> **Note** Although the videos and samples accessible through these links were developed for previous versions of Integration Services, the principles remain applicable to the latest version. When opening a sample project in SSDT, you will be prompted to convert the project.

You can customize the Getting Started window by adding your own links to the SampleSites.xml file located in the Program Files (x86)\Microsoft SQL Server\110\DTS\Binn folder.

SSIS Toolbox

Another new window for the package designer is the SSIS Toolbox. Not only has the overall interface been improved, but you will find there is also added functionality for arranging items in the toolbox.

Interface Improvement

The first thing you notice in the SSIS Toolbox is the updated icons for most items. Furthermore, the SSIS Toolbox includes a description for the item that is currently selected, allowing you to see what it does without needing to add it first to the design surface. You can continue to use drag-and-drop to place items on the design surface, or you can double-click the item. However, the new behavior when you double-click is to add the item to the container that is currently selected, which is a welcome time-saver for the development process. If no container is selected, the item is added directly to the design surface.

Item Arrangement

At the top of the SSIS Toolbox, you will see two new categories, Favorites and Common, as shown in Figure 6-3. All categories are populated with items by default, but you can move items into another category at any time. To do this, right-click the item and select Move To Favorites or Move To Common. If you are working with control flow items, you have Move To Other Tasks as another choice, but if you are working with data flow items, you can choose Move To Other Sources, Move To Other Transforms, or Move To Other Destinations. You will not see the option to move an item to the category in which it already exists, nor are you able to use drag-and-drop to move items manually. If you decide to start over and return the items to their original locations, select Restore Toolbox Defaults.

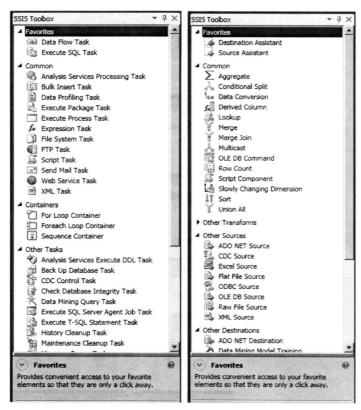

FIGURE 6-3 SSIS Toolbox for control flow and data flow

Shared Connection Managers

If you look carefully at the Solution Explorer window, you will notice that the Data Sources and Data Source Views folders are missing, and have been replaced by a new file and a new folder. The new file is Project.params, which is used for package parameters and is discussed in the "Package Parameters" section of this chapter. The Connections Managers folder is the new container for connection managers that you want to share among multiple packages.

> **Note** If you create a Cache Connection Manager, Integration Services shares the in-memory cache with child packages using the same cache as the parent package. This feature is valuable for optimizing repeated lookups to the same source across multiple packages.

To create a shared connection manager, follow these steps:

1. Right-click the Connections Managers folder, and select New Connection Manager.

2. In the Add SSIS Connection Manager dialog box, select the desired connection-manager type and then click the Add button.

3. Supply the required information in the editor for the selected connection-manager type, and then click OK until all dialog boxes are closed.

A file with the CONMGR file extension displays in the Solution Explorer window within the Connections Managers folder. In addition, the file also appears in the Connections Managers tray in the package designer in each package contained in the same project. It displays with a (project) prefix to differentiate it from package connections. If you select the connection manager associated with one package and change its properties, the change affects the connection manager in all other packages.

If you change your mind about using a shared connection manager, you can convert it to a package connection. To do this, right-click the connection manager in the Connection Managers tray, and select Convert To Package Connection. The conversion removes the CONMGR file from the Connections Manager folder in Solution Explorer and from all other packages. Only the package in which you execute the conversion contains the connection. Similarly, you can convert a package connection to a shared connection manager by right-clicking the connection manager in Solution Explorer and selecting Convert To Project Connection.

Scripting Engine

The scripting engine in SSIS is an upgrade to Visual Studio Tools for Applications (VSTA) 3.0 and includes support for the Microsoft .NET Framework 4.0. When you edit a script task in the control flow or a script component in the data flow, the VSTA integrated development environment (IDE) continues to open in a separate window, but now it uses a Visual Studio 2010 shell. A significant improvement to the scripting engine is the ability to use the VSTA debug features with a Script component in the data flow.

> **Note** As with debugging the Script task in the control flow, you must set the *Run64BitRunTime* project property to *False* when you are debugging on a 64-bit computer.

Expression Indicators

The use of expressions in Integration Services allows you, as a developer, to create a flexible package. Behavior can change at run-time based on the current evaluation of the expression. For example, a common reason to use expressions with a connection manager is to dynamically change connection strings to accommodate the movement of a package from one environment to another, such as from development to production. However, earlier versions of Integration Services did not provide an easy way to determine whether a connection manager relies on an expression. In the latest version, an extra icon appears beside the connection manager icon as a visual cue that the connection manager uses expressions, as you can see in Figure 6-4.

 AdventureWorks

FIGURE 6-4 A visual cue that the connection manager uses an expression

This type of expression indicator also appears with other package objects. If you add an expression to a variable or a task, the expression indicator will appear on that object.

Undo and Redo

A minor feature, but one you will likely appreciate greatly, is the newly added ability to use Undo and Redo while developing packages in SSDT. You can now make edits in either the control flow or data flow designer surface, and you can use Undo to reverse a change or Redo to restore a change you had just reversed. This capability also works in the Variables window, and on the Event Handlers and Parameters tabs. You can also use Undo and Redo when working with project parameters.

To use Undo and Redo, click the respective buttons in the standard toolbar. You can also use Ctrl+Z and Ctrl+Y, respectively. Yet another option is to access these commands on the Edit menu.

> **Note** The Undo and Redo actions will not work with changes you make to the SSIS Toolbox, nor will they work with shared connection managers.

Package Sort By Name

As you add multiple packages to a project, you might find it useful to see the list of packages in Solution Explorer display in alphabetical order. In previous versions of Integration Services, the only way to re-sort the packages was to close the project and then reopen it. Now you can easily sort the list of packages without closing the project by right-clicking the SSIS Packages folder and selecting Sort By Name.

Status Indicators

After executing a package, the status of each item in the control flow and the data flow displays in the package designer. In previous versions of Integration Services, the entire item was filled with green to indicate success or red to indicate failure. However, for people who are color-blind, this use of color was not helpful for assessing the outcome of package execution. Consequently, the user interface now displays icons in the upper-right corner of each item to indicate success or failure, as shown in Figure 6-5.

FIGURE 6-5 Item status indicators appear in the upper-right corner

Control Flow

Apart from the general enhancements to the package-designer interface, there are three notable updates for the control flow. The Expression Task is a new item available to easily evaluate an expression during the package workflow. In addition, the Execute Package Task has some changes to make it easier to configure the relationship between a parent package and child package. Another new item is the Change Data Capture Task, which we discuss in the "Change Data Capture Support" section of this chapter.

Expression Task

Many of the developer experience enhancements in Integration Services affect both control flow and data flow, but there is one new feature that is exclusive to control flow. The Expression Task is a new item available in the SSIS Toolbox when the control flow tab is in focus. The purpose of this task is to make it easier to assign a dynamic value to a variable.

Rather than use a Script Task to construct a variable value at runtime, you can now add an Expression Task to the workflow and use the SQL Server Integration Services Expression Language. When you edit the task, the Expression Builder opens. You start by referencing the variable and including the equals sign (=) as an assignment operator. Then provide a valid expression that resolves to a single value with the correct data type for the selected variable. Figure 6-6 illustrates an example of a variable assignment in an Expression Task.

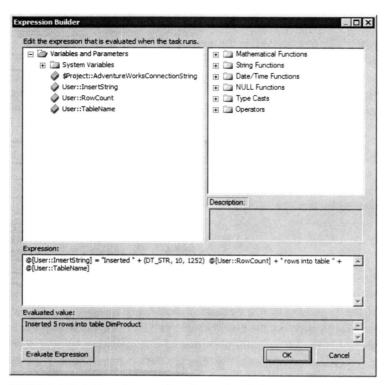

FIGURE 6-6 Variable assignment in an Expression Task

Note The Expression Builder is an interface commonly used with other tasks and data flow components. Notice in Figure 6-6 that the list on the left side of the dialog box includes both variables and parameters. In addition, system variables are now accessible from a separate folder rather than listed together with user variables.

Execute Package Task

The Execute Package Task has been updated to include a new property, *ReferenceType*, which appears on the Package page of the Execute Package Task Editor. You use this property to specify the location of the package to execute. If you select External Reference, you configure the path to the child package just as you do in earlier versions of Integration Services. If you instead select Project Reference, you then choose the child package from the drop-down list.

In addition, the Execute Package Task Editor has a new page for parameter bindings, as shown in Figure 6-7. You use this page to map a parameter from the child package to a parameter value or variable value in the parent package.

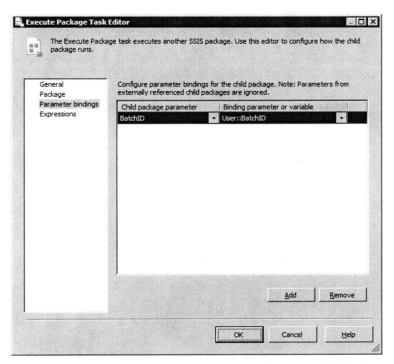

FIGURE 6-7 Parameter bindings between a parent package and a child package

Data Flow

The data flow also has some significant updates. It has some new items, such as the Source and Destination assistants and the DQS Cleansing transformation, and there are some improved items such as the Merge and Merge Join transformation. In addition, there are several new data flow components resulting from a partnership between Microsoft and Attunity for use when accessing Open Database Connectivity (ODBC) connections and processing change data capture logs. We describe the change data capture components in the "Change Data Capture Support" section of this chapter. Some user interface changes have also been made to simplify the process and help you get your job done faster when designing the data flow.

Sources and Destinations

Let's start exploring the changes in the data flow by looking at sources and destinations.

Source and Destination Assistants

The Source Assistant and Destination Assistant are two new items available by default in the Favorites folder of the SSIS Toolbox when working with the data flow designer. These assistants help you easily create a source or a destination and its corresponding connection manager.

To create a SQL Server source in a data flow task, perform the following steps:

1. Add the Source Assistant to the data flow design surface by using drag-and-drop or by double-clicking the item in the SSIS Toolbox, which opens the Source Assistant - Add New Source dialog box as shown here:

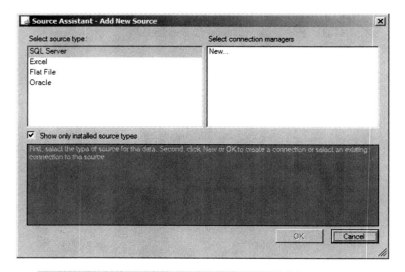

 Note Clear the Show Only Installed Source Types check box to display the additional available source types that require installation of one of the following client providers: DB2, SAP BI, Sybase, or Teradata.

2. In the Select Connection Managers list, select an existing connection manager or select New to create a new connection manager, and click OK.

3. If you selected the option to create a new connection manager, specify the server name, authentication method, and database for your source data in the Connection Manager dialog box, and click OK.

    The new data source appears on the data flow design surface, and the connection manager appears in the Connection Managers tray. You next need to edit the data source to configure the data-access mode, columns, and error output.

ODBC Source and Destination

The ODBC Source and ODBC Destination components, shown in Figure 6-8, are new to Integration Services in this release and are based on technology licensed by Attunity to Microsoft. Configuration of these components is similar to that of OLE DB sources and destinations. The ODBC Source supports Table Name and SQL Command as data-access modes, whereas data-access modes for the ODBC Destination are Table Name – Batch and Table Name – Row By Row.

FIGURE 6-8 ODBC Source and ODBC Destination data flow components

Flat File Source

You use the Flat File source to extract data from a CSV or TXT file, but there were some data formats that this source did not previously support without requiring additional steps in the extraction process. For example, you could not easily use the Flat File source with a file containing a variable number of columns. Another problem was the inability to use a character that was designated as a qualifier as a literal value inside a string. The current version of Integration Services addresses both of these problems.

- **Variable columns**   A file layout with a variable number of columns is also known as a *ragged-right delimited file*. Although Integration Services supports a ragged-right format, a problem arises when one or more of the rightmost columns do not have values and the column delimiters for the empty columns are omitted from the file. This situation commonly occurs when the flat file contains data of mixed granularity, such as header and detail transaction records. Although a row delimiter exists on each row, Integration Services ignored the row delimiter and included data from the next row until it processed data for each expected column. Now the Flat File source correctly recognizes the row delimiter and handles the missing columns as NULL values.

 Note If you expect data in a ragged-right format to include a column delimiter for each missing column, you can disable the new processing behavior by changing the *AlwaysCheckForRowDelimiters* property of the Flat File connection manager to *False*.

- **Embedded qualifiers**   Another challenge with the Flat File source in previous versions of Integration Services was the use of a qualifier character inside a string encapsulated within qualifiers. For example, consider a flat file that contains the names of businesses. If a single quote is used as a text qualifier but also appears within the string as a literal value, the common practice is to use another single quote as an escape character, as shown here.

```
ID,BusinessName
404,'Margie''s Travel'
406, 'Kickstand Sellers'
```

In the first data row in this example, previous versions of Integration Services would fail to interpret the second apostrophe in the *BusinessName* string as an escape character, and instead would process it as the closing text qualifier for the column. As a result, processing of the flat file returned an error because the next character in the row is not a column delimiter. This problem is now resolved in the current version of Integration Services with no additional configuration required for the Flat File source.

Transformations

Next we turn our attention to transformations.

Pivot Transformation

The user interface of the Pivot transformation in previous versions of Integration Services was a generic editor for transformations, and it was not intuitive for converting input rows into a set of columns for each row. The new custom interface, shown in Figure 6-9, provides distinctly named fields and includes descriptions describing how each field is used as input or output for the pivot operation.

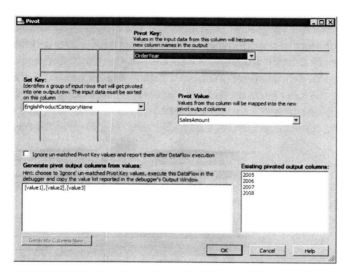

FIGURE 6-9 Pivot transformation editor for converting a set of rows into columns of a single row

Row Count Transformation

Another transformation having a generic editor in previous versions is the Row Count transformation. The sole purpose of this transformation is to update a variable with the number of rows passing through the transformation. The new editor makes it very easy to change the one property for this transformation that requires configuration, as shown in Figure 6-10.

FIGURE 6-10 Row Count transformation editor for storing the current row count in a variable

Merge and Merge Join Transformations

Both the Merge transformation and the Merge Join transformation allow you to collect data from two inputs and produce a single output of combined results. In earlier versions of Integration Services, these transformations could result in excessive memory consumption by Integration Services when data arrives from each input at different rates of speed. The current version of Integration Services better accommodates this situation by introducing a mechanism for these two transformations to better manage memory pressure in this situation. This memory-management mechanism operates automatically, with no additional configuration of the transformation necessary.

Note If you develop custom data flow components for use in the data flow and if these components accept multiple inputs, you can use new methods in the *Microsoft.SqlServer.Dts.Pipeline* namespace to provide similar memory pressure management to your custom components. You can learn more about implementing these methods by reading "Developing Data Flow Components with Multiple Inputs," located at *http://msdn.microsoft.com/en-us/library/ff877983(v=sql.110).aspx*.

DQS Cleansing Transformation

The DQS Cleansing transformation is a new data flow component you use in conjunction with Data Quality Services (DQS). Its purpose is to help you improve the quality of data by using rules that are established for the applicable knowledge domain. You can create rules to test data for common misspellings in a text field or to ensure that the column length conforms to a standard specification.

To configure the transformation, you select a data-quality-field schema that contains the rules to apply and then select the input columns in the data flow to evaluate. In addition, you configure error handling. However, before you can use the DQS Cleansing transformation, you must first install and configure DQS on a server and create a knowledge base that stores information used to detect data anomalies and to correct invalid data, which deserves a dedicated chapter. We explain not only how DQS works and how to get started with DQS, but also how to use the DQS Cleansing transformation in Chapter 7, "Data Quality Services."

Column References

The pipeline architecture of the data flow requires precise mapping between input columns and output columns of each data flow component that is part of a Data Flow Task. The typical workflow during data flow development is to begin with one or more sources, and then proceed with the addition of new components in succession until the pipeline is complete. As you plug each subsequent component into the pipeline, the package designer configures the new component's input columns to match the data type properties and other properties of the associated output columns from the preceding component. This collection of columns and related property data is also known as *metadata*.

If you later break the path between components to add another transformation to pipeline, the metadata in some parts of the pipeline could change because the added component can add columns, remove columns, or change column properties (such as convert a data type). In previous versions of Integration Services, an error would display in the data flow designer whenever metadata became invalid. On opening a downstream component, the Restore Invalid Column References editor displayed to help you correct the column mapping, but the steps to perform in this editor were not always intuitive. In addition, because of each data flow component's dependency on access to metadata, it was often not possible to edit the component without first attaching it to an existing component in the pipeline.

Components Without Column References

Integration Services now makes it easier to work with disconnected components. If you attempt to edit a transformation or destination that is not connected to a preceding component, a warning message box displays: "This component has no available input columns. Do you want to continue editing the available properties of this component?"

After you click Yes, the component's editor displays and you can configure the component as needed. However, the lack of input columns means that you will not be able to fully configure the component using the basic editor. If the component has an advanced editor, you can manually add input columns and then complete the component configuration. However, it is usually easier to use the interface to establish the metadata than to create it manually.

Resolve References Editor

The current version of Integration Services also makes it easier to manage the pipeline metadata if you need to add or remove components to an existing data flow. The data flow designer displays an error indicator next to any path that contains unmapped columns. If you right-click the path between components, you can select Resolve References to open a new editor that allows you to map the output columns to input columns by using a graphical interface, as shown in Figure 6-11.

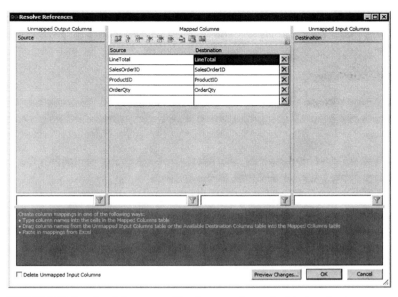

FIGURE 6-11 Resolve References editor for mapping output to input columns

In the Resolve References editor, you can drag a column from the Unmapped Output Columns list and add it to the Source list in the Mapped Columns area. Similarly, you can drag a column from the Unmapped Input Columns area to the Destination list to link the output and input columns. Another option is to simply type or paste in the names of the columns to map.

> **Tip** When you have a long list of columns in any of the four groups in the editor, you can type a string in the filter box below the list to view only those columns matching the criteria you specify. For example, if your input columns are based on data extracted from the Sales.SalesOrderDetail table in the AdventureWorks2008R2 database, you can type **unit** in the filter box to view only the UnitPrice and UnitPriceDiscount columns.

You can also manually delete a mapping by clicking the Delete Row button to the right of each mapping. After you have completed the mapping process, you can quickly delete any remaining unmapped input columns by selecting the Delete Unmapped Input Columns check box at the bottom of the editor. By eliminating unmapped input columns, you reduce the component's memory requirements during package execution.

Collapsible Grouping

Sometimes the data flow contains too many components to see at one time in the package designer, depending on your screen size and resolution. Now you can consolidate data flow components into groups and expand or collapse the groups. A group in the data flow is similar in concept to a sequence container in the control flow, although you cannot use the group to configure a common property for all components that it contains, nor can you use it to set boundaries for a transaction or to set scope for a variable.

To create a group, follow these steps:

1. On the data flow design surface, use your mouse to draw a box around the components that you want to combine as a group. If you prefer, you can click each component while pressing the Ctrl key.

2. Right-click one of the selected components, and select Group. A group containing the components displays in the package designer, as shown here:

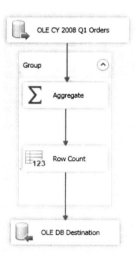

3. Click the arrow at the top right of the Group label to collapse the group.

Data Viewer

The only data viewer now available in Integration Services is the grid view. The histogram, scatter plot, and chart views have been removed.

To use the data viewer, follow these steps:

1. Right-click the path, and select Enable Data Viewer. All columns in the pipeline are automatically included.

2. If instead you want to display a subset of columns, right-click the new Data Viewer icon (a magnifying glass) on the data flow design surface, and select Edit.

3. In the Data Flow Path Editor, select Data Viewer in the list on the left.

4. Move columns from the Displayed Columns list to the Unused Columns list as applicable (shown next), and click OK.

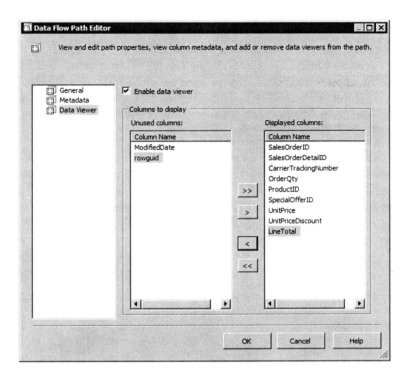

Change Data Capture Support

Change data capture (CDC) is a feature introduced in the SQL Server 2008 database engine. When you configure a database for change data capture, the Database Engine stores information about insert, update, and delete operations on tables you are tracking in corresponding change data capture tables. One purpose for tracking changes in separate tables is to perform extract, transform, and load (ETL) operations without adversely impacting the source table.

In the previous two versions of Integration Services, there were multiple steps required to develop packages that retrieve data from change data capture tables and load the results into destination. To expand Integration Services' data-integration capabilities in SQL Server 2012 by supporting change data capture for SQL Server, Microsoft partnered with Attunity, a provider of real-time data-integration software. As a result, new change data capture components are available for use in the control flow and data flow, simplifying the process of package development for change data capture.

Note Change data capture support in Integration Services is available only in Enterprise, Developer, and Evaluation editions. To learn more about the change data capture feature in the Database Engine, see "Basics of Change Data Capture" at *http://msdn.microsoft.com /en-us/library/cc645937(SQL.110).aspx*.

CDC Control Flow

There are two types of packages you must develop to manage change data processing with Integration Services: an initial load package for one-time execution, and a trickle-feed package for ongoing execution on a scheduled basis. You use the same components in each of these packages, but you configure the control flow differently. In each package type, you include a package variable with a string data type for use by the CDC components to reflect the current state of processing.

As shown in Figure 6-12, you begin the control flow with a CDC Control Task to mark the start of an initial load or to establish the Log Sequence Number (LSN) range to process during a trickle-feed package execution. You then add a Data Flow Task that contains CDC components to perform the processing of the initial load or changed data. (We describe the components to use in this Data Flow Task later in this section.) Then you complete the control flow with another CDC Control Task to mark the end of the initial load or the successful processing of the LSN range for a trickle-feed package.

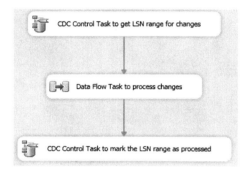

FIGURE 6-12 Trickle-feed control flow for change data capture processing

Figure 6-13 shows the configuration of the CDC Control Task for the beginning of a trickle-feed package. You use an ADO.NET Connection Manager to define the connection to a SQL Server database for which change data capture is enabled. You also specify a CDC control operation and the name of the CDC state variable. Optionally, you can use a table to persist the CDC state. If you do not use a table for state persistency, you must include logic in the package to write the state to a persistent store when change data processing completes and to read the state before beginning the next execution of change data processing.

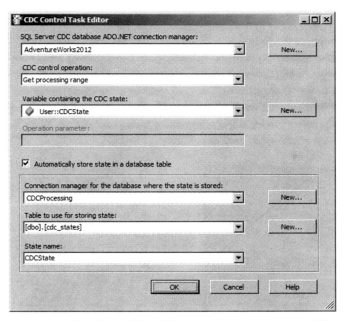

FIGURE 6-13 CDC Control Task Editor for retrieving the current LSN range for change data to process

CDC Data Flow

To process changed data, you begin a Data Flow Task with a CDC Source and a CDC Splitter, as shown in Figure 6-14. The CDC Source extracts the changed data according to the specifications defined by the CDC Control Task, and then the CDC Splitter evaluates each row to determine whether the changed data is a result of an insert, update, or delete operation. Then you add data flow components to the each output of the CDC Splitter for downstream processing.

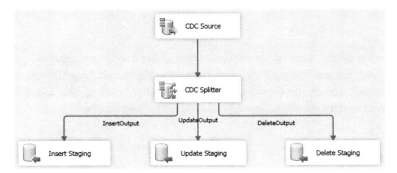

FIGURE 6-14 CDC Data Flow Task for processing changed data

CDC Source

In the CDC Source editor (shown in Figure 6-15), you specify an ADO.NET connection manager for the database and select a table and a corresponding capture instance. Both the database and table must be configured for change data capture in SQL Server. You also select a processing mode to control whether to process all change data or net changes only. The CDC state variable must match the variable you define in the CDC Control Task that executes prior to the Data Flow Task containing the CDC Source. Last, you can optionally select the Include Reprocessing Indicator Column check box to identify reprocessed rows for separate handling of error conditions.

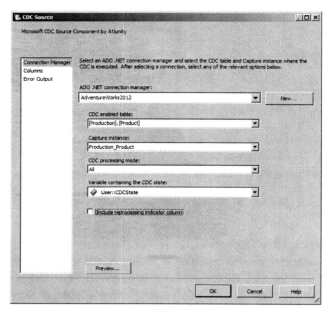

FIGURE 6-15 CDC Source editor for extracting change data from a CDC-enabled table

CDC Splitter

The CDC Splitter uses the value of the _$operation column to determine the type of change associated with each incoming row and assigns the row to the applicable output: InsertOutput, UpdateOutput, or DeleteOutput. You do not configure this transformation. Instead, you add downstream data flow components to manage the processing of each output separately.

Flexible Package Design

During the initial development stages of a package, you might find it easiest to work with hard-coded values in properties and expressions to ensure that your logic is correct. However, for maximum flexibility, you should use variables. In this section, we review the enhancements for variables and expressions—the cornerstones of flexible package design.

Variables

A common problem for developers when adding a variable to a package has been the scope assignment. If you inadvertently select a task in the control flow designer and then add a new variable in the Variables window, the variable is created within the scope of that task and cannot be changed. In these cases, you were required to delete the variable, clear the task selection on the design surface, and then add the variable again within the scope of the package.

Integration Services now creates new variables with scope set to the package by default. To change the variable scope, follow these steps:

1. In the Variables window, select the variable to change and then click the Move Variable button in the Variables toolbar (the second button from the left), as shown here:

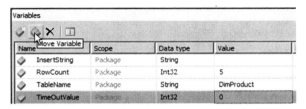

2. In the Select New Scope dialog box, select the executable to have scope—the package, an event handler, container, or task—as shown here, and click OK:

Expressions

The expression enhancements in this release address a problem with expression size limitations and introduce new functions in the SQL Server Integration Services Expression Language.

Expression Result Length

Prior to the current version of Integration Services, if an expression result had a data type of DT_WSTR or DT_STR, any characters above a 4000-character limit would be truncated. Furthermore, if an expression contained an intermediate step that evaluated a result exceeding this 4000-character limit, the intermediate result would similarly be truncated. This limitation is now removed.

New Functions

The SQL Server Integration Services Expression Language now has four new functions:

- **LEFT** You can now more easily return the leftmost portion of a string rather than use the SUBSTRING function:

  ```
  LEFT(character_expression,number)
  ```

- **REPLACENULL** You can use this function to replace NULL values in the first argument with the expression specified in the second expression:

  ```
  REPLACENULL(expression, expression)
  ```

- **TOKEN** This function allows you to return a substring by using delimiters to separate a string into tokens and then specifying which occurrence to return:

  ```
  TOKEN(character_expression, delimiter_string, occurrence)
  ```

- **TOKENCOUNT** This function uses delimiters to separate a string into tokens and then returns the count of tokens found within the string:

  ```
  TOKENCOUNT(character_expression, delimiter_string)
  ```

Deployment Models

Up to now in this chapter, we have explored the changes to the package-development process in SSDT, which have been substantial. Another major change to Integration Services is the concept of deployment models.

Supported Deployment Models

The latest version of Integration Services supports two deployment models:

- **Package deployment model** The package deployment model is the deployment model used in previous versions of Integration Services, in which the unit of deployment is an individual package stored as a DTSX file. A package can be deployed to the file system or to the MSDB database in a SQL Server database instance. Although packages can be deployed as a group and dependencies can exist between packages, there is no unifying object in Integration Services that identifies a set of related packages deployed using the package model. To modify properties of package tasks at runtime, which is important when running a package in different environments such as development or production, you use configurations saved as DTSCONFIG files on the file system. You use either the DTExec or the DTExecUI utilities to execute a package on the Integration Services server, providing arguments on the command line or in the graphical interface when you want to override package property values at run time manually or by using configurations.

■ **Project deployment model** With this deployment model, the unit of deployment is a project, stored as an ISPAC file, which in turn is a collection of packages and parameters. You deploy the project to the Integration Services catalog, which we describe in a separate section of this chapter. Instead of configurations, you use parameters (as described later in the "Parameters" section) to assign values to package properties at runtime. Before executing a package, you create an execution object in the catalog and, optionally, assign parameter values or environment references to the execution object. When ready, you start the execution object by using a graphical interface in SQL Server Management Studio by executing a stored procedure or by running managed code.

In addition to the characteristics just described, there are additional differences between the package deployment model and the project deployment model. Table 6-1 compares these differences.

TABLE 6-1 Deployment Model Comparison

Characteristic	Package Deployment Model	Project Deployment Model
Unit of deployment	Package	Project
Deployment location	File system or MSDB database	Integration Services catalog
Run-time property value assignment	Configurations	Parameters
Environment-specific values for use in property values	Configurations	Environment variables
Package validation	Just before execution using: • DTExec • Managed code	Independent of execution using: • SQL Server Management Studio interface • Stored procedure • Managed code
Package execution	DTExec DTExecUI	SQL Server Management Studio interface Stored procedure Managed code
Logging	Configure log provider or implement custom logging	No configuration required
Scheduling	SQL Server Agent job	SQL Server Agent job
CLR integration	Not required	Required

When you create a new project in SSDT, the project is by default established as a project deployment model. You can use the Convert To Package Deployment Model command on the Project menu (or choose it from the context menu when you right-click the project in Solution Explorer) to switch to the package deployment model. The conversion works only if your project is compatible with the package deployment model. For example, it cannot use features that are exclusive to the project deployment model, such as parameters. After conversion, Solution Explorer displays an additional label after the project name to indicate the project is now configured as a package deployment model, as shown in Figure 6-16. Notice that the Parameters folder is no longer available in the project, while the Data Sources folder is now available in the project.

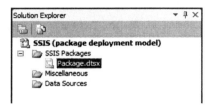

FIGURE 6-16 Package deployment model

Tip You can reverse the process by using the Project menu, or the project's context menu in Solution Explorer, to convert a package deployment model project to a project deployment model.

Project Deployment Model Features

In this section, we provide an overview of the project deployment model features to help you understand how you use these features in combination to manage deployed projects. Later in this chapter, we explain each of these features in more detail and provide links to additional information available online.

Although you can continue to work with the package deployment model if you prefer, the primary advantage of using the new project deployment model is the improvement in package management across multiple environments. For example, a package is commonly developed on one server, tested on a separate server, and eventually implemented on a production server. With the package deployment model, you can use a variety of techniques to provide connection strings for the correct environment at runtime, each of which requires you to create at least one configuration file and, optionally, maintain SQL Server tables or environment variables. Although this approach is flexible, it can also be confusing and prone to error. The project deployment model continues to separate run-time values from the packages, but it uses object collections in the Integration Services catalog to store these values and to define relationships between packages and these object collections, known as parameters, environments, and environment variables.

- **Catalog**   The catalog is a dedicated database that stores packages and related configuration information accessed at package runtime. You can manage package configuration and execution by using the catalog's stored procedures and views or by using the graphical interface in SQL Server Management Studio.

- **Parameters**   As Table 6-1 shows, the project deployment model relies on parameters to change task properties during package execution. Parameters can be created within a project scope or within a package scope. When you create parameters within a project scope, you apply a common set of parameter values across all the packages contained in the project. You can then use parameters in expressions or tasks, much the same way that you use variables.

- **Environments**   Each environment is a container of variables you associate with a package at runtime. You can create multiple environments to use with a single package, but the package can use variables from only one environment during execution. For example, you can create environments for development, test, and production, and then execute a package using one of the applicable environments.

- **Environment variables**   An environment variable contains a literal value that Integration Services assigns to a parameter during package execution. After deploying a project, you can associate a parameter with an environment variable. The value of the environment variable resolves during package execution.

Project Deployment Workflow

The project deployment workflow includes not only the process of converting design-time objects in SSDT into database objects stored in the Integration Services catalog, but also the process of retrieving database objects from the catalog to update a package design or to use an existing package as a template for a new package. To add a project to the catalog or to retrieve a project from the catalog, you use a project-deployment file that has an ISPAC file extension. There are four stages of the project deployment workflow in which the ISPAC file plays a role: build, deploy, import, and convert. In this section, we review each of these stages.

Build

When you use the project deployment model for packages, you use SSDT to develop one or more packages as part of an Integration Services project. In preparation for deployment to the catalog, which serves as a centralized repository for packages and related objects, you build the Integration Services project in SSDT to produce an ISPAC file. The ISPAC file is the project deployment file that contains project information, all packages in the Integration Services project, and parameters.

Before performing the build, there are two additional tasks that might be necessary:

- **Identify entry-point package**   If one of the packages in the project is the package that triggers the execution of the other packages in the project, directly or indirectly, you should flag that package as an entry-point package. You can do this by right-clicking the package in

Solution Explorer and selecting Entry-Point Package. An administrator uses this flag to identify the package to start when a package contains multiple projects.

- **Create project and package parameters**   You use project-level or package-level parameters to provide values for use in tasks or expressions at runtime, which you learn more about how to do later in this chapter in the "Parameters" section. In SSDT, you assign parameter values to use as a default. You also mark a parameter as required, which prevents a package from executing until you assign a value to the variable.

During the development process in SSDT, you commonly execute a task or an entire package within SSDT to test results before deploying the project. SSDT creates an ISPAC file to hold the information required to execute the package and stores it in the bin folder for the Integration Services project. When you finish development and want to prepare the ISPAC file for deployment, use the Build menu or press F5.

Deploy

The deployment process uses the ISPAC file to create database objects in the catalog for the project, packages, and parameters, as shown in Figure 6-17. To do this, you use the Integration Services Deployment Wizard, which prompts you for the project to deploy and the project to create or update as part of the deployment. You can also provide literal values or specify environment variables as default parameter values for the current project version. These parameter values that you provide in the wizard are stored in the catalog as server defaults for the project, and they override the default parameter values stored in the package.

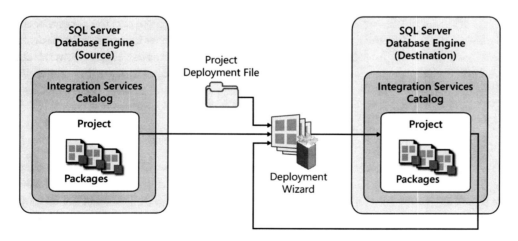

FIGURE 6-17 Deployment of the ISPAC file to the catalog

You can launch the wizard from within SSDT by right-clicking the project in Solution Explorer and selecting Deploy. However, if you have an ISPAC file saved to the file system, you can double-click the file to launch the wizard.

Import

When you want to update a package that has already been deployed or to use it as basis for a new package, you can import a project into SSDT from the catalog or from an ISPAC file, as shown in Figure 6-18. To import a project, you use the Integration Services Import Project Wizard, which is available in the template list when you create a new project in SSDT.

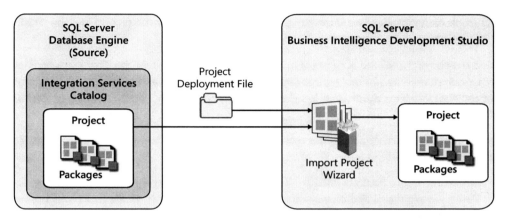

FIGURE 6-18 Import a project from the catalog or an ISPAC file

Convert

If you have legacy packages and configuration files, you can convert them to the latest version of Integration Services, as shown in Figure 6-19. The Integration Services Project Conversion Wizard is available in both SSDT and in SQL Server Management Studio. Another option is to use the Integration Services Package Upgrade Wizard available on the Tools page of the SQL Server Installation Center.

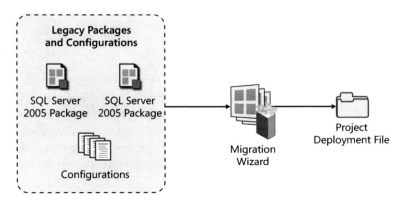

FIGURE 6-19 Convert existing DTSX files and configurations to an ISPAC file

Note You can use the Conversion Wizard to migrate packages created using SQL Server 2005 Integration Services and later. If you use SQL Server Management Studio, the original DTSX files are not modified, but used only as a source to produce the ISPAC file containing the upgraded packages.

In SSDT, open a package project, right-click the project in Solution Explorer, and select Convert To Project Deployment Model. The wizard upgrades the DTPROJ file for the project and the DTSX files for the packages.

The behavior of the wizard is different in SQL Server Management Studio. There you right-click the Projects node of the Integration Services catalog in Object Explorer and select Import Packages. The wizard prompts you for a destination location and produces an ISPAC file for the new project and the upgraded packages.

Regardless of which method you use to convert packages, there are some common steps that occur as packages are upgraded:

- **Update Execute Package tasks** If a package in a package project contains an Execute Package task, the wizard changes the external reference to a DTSX file to a project reference to a package contained within the same project. The child package must be in the same package project you are converting and must be selected for conversion in the wizard.

- **Create parameters** If a package in a package project uses a configuration, you can choose to convert the configuration to parameters. You can add configurations belonging to other projects to include them in the conversion process. Additionally, you can choose to remove configurations from the upgraded packages. The wizard uses the configurations to prompt you for properties to convert to parameters, and it also requires you to specify project scope or package scope for each parameter.

- **Configure parameters** The Conversion Wizard allows you to specify a server value for each parameter and whether to require the parameter at runtime.

Parameters

As we explained in the previous section, parameters are the replacement for configurations in legacy packages, but only when you use the project deployment model. The purpose of configurations was to provide a way to change values in a package at runtime without requiring you to open the package and make the change directly. You can establish project-level parameters to assign a value to one or more properties across multiple packages, or you can have a package-level parameter when you need to assign a value to properties within a single package.

Project Parameters

A project parameter shares its values with all packages within the same project. To create a project parameter in SSDT, follow these steps:

1. In Solution Explorer, double-click Project.params.

2. Click the Add Parameter button on the toolbar in the Project.params window.

3. Type a name for the parameter in the Name text box, select a data type, and specify a value for the parameter as shown here. The parameter value you supply here is known as the *design default value*.

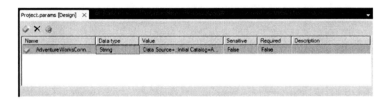

 Note The parameter value is a design-time value that can be overwritten during or after deployment to the catalog. You can use the Add Parameters To Configuration button on the toolbar (the third button from the left) to add selected parameters to Visual Studio project configurations, which is useful for testing package executions under a variety of conditions.

4. Save the file.

Optionally, you can configure the following properties for each parameter:

- **Sensitive** By default, this property is set to *False*. If you change it to *True*, the parameter value is encrypted when you deploy the project to the catalog. If anyone attempts to view the parameter value in SQL Server Management Studio or by accessing Transact-SQL views, the parameter value will display as NULL. This setting is important when you use a parameter to set a connection string property and the value contains specific credentials.

- **Required** By default, this property is also set to *False*. When the value is *True*, you must configure a parameter value during or after deployment before you can execute the package. The Integration Services engine will ignore the parameter default value that you specify on this screen when the *Required* property is *True* and deploy the package to the catalog.

- **Description** This property is optional, but it allows you to provide documentation to an administrator responsible for managing packages deployed to the catalog.

Package Parameters

Package parameters apply only to the package in which they are created and cannot be shared with other packages. The center tab in the package designer allows you to access the Parameters window for your package. The interface for working with package parameters is identical to the project parameters interface.

Parameter Usage

After creating project or package parameters, you are ready to implement the parameters in your package much like you implement variables. That is, anywhere you can use variables in expressions for tasks, data flow components, or connection managers, you can also use parameters.

As one example, you can reference a parameter in expressions, as shown in Figure 6-20. Notice the parameter appears in the Variables And Parameters list in the top left pane of the Expression Builder. You can drag the parameter to the Expression text box and use it alone or as part of a more complex expression. When you click the Evaluate Expression button, you can see the expression result based on the design default value for the parameter.

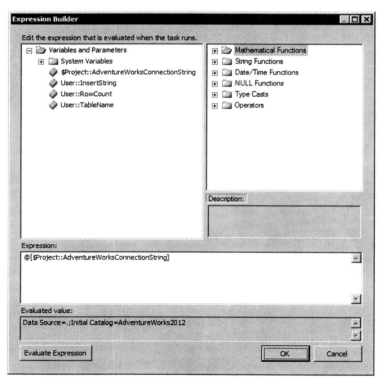

FIGURE 6-20 Parameter usage in an expression

> **Note** This expression uses a project parameter that has a prefix of *$Project*. To create an expression that uses a package parameter, the parameter prefix is *$Package*.

You can also directly set a task property by right-clicking the task and selecting Parameterize on the context menu. The Parameterize dialog box displays as shown in Figure 6-21. You select a property, and then choose whether to create a new parameter or use an existing parameter. If you create a new parameter, you specify values for each of the properties you access in the Parameters window. Additionally, you must specify whether to create the parameter within package scope or project scope.

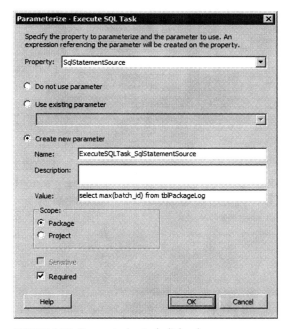

FIGURE 6-21 Parameterize task dialog box

Post-Deployment Parameter Values

The design default values that you set for each parameter in SSDT are typically used only to supply a value for testing within the SSDT environment. You can replace these values during deployment by specifying server default values when you use the Deployment Wizard or by configuring execution values when creating an execution object for deployed projects.

Figure 6-22 illustrates the stage at which you create each type of parameter value. If a parameter has no execution value, the Integration Services engine uses the server default value when executing the package. Similarly, if there is no server default value, package execution uses the design default value. However, if a parameter is marked as required, you must provide either a server default value or an execution value.

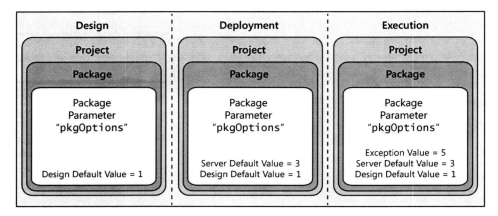

FIGURE 6-22 Parameter values by stage

Note A package will fail when the Integration Services engine cannot resolve a parameter value. For this reason, it is recommended that you validate projects and packages as described in the "Validation" section of this chapter.

Server Default Values

Server default values can be literal values or environment variable references (explained later in this chapter), which in turn are literal values. To configure server defaults in SQL Server Management Studio, you right-click the project or package in the Integration Services node in Object Explorer, select Configure, and change the Value property of the parameter, as shown in Figure 6-23. This server default value persists even if you make changes to the design default value in SSDT and redeploy the project.

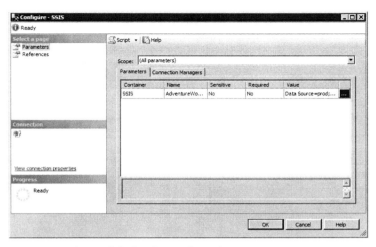

FIGURE 6-23 Server default value configuration

Execution Parameter Values

The execution parameter value applies only to a specific execution of a package and overrides all other values. You must explicitly set the execution parameter value by using the *catalog.set_execution_ parameter_value* stored procedure. There is no interface available in SQL Server Management Studio to set an execution parameter value.

```
set_execution_parameter_value [ @execution_id = execution_id
      , [ @object_type = ] object_type
      , [ @parameter_name = ] parameter_name
      , [ @parameter_value = ] parameter_value
```

To use this stored procedure, you must supply the following arguments:

- **execution_id**   You must obtain the *execution_id* for the instance of the execution. You can use the *catalog.executions* view to locate the applicable *execution_id*.

- **object_type**   The object type specifies whether you are setting a project parameter or a package parameter. Use a value of *20* for a project parameter and a value of *30* for a package parameter.

- **parameter_name**   The name of the parameter must match the parameter stored in the catalog.

- **parameter_value**   Here you provide the value to use as the execution parameter value.

Integration Services Catalog

The Integration Services catalog is a new feature to support the centralization of storage and the administration of packages and related configuration information. Each SQL Server instance can host only one catalog. When you deploy a project using the project deployment model, the project and its components are added to the catalog and, optionally, placed in a folder that you specify in the Deployment Wizard. Each folder (or the root level if you choose not to use folders) organizes its contents into two groups: projects and environments, as shown in Figure 6-24.

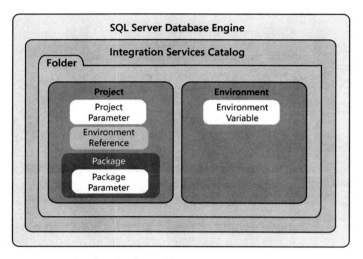

FIGURE 6-24 Catalog database objects

Catalog Creation

Installation of Integration Services on a server does not automatically create the catalog. To do this, follow these steps:

1. In SQL Server Management Studio, connect to the SQL Server instance, right-click the Integration Services Catalogs folder in Object Explorer, and select Create Catalog.

2. In the Create Catalog dialog box, you can optionally select the Enable Automatic Execution Of Integration Services Stored Procedure At SQL Server Startup check box. This stored procedure performs a cleanup operation when the service restarts and adjusts the status of packages that were executing when the service stopped.

3. Notice that the catalog database name cannot be changed from SSISDB, as shown in the following figure, so the final step is to provide a strong password and then click OK. The password creates a database master key that Integration Services uses to encrypt sensitive data stored in the catalog.

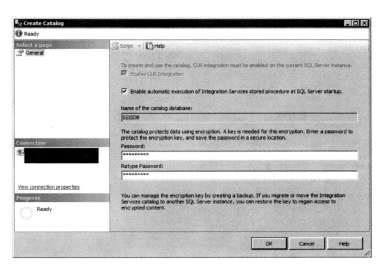

After you create the catalog, you will see it appear twice as the SSISDB database in Object Explorer. It displays under both the Databases node as well as the Integration Services node. In the Databases node, you can interact with it as you would any other database, using the interface to explore database objects. You use the Integration Services node to perform administrative tasks.

Note In most cases, multiple options are available for performing administrative tasks with the catalog. You can use the graphical interface by opening the applicable dialog box for a selected catalog object, or you can use Transact-SQL views and stored procedures to view and modify object properties. For more information about the Transact-SQL API, see *http://msdn.microsoft.com/en-us/library/ff878003(v=SQL.110).aspx*. You can also use Windows PowerShell to perform administrative tasks by using the SSIS Catalog Managed Object Model. Refer to *http://msdn.microsoft.com/en-us/library/microsoft.sqlserver.management.integrationservices(v=sql.110).aspx* for details about the API.

Catalog Properties

The catalog has several configurable properties. To access these properties, right-click SSISDB under the Integration Services node and select Properties. The Catalog Properties dialog box, as shown in Figure 6-25, displays several properties.

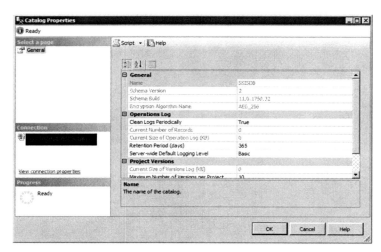

FIGURE 6-25 Catalog Properties dialog box

Encryption

Notice in Figure 6-25 that the default encryption algorithm is AES_256. If you put the SSISDB database in single-user mode, you can choose one of the other encryption algorithms available:

- DES

- TRIPLE_DES

- TRIPLE_DES_3KEY

- DESX

- AES_128

- AES_192

Integration Services uses encryption to protect sensitive parameter values. When anyone uses the SQL Server Management Studio interface or the Transact-SQL API to query the catalog, the parameter value displays only a NULL value.

Operations

Operations include activities such as package execution, project deployment, and project validation, to name a few. Integration Services stores information about these operations in tables in the catalog. You can use the Transact-SQL API to monitor operations, or you can right-click the SSISDB database on the Integration Services node in Object Explorer and select Active Operations. The Active Operations dialog box displays the operation identifier, its type, name, the operation start time, and the caller of the operation. You can select an operation and click the Stop button to end the operation.

Periodically, older data should be purged from these tables to keep the catalog from growing unnecessarily large. By configuring the catalog properties, you can control the frequency of the SQL Server Agent job that purges the stale data by specifying how many days of data to retain. If you prefer, you can disable the job.

Project Versioning

Each time you redeploy a project with the same name to the same folder, the previous version remains in the catalog until ten versions are retained. If necessary, you can restore a previous version by following these steps:

1. In Object Explorer, locate the project under the SSISDB node.

2. Right-click the project, and select Versions.

3. In the Project Versions dialog box, shown here, select the version to restore and click the Restore To Selected Version button:

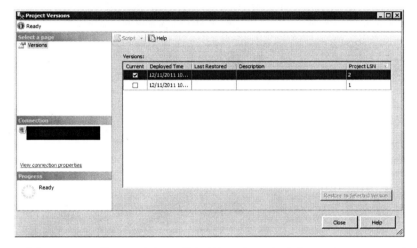

4. Click Yes to confirm, and then click OK to close the information message box. Notice the selected version is now flagged as the current version, and that the other version remains available as an option for restoring.

You can modify the maximum number of versions to retain by updating the applicable catalog property. If you increase this number above the default value of ten, you should continually monitor the size of the catalog database to ensure that it does not grow too large. To manage the size of the catalog, you can also decide whether to remove older versions periodically with a SQL Server agent job.

Environment Objects

After you deploy projects to the catalog, you can create environments to work in tandem with parameters to change parameter values at execution time. An environment is a collection of environment variables. Each environment variable contains a value to assign to a parameter. To connect an environment to a project, you use an environment reference. Figure 6-26 illustrates the relationship between parameters, environments, environment variables, and environment references.

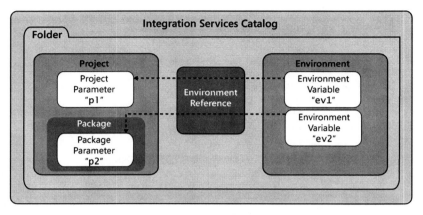

FIGURE 6-26 Environment objects in the catalog

Environments

One convention you can use is to create one environment for each server you will use for package execution. For example, you might have one environment for development, one for testing, and one for production. To create a new environment using the SQL Server Management Studio interface, follow these steps:

1. In Object Explorer, expand the SSISDB node and locate the Environments folder that corresponds to the Projects folder containing your project.

2. Right-click the Environments folder, and select Create Environment.

3. In the Create Environment dialog box, type a name, optionally type a description, and click OK.

Environment Variables

For each environment, you can create a collection of environment variables. The properties you configure for an environment variable are the same ones you configure for a parameter, which is understandable when you consider that you use the environment variable to replace the parameter value at runtime. To create an environment variable, follow these steps:

1. In Object Explorer, locate the environment under the SSISDB node.

2. Right-click the environment, and select Properties to open the Environment Properties dialog box.

3. Click Variables to display the list of existing environment variables, if any, as shown here:

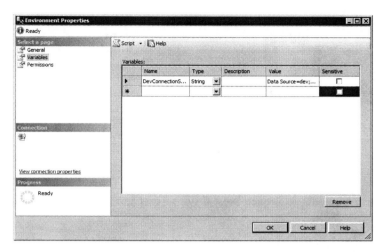

4. On an empty row, type a name for the environment variable in the Name text box, select a data type in the Type column, type a description (optional), type a value in the Value column for the environment variable, and select the Sensitive check box if you want the value to be encrypted in the catalog. Continue adding environment variables on this page, and click OK when you're finished.

5. Repeat this process by adding the same set of environment variables to other environments you intend to use with the same project.

Environment References

To connect environment variables to a parameter, you create an environment reference. There are two types of environment references: relative and absolute. When you create a relative environment reference, the parent folder for the environment folder must also be the parent folder for the project folder. If you later move the package to another without also moving the environment, the package execution will fail. An alternative is to use an absolute reference, which maintains the relationship between the environment and the project without requiring them to have the same parent folder.

The environment reference is a property of the project. To create an environment reference, follow these steps:

1. In Object Explorer, locate the project under the SSISDB node.

2. Right-click the project, and select Configure to open the Configure <Project> dialog box.

3. Click References to display the list of existing environment references, if any.

4. Click the Add button and select an environment in the Browse Environments dialog box. Use the Local Folder node for a relative environment reference, or use the SSISDB node for an absolute environment reference.

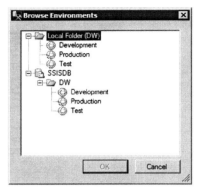

5. Click OK twice to create the reference. Repeat steps 4 and 5 to add reference for all other applicable environments.

6. In the Configure <Project> dialog box, click Parameters to switch to the parameters page.

7. Click the ellipsis button to the right of the Value text box to display the Set Parameter Value dialog box, select the Use Environment Variable option, and select the applicable variable in the drop-down list, as shown here:

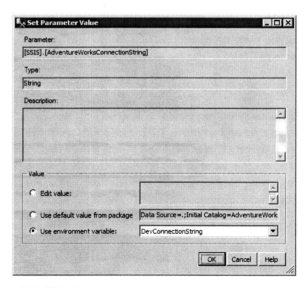

8. Click OK twice.

You can create multiple references for a project, but only one environment will be active during package execution. At that time, Integration Services will evaluate the environment variable based on the environment associated with the current execution instance as explained in the next section.

Administration

After the development and deployment processes are complete, it's time to become familiar with the administration tasks that enable operations on the server to keep running.

Validation

Before executing packages, you can use validation to verify that projects and packages are likely to run successfully, especially if you have configured parameters to use environment variables. The validation process ensures that server default values exist for required parameters, that environment references are valid, and that data types for parameters are consistent between project and package configurations and their corresponding environment variables, to name a few of the validation checks.

To perform the validation, right-click the project or package in the catalog, click Validate, and select the environments to include in the validation: all, none, or a specific environment. Validation occurs asynchronously, so the Validation dialog box closes while the validation processes. You can open the Integration Services Dashboard report to check the results of validation. Your other options are to right-click the SSISDB node in Object Explorer and select Active Operations or to use of the Transact-SQL API to monitor an executing package.

Package Execution

After deploying a project to the catalog and optionally configuring parameters and environment references, you are ready to prepare your packages for execution. This step requires you to create a SQL Server object called an execution. An *execution* is a unique combination of a package and its corresponding parameter values, whether the values are server defaults or environment references. To configure and start an execution instance, follow these steps:

1. In Object Explorer, locate the entry-point package under the SSISDB node.

2. Right-click the project, and select Execute to open the Execute Package dialog box, shown here:

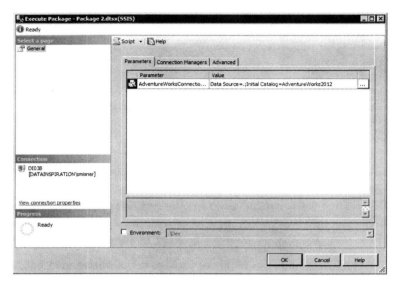

3. Here you have two choices. You can either click the ellipsis button to the right of the value and specify a literal execution value for the parameter, or you can select the Environment check box at the bottom of the dialog box and select an environment in the corresponding drop-down list.

You can continue configuring the execution instance by updating properties on the Connection Managers tab and by overriding property values and configuring logging on the Advanced tab. For more information about the options available in this dialog box, see *http://msdn.microsoft.com/en-us /library/hh231080(v=SQL.110).aspx*.

When you click OK to close the Execute Package dialog box, the package execution begins. Because package execution occurs asynchronously, the dialog box does not need to stay open during execution. You can use the Integration Services Dashboard report to monitor the execution status, or right-click the SSISDB node and select Active Operations. Another option is the use of the Transact-SQL API to monitor an executing package.

More often, you will schedule package execution by creating a Transact-SQL script that starts execution and save the script to a file that you can then schedule using a SQL Server agent job. You add a job step using the Operating System (CmdExec) step type, and then configure the step to use the sqlcmd.exe utility and pass the package execution script to the utility as an argument. You run the job using the SQL Server Agent service account or a proxy account. Whichever account you use, it must have permissions to create and start executions.

Logging and Troubleshooting Tools

Now that Integration Services centralizes package storage and executions on the server and has access to information generated by operations, server-based logging is supported and operations reports are available in SQL Server Management Studio to help you monitor activity on the server and troubleshoot problems when they occur.

Package Execution Logs

In legacy Integration Services packages, there are two options you can use to obtain logs during package execution. One option is to configure log providers within each package and associate log providers with executables within the package. The other option is to use a combination of Execute SQL statements or script components to implement a custom logging solution. Either way, the steps necessary to enable logging are tedious in legacy packages.

With no configuration required, Integration Services stores package execution data in the [catalog].[executions] table. The most important columns in this table include the start and end times of package execution, as well as the status. However, the logging mechanism also captures information related to the Integration Services environment, such as physical memory, the page file size, and available CPUs. Other tables provide access to parameter values used during execution, the duration of each executable within a package, and messages generated during package execution. You can easily write ad hoc queries to explore package logs or build your own custom reports using Reporting Services for ongoing monitoring of the log files.

> **Note** For a thorough walkthrough of the various tables in which package execution log data is stored, see "SSIS Logging in Denali," a blog post by Jamie Thomson at *http://sqlblog.com/blogs/jamie_thomson/archive/2011/07/16/ssis-logging-in-denali.aspx*.

Data Taps

A data tap is similar in concept to a data viewer, except that it captures data at a specified point in the pipeline during package execution outside of SSDT. You can use the T-SQL stored procedure *catalog.add_data_tap* to tap into the data flow during execution if the package has been deployed to SSIS. The captured data from the data flow is stored in a CSV file you can review after package execution completes. No changes to your package are necessary to use this feature.

Reports

Before you build custom reports from the package execution log tables, review the built-in reports now available in SQL Server Management Studio for Integration Services. These reports provide information on package execution results for the past 24 hours (as shown in Figure 6-27), performance, and error messages from failed package executions. Hyperlinks in each report allow you to drill through from summary to detailed information to help you diagnose package execution problems.

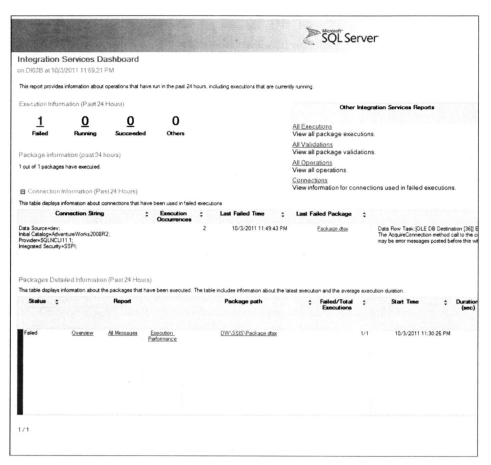

FIGURE 6-27 Integration Services operations dashboard.

To view the reports, you right-click the SSISDB node in Object Explorer, point to Reports, point to Standard Reports, and then choose from the following list of reports:

- All Executions

- All Validations

- All Operations

- Connections

Security

Packages and related objects are stored securely in the catalog using encryption. Only members of the new SQL Server database role ssis_admin or members of the existing sysadmin role have permissions to all objects in the catalog. Members of these roles can perform operations such as creating the catalog, creating folders in the catalog, and executing stored procedures, to name a few.

Members of the administrative roles delegate administrative permissions to users who need to manage a specific folder. Delegation is useful when you do not want to give these users access to the higher privileged roles. To give a user folder-level access, you grant the MANAGE_OBJECT_PERMISSIONS permission to the user.

For general permissions management, open the Properties dialog box for a folder (or any other securable object) and go to the Permissions page. On that page, you can select a security principal by name and then set explicit Grant or Deny permissions as appropriate. You can use this method to secure folders, projects, environments, and operations.

Package File Format

Although legacy packages stored as DTSX files are formatted as XML, their structure is not compatible with differencing tools and source-control systems you might use to compare packages. In the current version of Integration Services, the package file format is pretty-printed, with properties formatted as attributes rather than as elements. (*Pretty-printing* is the enhancement of code with syntax conventions for easier viewing.) Moreover, attributes are listed alphabetically and attributes configured with default values have been eliminated. Collectively, these changes not only help you more easily locate information in the file, but you can more easily compare packages with automated tools and more reliably merge packages that have no conflicting changes.

Another significant change to the package file format is the replacement of the meaningless numeric lineage identifiers with a *refid* attribute with a text value that represents the path to the referenced object. For example, a *refid* for the first input column of an Aggregate transformation in a data flow task called Data Flow Task in a package called Package looks like this:

```
Package\Data Flow Task\Aggregate.Inputs[Aggregate Input 1].Columns[LineTotal]
```

Last, annotations are no longer stored as binary streams. Instead, they appear in the XML file as clear text. With better access to annotations in the file, the more likely it is that annotations can be programmatically extracted from a package for documentation purposes.

CHAPTER 7

Data Quality Services

The quality of data is a critical success factor for many data projects, whether for general business operations or business intelligence. Bad data creeps into business applications as a result of user entry, corruption during transmission, business processes, or even conflicting data standards across data sources. The Data Quality Services (DQS) feature of Microsoft SQL Server 2012 is a set of technologies you use to measure and manage data quality through a combination of computer-assisted and manual processes. When your organization has access to high-quality data, your business process can operate more effectively and managers can rely on this data for better decision-making. By centralizing data quality management, you also reduce the amount of time that people spend reviewing and correcting data.

Data Quality Services Architecture

In this section, we describe the two primary components of DQS: the Data Quality Server and Data Quality Client. The DQS architecture also includes components that are built into other SQL Server 2012 features. For example, Integration Services has the DQS Cleansing transformation you use to apply data-cleansing rules to a data flow pipeline. In addition, Master Data Services supports DQS matching so that you can de-duplicate data before adding it as master data. We explain more about these components in the "Integration" section of this chapter. All DQS components can coexist on the same server, or they can be installed on separate servers.

Data Quality Server

The Data Quality Server is the core component of the architecture that manages the storage of knowledge and executes knowledge-related processes. It consists of a DQS engine and multiple databases stored in a local SQL Server 2012 instance. These databases contain knowledge bases, stored procedures for managing the Data Quality Server and its contents, and data about cleansing, matching, and data-profiling activities.

Installation of the Data Quality Server is a multistep process. You start by using SQL Server Setup and, at minimum, selecting the Database Engine and Data Quality Services on the Feature Selection page. Then you continue installation by opening the Data Quality Services folder in the Microsoft SQL Server 2012 program group on the Start menu, and launching Data Quality Server Installer. A command window opens, and a prompt appears for the database master key password. You must supply a strong password having at least eight characters and including at least one uppercase letter, one lowercase letter, and one special character.

After you provide a valid password, installation of the Data Quality Server continues for several minutes. In addition to creating and registering assemblies on the server, the installation process creates the following databases on a local instance of SQL Server 2012:

- **DQS_MAIN**   As its name implies, this is the primary database for the Data Quality Server. It contains the published knowledge bases as well as the stored procedures that support the DQS engine. Following installation, this database also contains a sample knowledge base called *DQS data*, which you can use to cleanse country data or data related to geographical locations in the United States.

- **DQS_PROJECTS**   This database is for internal use by the Data Quality Server to store data related to managing knowledge bases and data quality projects.

- **DQS_STAGING_DATA**   You can use this database as intermediate storage for data that you want to use as source data for DQS operations. DQS can also use this database to store processed data that you can later export.

Before users can use client components with the Data Quality Server, a user with sysadmin privileges must create a SQL Server login for each user and map each user to the DQS_MAIN database using one of the following database roles created at installation of the Data Quality Server:

- *dqs_administrator*   A user assigned to this role has all privileges available to the other roles plus full administrative privileges, with the exception of adding new users. Specifically, a member of this role can stop any activity or stop a process within an activity and perform any configuration task using Data Quality Client.

- *dqs_kb_editor*   A member of this role can perform any DQS activity except administration. A user must be a member of this role to create or edit a knowledge base.

- *dqs_kb_operator*   This role is the most limited of the database roles, allowing its members only to edit and execute data quality projects and to view activity-monitoring data.

> **Important** You must use SQL Server Configuration Manager to enable the TCP/IP protocol for the SQL Server instance hosting the DQS databases before remote clients can connect to the Data Quality Server.

Data Quality Client

Data Quality Client is the primary user interface for the Data Quality Server that you install as a stand-alone application. Business users can use this application to interactively work with data quality projects, such as cleansing or data profiling. Data stewards use Data Quality Client to create or maintain knowledge bases, and DQS administrators use it to configure and manage the Data Quality Server.

To install this application, use SQL Server Setup and select Data Quality Client on the Feature Selection page. It requires the Microsoft .NET Framework 4.0, which installs automatically if necessary.

> **Note** If you plan to import data from Microsoft Excel, you must install Excel on the Data Quality Client computer. DQS supports both 32-bit and 64-bit versions of Excel 2003, but it supports only the 32-bit version of Excel 2007 or 2010 unless you save the workbook as an XLS or CSV file.

If you have been assigned to one of the DQS database roles, or if you have sysadmin privileges on the SQL Server instance hosting the Data Quality Server, you can open Data Quality Client, which is found in the Data Quality Services folder of the Microsoft SQL Server 2012 program group on the Start menu. You must then identify the Data Quality Server to establish the client-server connection. If you click the Options button, you can select a check box to encrypt the connection.

After opening Data Quality Client, the home screen provides access to the following three types of tasks:

- **Knowledge Base Management** You use this area of Data Quality Client to create a new knowledge base, edit an existing knowledge base, use knowledge discovery to enhance a knowledge base with additional values, or create a matching policy for a knowledge base.

- **Data Quality Projects** In this area, you create and run data quality projects to perform data-cleansing or data-matching tasks.

- **Administration** This area allows you to view the status of knowledge base management activities, data quality projects, and DQS Cleansing transformations used in Integration Services packages. In addition, it provides access to configuration properties for the Data Quality Server, logging, and reference data services.

Knowledge Base Management

In DQS, you create a knowledge base to store information about your data, including valid and invalid values and rules to apply for validating and correcting data. You can generate a knowledge base from sample data, or you can manually create one. You can reuse a knowledge base with multiple data quality projects and enhance it over time with the output of cleansing and matching projects. You can give responsibility for maintaining the knowledge base to data stewards. There are three activities that you or data stewards perform using the Knowledge Base Management area of Data Quality Client: Domain Management, Knowledge Discovery, and Matching Policy.

Domain Management

After creating a knowledge base, you manage its contents and rules through the Domain Management activity. A knowledge base is a logical collection of domains, with each domain corresponding to a single field. You can create separate knowledge bases for customers and products, or you can combine these subject areas into a single knowledge base. After you create a domain, you define trusted values, invalid values, and examples of erroneous data. In addition to this set of values, you also manage properties and rules for a domain.

To prevent potential conflicts resulting from multiple users working on the same knowledge base at the same time, DQS locks the knowledge base when you begin a new activity. To unlock an activity, you must publish or discard the results of your changes.

> **Note** If you have multiple users who have responsibility for managing knowledge, keep in mind that only one user at a time can perform the Domain Management activity for a single knowledge base. Therefore, you might consider using separate knowledge bases for each area of responsibility.

DQS Data Knowledge Base

Before creating your own knowledge base, you can explore the automatically installed knowledge base, DQS Data, to gain familiarity with the Data Quality Client interface and basic knowledge-base concepts. By exploring DQS Data, you can learn about the types of information that a knowledge base can contain.

To get started, open Data Quality Client and click the Open Knowledge Base button on the home page. DQS Data displays as the only knowledge base on the Open Knowledge Base page. When you select DQS Data in the list of existing knowledge bases, you can see the collection of domains associated with this knowledge base, as shown in Figure 7-1.

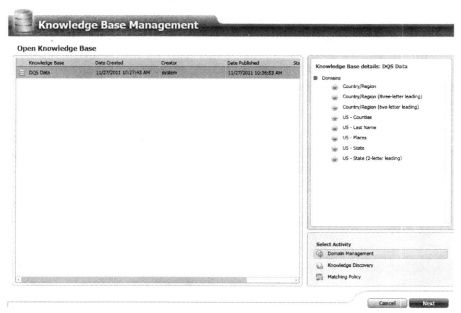

FIGURE 7-1 Knowledge base details for DQS Data

Choose the Domain Management activity in the bottom right corner of the window, and click Next to explore the domains in this knowledge base. In the Domain list on the Domain Management page, you choose a domain, such as Country/Region, and access separate tabs to view or change the knowledge associated with that domain. For example, you can click on the Domain Values tab to see how values that represent a specific country or region will be corrected when you use DQS to perform data cleansing, as shown in Figure 7-2.

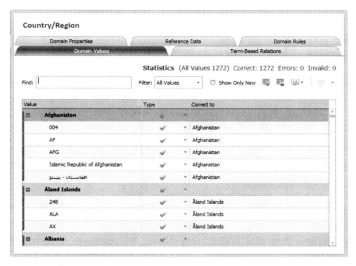

FIGURE 7-2 Domain values for the Country/Region domain

The DQS Data knowledge base, by default, contains only domain values. You can add other knowledge to make this data more useful for your own data quality projects. For example, you could add domain rules to define conditions that identify valid data or create term-based relations to define how to make corrections to terms found in a string value. More information about these other knowledge categories is provided in the "New Knowledge Base" section of this chapter.

Tip When you finish reviewing the knowledge base, click the Cancel button and click Yes to confirm that you do not want to save your work.

New Knowledge Base

On the home page of Data Quality Client, click the New Knowledge Base button to start the process of creating a new knowledge base. At a minimum, you provide a name for the knowledge base, but you can optionally add a description. Then you must specify whether you want to create an empty knowledge base or create your knowledge base from an existing one, such as DQS Data. Another option is to create a knowledge base by importing knowledge from a DQS file, which you create by using the export option from any existing knowledge base.

After creating the knowledge base, you select the Domain Management activity, and click Next so that you can add one or more domains in the knowledge base. To add a new domain, you can create the domain manually or import a domain from an existing knowledge base using the applicable button in the toolbar on the Domain Management page. As another option, you can create a domain from the output of a data quality project.

Domain   When you create a domain manually, you start by defining the following properties for the domain (as shown in Figure 7-3):

- **Domain Name**   The name you provide for the domain must be unique within the knowledge base and must be 256 characters or less.

- **Description**   You can optionally add a description to provide more information about the contents of the domain. The maximum number of characters for the description is 2048.

- **Data Type**   Your options here are String, Date, Integer, or Decimal.

- **Use Leading Values**   When you select this option, the output from a cleansing or matching data quality project will use the leading value in a group of synonyms. Otherwise, the output will be the input value or its corrected value.

- **Normalize String**   This option appears only when you select String as the Data Type. You use it to remove special characters from the domain values during the data-processing stage of knowledge discovery, data cleansing, and matching activities. Normalization might be helpful for improving the accuracy of matches when you want to de-duplicate data because punctuation might be used inconsistently in strings that otherwise are a match.

- **Format Output To**   When you output the results of a data quality project, you can apply formatting to the domain values if you change this setting from None to one of the available format options, which will depend on the domain's data type. For example, you could choose Mon-yyyy for a Date data type, #,##0.00 for a Decimal data type, #,##0 for an Integer data type, or Capitalize for a String data type.

- **Language**   This option applies only to String data types. You use it to specify the language to apply when you enable the Speller.

- **Enable Speller**   You can use this option to allow DQS to check the spelling of values for a domain with a String data type. The Speller will flag suspected syntax, spelling, and sentence-structure errors with a red underscore when you are working on the Domain Values or Term-Based Relations tabs of the Domain Management activity, the Manage Domain Values step of the Knowledge Discovery activity, or the Manage And View Results step of the Cleansing activity.

- **Disable Syntax Error Algorithms**   DQS can check string values for syntax errors before adding each value to the domain during data cleansing.

FIGURE 7-3 Domain properties in the Create Domain dialog box

Domain Values   After you create the domain, you can add knowledge to the domain by setting domain values. Domain values represent the range of possible values that might exist in a data source for the current domain, including both correct and incorrect values. The inclusion of incorrect domain values in a knowledge base allows you to establish rules for correcting those values during cleansing activities.

You use buttons on the Domain Values tab to add a new domain value manually, import new valid values from Excel, or import new string values with type Correct or Error from a cleansing data quality project.

> **Tip** To import data from Excel, you can use any of the following file types: XLS, XLSX, or CSV. DQS attempts to add every value found in the file, but only if the value does not already exist in the domain. DQS imports values in the first column as domain values and values in other columns as synonyms, setting the value in the first column as the leading value. DQS will not import a value if it violates a domain rule, if the data type does not match that of the domain, or if the value is null.

When you add or import values, you can adjust the Type to one of the following settings for each domain value:

- **Correct**   You use this setting for domain values that you know are members of the domain and have no syntax errors.

- **Error** You assign a Type of Error to a domain value that you know is a member of the domain but has an incorrect value, such as a misspelling or undesired abbreviation. For example, in a Product domain, you might add a domain value of *Mtn 500 Silver 52* with the Error type and include a corrected value of *Mountain-500 Silver, 52*. By adding known error conditions to the domain, you can speed up the data cleansing process by having DQS automatically identify and fix known errors, which allows you to focus on new errors found during data processing. However, you can flag a domain value as an Error value without providing a corrected value.

- **Invalid** You designate a domain value as Invalid when it is not a member of the domain and you have no correction to associate with it. For example, a value of *United States* would be an invalid value in a Product domain.

After you publish your domain changes to the knowledge base and later return to the Domain Values tab, you can see the relationship between correct and incorrect values in the domain values list, as shown in Figure 7-4 for the product Adjustable Race. Notice also the underscore in the user interface to identify a potential misspelling of "Adj Race."

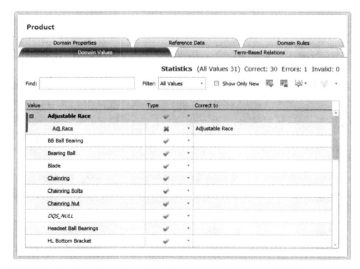

FIGURE 7-4 Domain value with Error state and corrected value

If there are multiple correct domain values that correspond to a single entity, you can organize them as a group of synonyms by selecting them and clicking the Set Selected Domain Values As Synonyms button in the Domain Values toolbar. Furthermore, you can designate one of the synonyms as a leading value by right-clicking the value and selecting Set As Leading in the context menu. When DQS encounters any of the other synonyms in a cleansing activity, it replaces the nonleading synonym values with the leading value. Figure 7-5 shows an example of synonyms for the leading value *Road-750 Black, 52* after the domain changes have been published.

Value	Type		Correct to
Mountain-500 Black, 52	✓	▾	
Mountain-500 Silver, 40	✓	▾	
Mountain-500 Silver, 42	✓	▾	
Mountain-500 Silver, 44	✓	▾	
Mountain-500 Silver, 48	✓	▾	
Mountain-500 Silver, 52	✓	▾	
Road-750 Black, 44	✓	▾	
Road-750 Black, 48	✓	▾	
Road-750 Black, 52	✓	▾	
Road 750 Black 52	✓	▾	Road-750 Black, 52
Road-750 Black 52	✓	▾	Road-750 Black, 52

FIGURE 7-5 Synonym values with designation of a leading value

Data Quality Client keeps track of the changes you make to domain values during your current session. To review your work, you click the Show/Hide The Domain Values Changes History Panel button, which is accessible by clicking the last button in the Domain Values toolbar.

Term-Based Relations Another option you have for adding knowledge to a domain is *term-based relations*, which you use to make it easier to find and correct common occurrences in your domain values. Rather than set up synonyms for variations of a domain value on the Domain Values tab, you can define a list of string values and specify the corresponding Correct To value on the Term-Based Relations tab. For example, in the product domain, you could have various products that contain the abbreviation Mtn, such as *Mtn-500 Silver, 40* and *Mtn End Caps*. To have DQS automatically correct any occurrence of *Mtn* within a domain value string to *Mountain*, you can create a term-based relation by specifying a Value/Correct To pair, as shown in Figure 7-6.

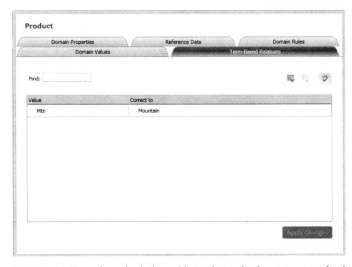

FIGURE 7-6 Term-based relation with a value paired to a corrected value

Reference Data You can subscribe to a reference data service (RDS) that DQS uses to cleanse, standardize, and enhance your data. Before you can set the properties on the Reference Data tab for your knowledge base, you must configure the RDS provider as described in the "Configuration" section of this chapter.

After you configure your DataMarket Account key in the Configuration area, you click the Browse button on the Reference Data tab to select a reference data service provider for which you have a current subscription. On the Online Reference Data Service Providers Catalog page, you map the domain to an RDS schema column. The letter *M* displays next to mandatory columns in the RDS schema that you must include in the mapping.

Next, you configure the following settings for the RDS (as shown in Figure 7-7):

- **Auto Correction Threshold** Specify the threshold for the confidence score. During data cleansing, DQS autocorrects records having a score higher than this threshold.

- **Suggested Candidates** Specify the number of candidates for suggested values to retrieve from the reference data service.

- **Min Confidence** Specify the threshold for the confidence score for suggestions. During data cleansing, DQS ignores suggestions with a score lower than this threshold.

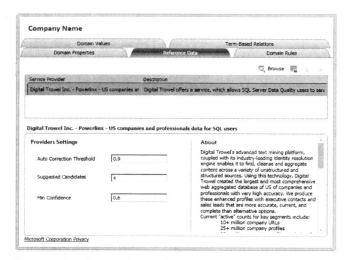

FIGURE 7-7 Reference data service provider settings

Domain Rules You use domain rules to establish the conditions that determine whether a domain value is valid. However, note that domain rules are not used to correct data.

After you click the Add A New Domain Rule button on the Domain Rules tab, you provide a name for the rule and an optional description. Then you define the conditions for the rule in the Build A Rule pane. For example, if there is a maximum length for a domain value, you can create a rule by selecting Length Is Less Than Or Equal To in the rule drop-down list and then typing in the condition value, as shown in Figure 7-8.

FIGURE 7-8 Domain rule to validate the length of domain values

You can create compound rules by adding multiple conditions to the rule and specifying whether the conditions have AND or OR logic. As you build the rule, you can use the Run The Selected Domain Rule On Test Data button. You must manually enter one or more values as test data for this procedure, and then click the Test The Domain Rule On All The Terms button. You will see icons display to indicate whether a value is correct, in error, or invalid. Then when you finish building the rule, you click the Apply All Rules button to update the status of domain values according to the new rule.

Note You can temporarily disable a rule by clearing its corresponding Active check box.

Composite Domain   Sometimes a complex string in your data source contains multiple terms, each of which has different rules or different data types and thus requires separate domains. However, you still need to validate the field as a whole. For example, with a product name like *Mountain-500 Black, 40*, you might want to validate the model of *Mountain-500*, the color *Black*, and the size *40* separately to confirm the validity of the product name. To address this situation, you can create a composite domain.

Before you can create a composite domain, you must have at least two domains in your knowledge base. Begin the Domain Management activity, and click the Create A Composite Domain button on the toolbar. Type a name for the composite domain, provide a description if you like, and then select the domains to include in the composite domain.

> **Note** After you add a domain to a composite domain, you cannot add it to a second composite domain.

CD Properties You can always change, add, or remove domains in the composite domain on the CD Properties tab. You can also select one of the following parsing methods in the Advanced section of this tab:

- **Reference Data** If you map the composite domain to an RDS, you can specify that DQS use the RDS for parsing each domain in the composite domain.

- **In Order** You use this setting when you want DQS to parse the field values in the same order that the domains are listed in the composite domain.

- **Delimiters** When your field contains delimiters, you can instruct DQS to parse values based on the delimiter you specify, such as a tab, comma, or space. When you use delimiters for parsing, you have the option to use knowledge-base parsing. With knowledge-base parsing, DQS identifies the domains for known values in the string and then uses domain knowledge to determine how to add unknown values to other domains. For example, let's say that you have a field in the data source containing the string *Mountain-500 Brown, 40*. If DQS recognizes *Mountain-500* as a value in the Model domain and *40* as a value in the Size domain, but it does not recognize *Brown* in the Color domain, it will add *Brown* to the Color domain.

Reference Data You use this tab to specify an RDS provider and map the individual domains of a composite domain to separate fields of the provider's RDS schema. For example, you might have company information for which you want to validate address details. You combine the domains Address, City, State, and Zip to create a composite domain that you map to the RDS schema. You then create a cleansing project to apply the RDS rules to your data.

CD Rules You use the CD Rules tab to define cross-domain rules for validating, correcting, and standardizing domain values for a composite domain. A cross-domain rule uses similar conditions available to domain rules, but this type of rule must hold true for all domains in the composite domain rather than for a single domain. Each rule contains an *If* clause and a *Then* clause, and each clause contains one or more conditions and is applicable to separate domains. For example, you can develop a rule that invalidates a record if the *Size* value is not *S, M,* or *L* when the Model value begins with *Mountain-*, as shown in Figure 7-9. As with domain rules, you can create rules with multiple conditions and you can test a rule before finalizing its definition.

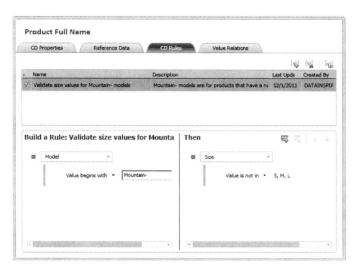

FIGURE 7-9 Cross-domain rule to validate corresponding size values in composite domain

Note If you create a *Then* clause that uses a definitive condition, DQS will not apply the rule to both domain values and their synonyms. Definitive conditions are Value Is Equal To, Value Is Not Equal To, Value Is In, or Value Is Not In. Furthermore, if you use the Value Is Equal To condition for the *Then* clause, DQS not only validates data, but also corrects data using this rule.

Value Relations After completing a knowledge-discovery activity, you can view the number of occurrences for each combination of values in a composite domain, as shown in Figure 7-10.

Model	Color	Size	Frequency
DQS_NULL	*DQS_NULL*	*DQS_NULL*	209

FIGURE 7-10 Value relations for a composite domain

Linked Domain You can use a linked domain to handle situations that a regular domain cannot support. For example, if you create a data quality project for a data source that has two fields that use the same domain values, you must set up two domains to complete the mapping of fields to domains. Rather than maintain two domains with the same values, you can create a linked domain that inherits the properties, values, and rules of another domain.

One way to create a linked domain is to open the knowledge base containing the source domain, right-click the domain, and select Create A Linked Domain. Another way to create a linked domain is during an activity that requires you to map fields. You start by mapping the first field to a domain and then attempt to map the second field to the same domain. Data Quality Client prompts you to create a linked domain, at which time you provide a domain name and description.

After you create the linked domain, you can use the Domain Management activity to complete tasks such as adding domain values or setting up domain rules by accessing either domain. The changes are made automatically in the other domain. However, you can change the domain properties in the original domain only.

End of Domain Management Activity

DQS locks the knowledge base when you begin the Domain Management activity to prevent others from making conflicting changes. If you cannot complete all the changes you need to make in a single session, you click the Close button to save your work and keep the knowledge base locked. Click the Finish button when your work is complete. Data Quality Client displays a prompt for you to confirm the action to take. Click Publish to make your changes permanent, unlock the database, and make the knowledge base available to others. Otherwise, click No to save your work, keep the database locked, and exit the Domain Management activity.

Knowledge Discovery

As an alternative to manually adding knowledge to your knowledge base, you can use the Knowledge Discovery activity to partially automate that process. You can perform this activity multiple times, as often as needed, to add domain values to the knowledge base from one or more data sources.

To start, you open the knowledge base in the Domain Management area of Data Quality Client and select the Knowledge Discovery activity. Then you complete a series of three steps: Map, Discover, and Manage Domain Values.

Map

In the Map step, you identify the source data you want DQS to analyze. This data must be available on the Data Quality Server, either in a SQL Server table or view or in an Excel file. However, it does not need to be from the same source that you intend to cleanse or de-duplicate with DQS.

The purpose of this step is to map columns in the source data to a domain or composite domain in the knowledge base, as shown in Figure 7-11. You can choose to create a new domain or composite domain at this point when necessary. When you finish mapping all columns, click the Next button to proceed to the Discover step.

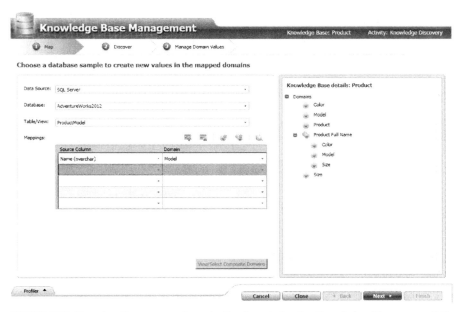

FIGURE 7-11 Mapping the source column to the domain for the Knowledge Discovery activity

Discover

In the Discover step, you use the Start button to begin the knowledge discovery process. As the process executes, the Discover step displays the current status for the following three phases of processing (as shown in Figure 7-12):

- **Pre-processing Records**   During this phase, DQS loads and indexes records from the source in preparation for profiling the data. The status of this phase displays as the number of pre-processed records compared to the total number of records in the source. In addition, DQS updates all data-profiling statistics except the Valid In Domain column. These statistics are visible in the Profiler tab and include the total number of records in the source, the total number of values for the domain by field, and the number of unique values by field. DQS also compares the values from the source with the values from the domain to determine which values are found only in the source and identified as new.

- **Running Domain Rules**   DQS uses the domain rules for each domain to update the Valid In Domain column in the Profiler, and it displays the status as a percentage of completion.

- **Running Discovery**   DQS analyzes the data to add to the Manage Domain Values step and identifies syntax errors. As this phase executes, the current status displays as a percentage of completion.

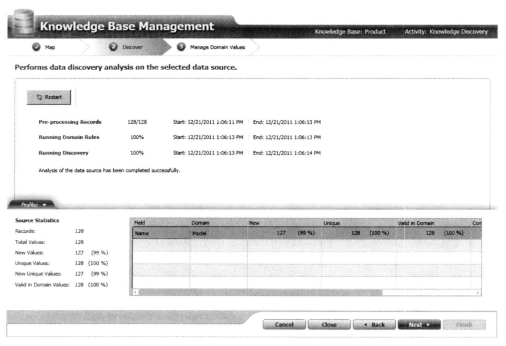

FIGURE 7-12 Source statistics resulting from data discovery analysis

You use the source statistics on the Profiler tab to assess the completeness and uniqueness of the source data. If the source yields few new values for a domain or has a high number of invalid values, you might consider using a different source. The Profiler tab might also display notifications, as shown in Figure 7-13, to alert you to such conditions.

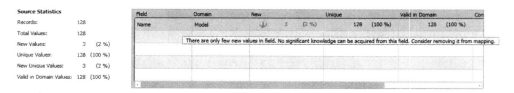

FIGURE 7-13 Notifications and source statistics display on the Profiler tab

Manage Domain Values

In the third step of the Knowledge Discovery activity, you review the results of the data-discovery analysis. The unique new domain values display in a list with a Type setting and suggested corrections, where applicable. You can make any necessary changes to the values, type, and corrected values, and you can add new domain values, delete values, and work with synonyms just like you can when working on the Doman Values tab of the Domain Management activity.

Notice in Figure 7-14 that the several product models beginning with *Mountain-* were marked as Error and DQS proposed a corrected value of *Mountain-500* for each of the new domain values. It did this because *Mountain-500* was the only pre-existing product model in the domain. DQS determined that similar product models found in the source must be misspellings and proposed corrections to the source values to match them to the pre-existing domain value. In this scenario, if the new product models are all correct, you can change the Type setting to Correct. When you make this change, Data Quality Client automatically removes the Correct To value.

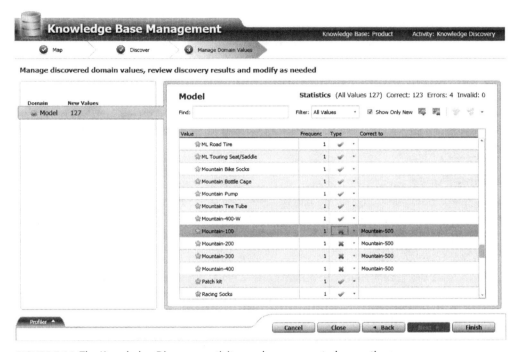

FIGURE 7-14 The Knowledge Discovery activity produces suggested corrections

After reviewing each domain and making corrections, click the Finish button to end the Knowledge Discovery activity. Then click the Publish button to complete the activity, update the knowledge base with the new domain values, and leave the knowledge base in an unlocked state. If you click the No button instead of the Publish button, the results of the activity are discarded and the knowledge base is unlocked.

Matching Policy

Another aspect of adding knowledge to a knowledge base is defining a matching policy. This policy is necessary for data quality projects that use matching to correct data problems such as misspelled customer names or inconsistent address formats. A matching policy contains one or more matching rules that DQS uses to determine the probability of a match between two records.

You begin by opening a knowledge base in the Domain Management area of Data Quality Client and selecting the Matching Policy activity. The process to create a matching policy consists of three steps: Map, Matching Policy, and Matching Results.

Tip You might consider creating a knowledge base that you use only for matching projects. In this matching-only knowledge base, include only domains that have values that are both discrete and uniquely identify a record, such as names and addresses.

Map

The first step of the Matching Policy activity is similar to the first step of the Knowledge Discovery activity. You start the creation of a matching policy by mapping a field from an Excel or SQL Server data source to a domain or composite domain in the selected knowledge base. If a corresponding domain does not exist in the knowledge base, you have the option to create one. You must select a source field in this step if you want to reference that field in a matching rule in the next step. Use the Next button to continue to the Discover step.

Matching Policy

In the Matching Policy step, you set up one or more matching rules that DQS uses to assign a matching score for each pair of records it compares. DQS considers the records to be a match when this matching score is greater than the minimum matching score you establish for the matching policy.

To begin, click the Create A Matching Rule button. Next, assign a name, an optional description, and a minimum matching score to the matching rule. The lowest minimum matching score you can assign is 80 percent, unless you change the DQS configuration on the Administration page. In the Rule Editor toolbar, click the Add A New Domain Element button, select a domain, and configure the matching rule parameters for the selected domain, as shown in Figure 7-15.

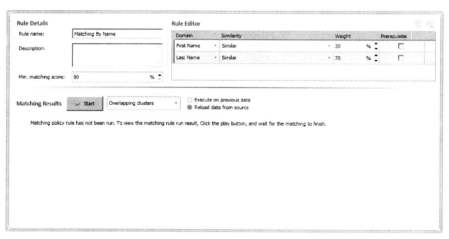

FIGURE 7-15 Creation of a matching rule for a matching policy

You can choose from the following values when configuring the Similarity parameter:

- **Similar** You select this value when you want DQS to calculate a matching score for a field in two records and set the similarity score to 0 (to indicate no similarity) when the matching score is less than 60. If the field has a numeric data type, you can set a threshold for similarity using a percentage or integer value. If the field has a date data type, you can set the threshold using a numeric value for day, month, or year.

- **Exact** When you want DQS to identify two records to be a match only when the same field in each record is identical, you select this value. DQS assigns a matching score of 100 for the domain when the fields are identical. Otherwise, it assigns a matching score of 0.

Whether you add one or more domains to a matching rule, you must configure the Weight parameter for each domain that you do not set as a prerequisite. DQS uses the weight to determine how the individual domain's matching score affects the overall matching score. The sum of the weight values must be equal to 100.

When you select the Prerequisite check box for a domain, DQS sets the Similarity parameter to Exact and considers values in a field to be a match only when they are identical in the two compared records. Regardless of the result, a prerequisite domain has no effect on the overall matching score for a record. Using the prerequisite option is an optimization that speeds up the matching process.

You can test the rule by clicking the Start button on the Matching Policy page. If the results are not what you expect, you can modify the rule and test the rule again. When you retest the matching policy, you can choose to either execute the matching policy on the processed matches from a previous execution or on data that DQS reloads from the source. The Matching Results tab, shown in Figure 7-16, displays the results of the current test and the previous test so that you can determine whether your changes improve the match results.

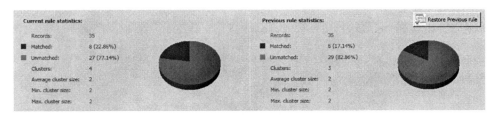

FIGURE 7-16 Comparison of results from consecutive executions of a matching rule

A review of the Profiler tab can help you decide how to modify a match rule. For example, if a field has a high percentage of unique records, you might consider eliminating the field from a match rule or lower the weight value. On the other hand, having a low percentage of unique records is useful only if the field has a high level of completeness. If both uniqueness and completeness are low, you should exclude the field from the matching policy.

You can click the Restore Previous Rule button to revert the rule settings to their prior state if you prefer. When you are satisfied with the results, click the Next button to continue to the next step.

Matching Results

In the Matching Results step, you choose whether to review results as overlapping clusters or nonoverlapping clusters. With overlapping clusters, you might see separate clusters that contain the same records, whereas with nonoverlapping clusters you see only clusters with records in common. Then you click the Start button to apply all matching rules to your data source.

When processing completes, you can view a table that displays a filtered list of matched records with a color code to indicate the applicable matching rule, as shown in Figure 7-17. Each cluster of records has a pivot record that DQS randomly selects from the cluster as the record to keep. Furthermore, each cluster includes one or more matched records along with its matching score. You can change the filter to display unmatched records, or you can apply a separate filter to view matched records having scores greater than or equal to 80, 85, 90, 95, or 100 percent.

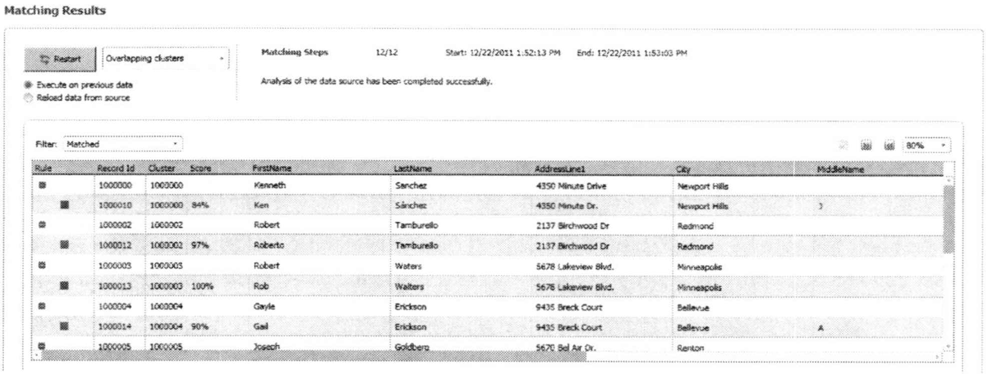

FIGURE 7-17 Matched records based on two matching rules

You can review the color codes on the Matching Rules tab, and you can evaluate statistics about the matching results on the Matching Results tab. You can also double-click a matched record in the list to see the Pivot and Matched Records fields side by side, the score for each field, and the overall score for the match, as shown in Figure 7-18.

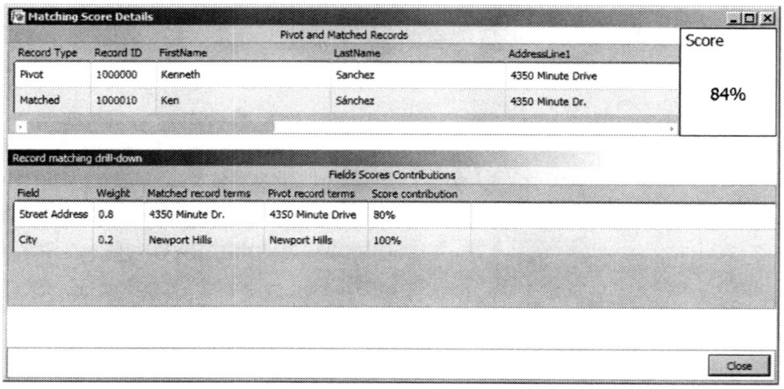

FIGURE 7-18 Matching-score details displaying field scores and an overall score

If necessary, you can return to the previous step to fine-tune a matching rule and then return to this step. Before you click the Restart button, you can choose the Reload Data From Source option to copy the source data into a staging table where DQS re-indexes it. Your other option is to choose Execute On Previous Data to use the data in the staging table without re-indexing it, which could process the matching policy more quickly.

Once you are satisfied with the results, click the Finish button. You then have the option to publish the matching policy to the knowledge base. At this point, you can use the matching policy with a matching data quality project.

Data Quality Projects

When you have a knowledge base in place, you can create a data quality project to use the knowledge it contains to cleanse source data or use its matching policy to find matching records in source data. After you run the data quality project, you can export its results to a SQL Server database or to a CSV file. As another option, you can import the results to a domain in the Domain Management activity.

Regardless of which type of data quality project you want to create, you start the project in the same way, by clicking the New Data Quality Project button on the home page of Data Quality Client. When you create a new project, you provide a name for the data quality project, provide an optional description, and select a knowledge base. You can then select the Cleansing activity for any knowledge base; you can select the Matching activity for a knowledge base only when that knowledge base has a matching policy. To launch the activity's wizard, click the Create button. At this point, the project is locked and inaccessible to other users.

Cleansing Projects

A cleansing data quality project begins with an analysis of source data using knowledge contained in a knowledge base and a categorization of that data into groups of correct and incorrect data. After DQS completes the analysis and categorization process, you can approve, reject, or change the proposed corrections.

When you create a cleansing data quality project, the wizard leads you through four steps: Map, Cleanse, Manage And View Results, and Export.

Map

The first step in the cleansing data quality project is to map the data source to domains in the selected knowledge base, following the same process you used for the Knowledge Discovery and Matching Policy activities. The data source can be either an Excel file or a table or view in a SQL Server database. When you finish mapping all columns, click the Next button to proceed to the Cleanse step.

Note If you map a field to a composite domain, only the rules associated with the composite domain will apply, rather than the rules for the individual domains assigned to the composite domain. Furthermore, if the composite domain is mapped to a reference data service, DQS sends the source data to the reference data service for parsing and cleansing. Otherwise, DQS performs the parsing using the method you specified for the composite domain.

Cleanse

To begin the cleansing process, click the Start button. When the analysis process completes, you can view the statistics in the Profiler tab, as shown in Figure 7-19. These statistics reflect the results of categorization that DQS performs: correct records, corrected records, suggested records, and invalid records. DQS uses advanced algorithms to cleanse data and calculates a confidence score to determine the category applicable to each record in the source data. You can configure confidence thresholds for auto-correction and auto-suggestion. If a record's confidence score falls below either of these thresholds and is neither correct nor invalid, DQS categorizes the record as new and leaves it for you to manually correct if necessary in the next step.

Profiler ▼					
Source Statistics		Field	Domain	Corrected Values	Suggested Values	Completeness
Records:	606	ProductName	Product	15 (2 %)	16 (3 %)	
Correct Records:	15 (2 %)					
Corrected Records:	15 (2 %)					
Suggested Records:	16 (3 %)					
Invalid Records:	4 (1 %)					

FIGURE 7-19 Profiler statistics after the cleansing process completes

Manage and View Results

In the next step of the cleansing data quality project, you see separate tabs for each group of records categorized by DQS: Suggested, New, Invalid, Corrected, and Correct. The tab labels show the number of records allocated to each group. When you open a tab, you can see a table of domain values for that group and the number of records containing each domain value, as shown in Figure 7-20.

When applicable, you can also see the proposed corrected value, confidence score, and reason for the proposed correction for each value. If you select a row in the table, you can see the individual records that contain the original value. You must use the horizontal scroll bar to see all the fields for the individual records.

When you enable the Speller feature for a domain, the cleansing process identifies potential spelling errors by displaying a wavy red underscore below the domain value. You can right-click the value to see suggestions and then select one or add the potential error to the dictionary.

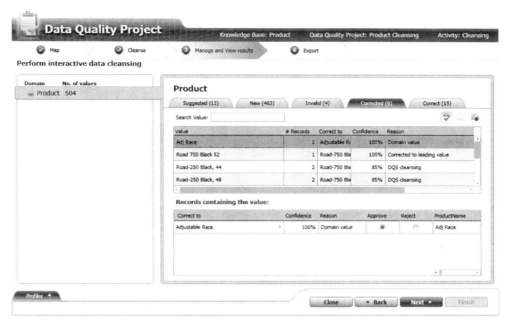

FIGURE 7-20 Categorized results after automated data cleansing

If DQS identifies a value in the source data as a synonym, it suggests a correction to the leading value. This feature is useful for standardization of your data. You must first enable the domain for leading values and define synonyms in the knowledge base before running a cleansing data quality project.

After reviewing the proposed corrections, you can either approve or reject the change for each value or for each record individually. Another option is to click the Approve All Terms button or the Reject All Terms button in the toolbar. You can also replace a proposed correction by typing a new value in the Correct To box, and then approve the manual correction. In most cases, approved values move to the Corrected tab and rejected values move to the Invalid tab. However, if you approve a value on the New tab, it moves to the Correct tab.

Export

At no time during the cleansing process does DQS change source data. Instead, you can export the results of the cleansing data quality project to a SQL Server table or to a CSV file. A preview of the output displays in the final step of the project, as shown in Figure 7-21.

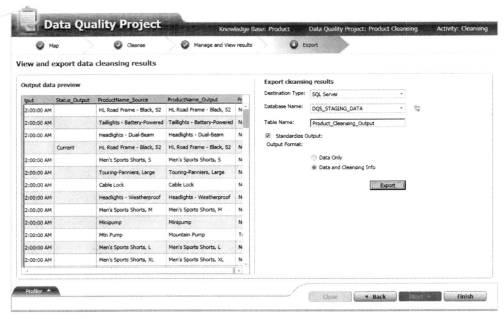

FIGURE 7-21 Review of the cleansing results to export

Before you export the data, you must decide whether you want to export the data only or export both the data and cleansing information. Cleansing information includes the original value, the cleansed value, the reason for a correction, a confidence score, and the categorization of the record. By default, DQS uses the output format for the domain as defined in the knowledge base unless you clear the Standardize Output check box. When you click the Export button, Data Quality Client exports the data to the specified destination. You can then click the Finish button to close and unlock the data quality project.

Matching Projects

By using a matching policy defined for a knowledge base, a matching data quality project can identify both exact and approximate matches in a data source. Ideally, you run the matching process after running the cleansing process and exporting the results. You can then specify the export file or destination table as the source for the matching project.

A matching data quality project consists of three steps: Map, Matching, and Export.

Map

The first step for a matching project begins in the same way as a cleansing project, by requiring you to map fields from the source to a domain. However, in a matching project, you must map a field to each domain specified in the knowledge base's matching policy.

Matching

In the Matching step, you choose whether to generate overlapping clusters or nonoverlapping clusters, and then click the Start button to launch the automated matching process. When the process completes, you can review a table of matching results by cluster. The interface is similar in functionality to the one you use when reviewing the matching results during the creation of a matching policy. However, in the matching project, an additional column includes a check box that you can select to reject a record as a match.

Export

After reviewing the matching results, you can export the results as the final step of the matching project. As shown in Figure 7-22, you must choose the destination and the content to export. You have the following two options for exporting content:

- **Matching Results**   This content type includes both matched and unmatched records. The matched records include several columns related to the matching process, including the cluster identifier, the matching rule that identified the match, the matching score, the approval status, and a flag to indicate the pivot record.

- **Survivorship Results**   This content type includes only the survivorship record and unmatched records. You must select a survivorship rule when choosing this export option to specify which of the matched records in a cluster are preserved in the export. All other records in a cluster are discarded. If more than one record satisfies the survivorship criteria, DQS keeps the record with the lowest record identifier.

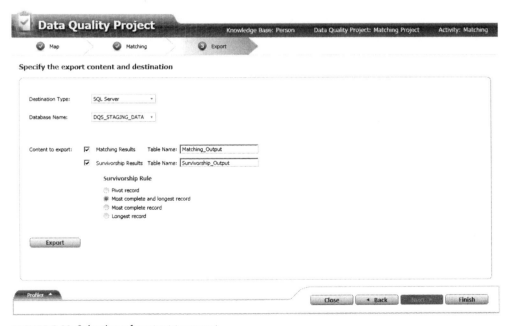

FIGURE 7-22 Selection of content to export

Important When you click the Finish button, the project is unlocked and available for later use. However, DQS uses the knowledge-base contents at the time that you finished the project and ignores any subsequent changes to the knowledge base. To access any changes to the knowledge base, such as a modified matching policy, you must create a new matching project.

Administration

In the Administration feature of Data Quality Client, you can perform activity-monitoring and configuration tasks. Activity monitoring is accessible by any user who can open Data Quality Client. On the other hand, only an administrator can access the configuration tasks.

Activity Monitoring

You can use the Activity Monitoring page to review the status of current and historic activities performed on the Data Quality Server, as shown in Figure 7-23. DQS administrators can terminate an activity or a step within an activity when necessary by right-clicking on the activity or step.

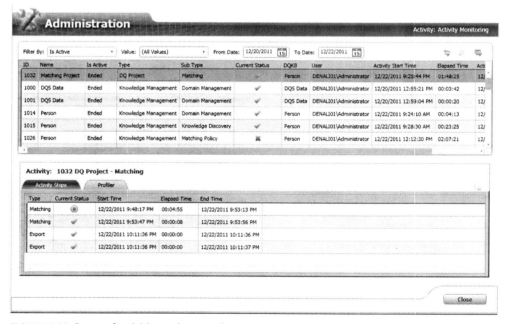

FIGURE 7-23 Status of activities and status of activity steps of the selected activity

Activities that appear on this page include knowledge discovery, domain management, matching policy, cleansing projects, matching projects, and the cleansing transformation in an Integration Services package. You can see who initiated each activity, the start and end time of the activity, and the elapsed time. To facilitate locating specific activities, you can use a filter to find activities by date range and by status, type, subtype, knowledge base, or user. When you select an activity on this page, you can view the related activity details, such as the steps and profiler information.

You can click the Export The Selected Activity To Excel button to export the activity details, process steps, and profiling information to Excel. The export file separates this information into four worksheets:

- **Activity**   This sheet includes the details about the activity, including the name, type, subtype, current status, elapsed time, and so on.

- **Processes**   This sheet includes information about each activity step, including current status, start and end time, and elapsed time.

- **Profiler – Source**   The contents of this sheet depend on the activity subtype. For the Cleansing subtype, you see the number of total records, correct records, corrected records, and invalid records. For the Knowledge Discovery, Domain Management, Matching Policy, and Matching subtypes, you see the number of records, total values, new values, unique value, and new unique values.

- **Profiler – Fields**   This sheet's contents also depend on the activity subtype. For the Cleansing and SSIS Cleansing subtypes, the sheet contains the following information by field: domain, corrected values, suggested values, completeness, and accuracy. For the Knowledge Discovery, Domain Management, Matching Policy, and Matching subtypes, the sheet contains the following information by field: domain, new value count, unique value count, count of values that are valid in the domain, and completeness.

Configuration

The Configuration area of Data Quality Client allows you to set up reference data providers, set properties for the Data Quality Server, and configure logging. You must be a DQS administrator to perform configuration tasks. You access this area from the Data Quality Client home page by clicking the Configuration button.

Reference Data

Rather than maintain domain values and rules in a knowledge base, you can subscribe to a reference data service through Windows Azure Marketplace. Most reference data services are available as a monthly paid subscription, but some providers offer a free trial. (Also, Digital Trowel provides a free service to cleanse and standardize data for US public and private companies.) When you subscribe to a service, you receive an account key that you must register in Data Quality Client before you can use reference data in your data-quality activities.

The Reference Data tab is the first tab that displays in the Configuration area, as shown in Figure 7-24. Here you type or paste your account key in the DataMarket Account ID box, and then click the Validate DataMarket Account ID button to the right of the box. You might need to provide a proxy server and port number if your DQS server requires a proxy server to connect to the Internet.

Note If you do not have a reference data service subscription, you can use the Create A DataMarket Account ID link to open the Windows Azure Marketplace site in your browser. You must have a Windows Live ID to access the site. Click the Data link at the top of the page, and then click the Data Quality Services link in the Category list. You can view the current list of reference data service providers at *https://datamarket.azure.com/browse /Data?Category=dqs*.

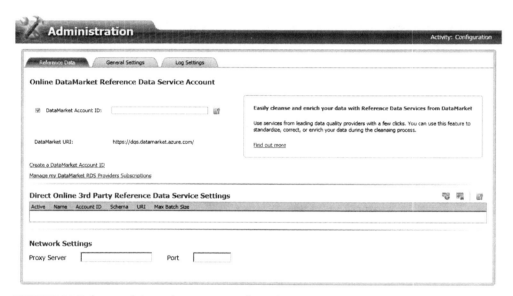

FIGURE 7-24 Reference data service account configuration

As an alternative to using a DataMarket subscription for reference data, you can configure settings for a third-party reference data service by clicking the Add New Reference Data Service Provider button and supplying the requisite details: a name for the service, a comma-delimited list of fields as a schema, a secure URI for the reference data service, a maximum number of records per batch, and a subscriber account identifier.

General Settings

You use the General Settings tab, shown in Figure 7-25, to configure the following settings:

- **Interactive Cleansing** Specify the minimum confidence score for suggestions and the minimum confidence score for auto-corrections. DQS uses these values as thresholds when determining how to categorize records for a cleansing data quality project.

- **Matching** Specify the minimum matching score for DQS to use for a matching policy.

- **Profiler** Use this check box to enable or disable profiling notifications. These notifications appear in the Profiler tab when you are performing a knowledge base activity or running a data quality project.

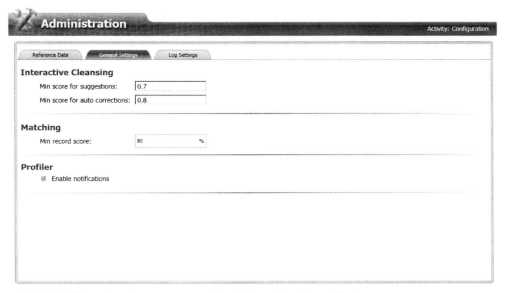

FIGURE 7-25 General settings to set score thresholds and enable notifications

Log Settings

Log files are useful for troubleshooting problems that might occur. By default, the DQS log files capture events with an Error severity level, but you can change the severity level to Fatal, Warn, Info, or Debug by activity, as shown in Figure 7-26.

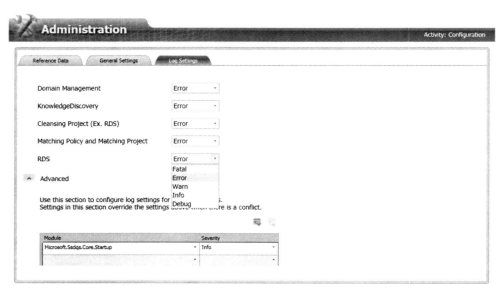

FIGURE 7-26 Log settings for the Data Quality Server

DQS generates the following three types of log files:

- **Data Quality Server**   You can find server-related activity in the DQServerLog.DQS_MAIN.log file in the Program Files\Microsoft SQL Server\MSSQL11.MSSQLSERVER\MSSQL\Log folder.

- **Data Quality Client**   You can view client-related activity in the DQClientLog.log file in the %APPDATA%\SSDQS\Log folder.

- **DQS Cleansing Transformation**   When you execute a package containing the DQS Cleansing transformation, DQS logs the cleansing activity in the DQSSSISLog.log file available in the %APPDATA%\SSDQS\Log folder.

In addition to configuring log severity settings by activity, you can configure them at the module level in the Advanced section of the Log Settings tab. By using a more granular approach to log settings, you can get better insight into a problem you are troubleshooting. The *Microsoft.Ssdqs.Core. Startup* is configured with a default severity of Info to track events related to starting and stopping the DQS service. You can use the drop-down list in the Advanced section to select another module and specify the log severity level you want.

Integration

DQS cleansing and matching functionality is built into two other SQL Server 2012 features—Integration Services and Master Data Services—so that you can more effectively manage data quality across your organization. In Integration Services, you can use DQS components to routinely perform data cleansing in a scheduled package. In Master Data Services, you can compare external data to master data to find matching records based on the matching policy you define for a knowledge base.

Integration Services

In earlier versions of SQL Server, you could use an Integration Services package to automate the process of cleansing data by using Derived Column or Script transformations, but the creation of a data flow to perform complex cleansing could be tedious. Now you can take advantage of DQS to use the rules or reference data in a knowledge base for data cleansing. The integration between Integration Services and DQS allows you to perform the same tasks that a cleansing data quality project supports, but on a scheduled basis. Another advantage of using the DQS Cleansing transformation in Integration Services is the ability to cleanse data from a source other than Excel or a SQL Server database.

Because the DQS functionality in Integration Services is built into the product, you can begin using it right away without additional installation or configuration. Of course, you must have both a Data Quality Server and a knowledge base available. To get started, you add a DQS connection manager to the package, add a Data Flow Task, and then add a DQS Cleansing transformation to the data flow.

DQS Connection Manager

You use the DQS connection manager to establish a connection from the Integration Services package to a Data Quality Server. When you add the connection manager to your package, you supply the server name. The connection manager interface includes a button to test the connection to the Data Quality Server. You can identify a DQS connection manager by its icon, as shown in Figure 7-27.

 DQS Cleansing

FIGURE 7-27 DQS connection manager

DQS Cleansing Transformation

As we explain in the "Cleansing Projects" section of this chapter, DQS uses advanced algorithms to cleanse data and calculates a confidence score to categorize records as Correct, Corrected, Suggested, or Invalid. The DQS Cleansing transformation in a data flow transfers data to the Data Quality Server, which in turn executes the cleansing process and sends the data back to the transformation with a corrected value, when applicable, and a status. You can then add a Conditional Split transformation to the data flow to route each record to a separate destination based on its status.

> **Note** If the knowledge base maps to a reference data service, the Data Quality Server might also forward the data to the service for cleansing and enhancement.

Configuration of the DQS Cleansing transformation begins with the selection of a connection manager and a knowledge base. After you select the knowledge base, the available domains and composite domains are displayed, as shown in Figure 7-28.

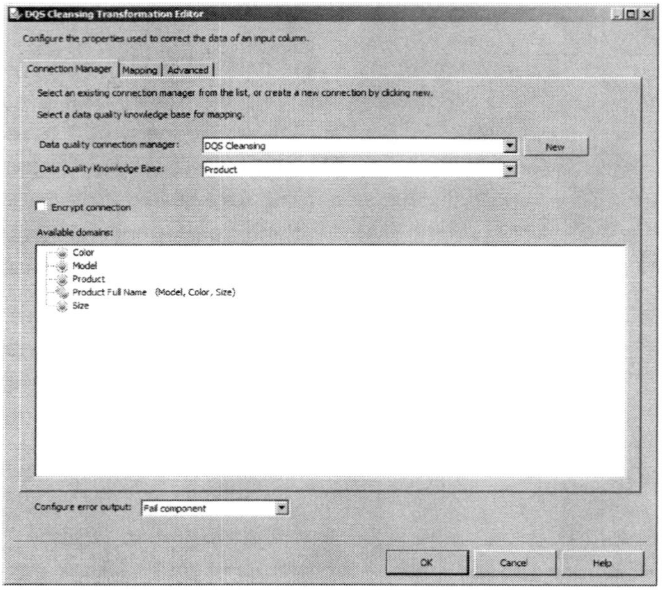

FIGURE 7-28 Connection manager configuration for the DQS Cleansing transformation

On the Mapping tab, you map each column in the data flow pipeline to its respective domain, as shown in Figure 7-29. If you are mapping a column to a composite domain, the column must contain the domain values as a comma-delimited string in the same order in which the individual domains appear in the composite domain.

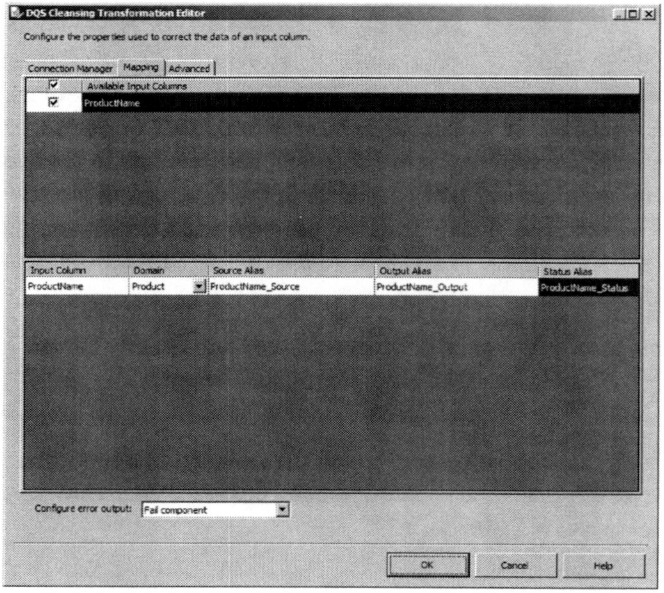

FIGURE 7-29 Mapping a pipeline column to a domain

For each input column, you also define the aliases for the following output columns: source, output, and status. The transformation editor supplies default values for you, but you can change these aliases if you like. During package execution, the column with the source alias contains the original value in the source, whereas the column with the output alias contains the same value for correct and invalid records or the corrected value for suggested or corrected records. The column with the status alias contains values to indicate the outcome of the cleansing process: Auto Suggest, Correct, Invalid, or New.

On the Advanced tab of the transformation editor, you can configure the following options:

- **Standardize Output**   This option, which is enabled by default, automatically standardizes the data in the Output Alias column according to the Format Output settings for each domain. In addition, this option changes synonyms to leading values if you enable Use Leading Values for the domain.

- **Enable Field-Level Columns**   You can optionally include the confidence score or the reason for a correction as additional columns in the transformation output.

- **Enable Record-Level Columns**   If a domain maps to a reference data service that returns additional data columns during the cleansing process, you can include this data as an appended column. In addition, you can include a column to contain the schema for the appended data.

Master Data Services

If you are using Master Data Services (MDS) for master data management, you can use the data-matching functionality in DQS to de-duplicate master data. You must first enable DQS integration on the Web Configuration page of the Master Data Services configuration manager, and you must create a matching policy for a DQS knowledge base. Then you add data to an Excel worksheet and use the MDS Add-in for Excel to combine that data with MDS-managed data in preparation for matching. The matching process adds columns to the worksheet similar to the columns you view during a matching-data-quality project, including the matching score. We provide more information about how to use the DQS matching with MDS in Chapter 8, "Master Data Services."

Master Data Services

The first release of Master Data Services (MDS) appeared in Microsoft SQL Server 2008 R2 to support master data management. In the current release, you find improvements in some areas of the user interface and a new feature for managing your master data, the *MDS Add-in for Excel*. In addition, there are deprecated features and discontinued features that change the way you work with MDS. Collectively, these changes to MDS simplify the implementation, workflows, and administration of MDS.

Getting Started

MDS is available as a feature in SQL Server 2012 Setup rather than as a separate installer as it was in SQL Server 2008. If you have an existing SQL Server 2008 MDS installation, you must decide whether to upgrade MDS with or without a Database Engine upgrade. In this section, we explain the considerations for each option. In addition, we describe the post-installation configuration steps to perform whether you have a new or upgraded MDS installation.

Upgrade Considerations

When you upgrade an existing MDS implementation, you can keep the MDS database in a SQL Server 2008 R2 database instance or you can migrate it to a SQL Server 2012 database instance. Regardless of which choice you make, you should back up your MDS database before you start the upgrade process.

If you choose not to upgrade the MDS database, you must install SQL Server 2012 side by side with SQL Server 2008 R2, although the two versions of SQL Server do not have to be on the same computer. Furthermore, when you install SQL Server 2012, you need to install only the MDS feature, which adds files to the Program Files\Microsoft SQL Server \110\Master Data Services. You must then use Master Data Services Configuration Manager to upgrade the MDS database. It will continue to reside in the SQL Server 2008 R2 instance, but the upgrade process modifies the schema of the MDS database to support the new features of MDS in SQL Server 2012.

On the other hand, if you choose to upgrade the Database Engine to SQL Server 2012, you must first uninstall MDS by using the Uninstall command in the Programs And Features area of Control Panel. Then you use the SQL Server 2012 Setup Wizard to perform the upgrade. After starting setup, choose Installation; select Upgrade from SQL Server 2005, SQL Server 2008, or SQL Server 2008 R2; and complete the wizard. Then use the SQL Server 2012 Setup Wizard again to add the MDS feature to your existing installation.

Configuration

Whether you perform a new installation of MDS or upgrade from a previous version, you must use the Master Data Services Configuration Manager. You can open this tool from the Master Data Services folder in the Microsoft SQL Server 2012 program group on the Start menu. You use it to create or upgrade the MDS database, configure MDS system settings, and create a web application for MDS.

> **Important** If you are upgrading from a previous version of MDS, you must log in using the Administrator account that was used to create the original MDS database. You can identify this account by finding the user with an ID value of *1* in the mdm.tblUser table in the MDS database.

The first configuration step to perform following installation is to configure the MDS database. On the Database Configuration page of Master Data Services Configuration Manager, perform one of the following tasks:

- **New installation**   Click the Create Database button, and complete the Database Wizard. In the wizard, you specify the SQL Server instance and authentication type and provide credentials having permissions to create a database on the selected instance. You also provide a database name and specify collation. Last, you specify a Microsoft Windows account to establish as the MDS administrator account.

> **Important** Before you begin a new installation, you must install Internet Information Services (IIS).

- **Upgrade**   If you want to keep your database in a SQL Server 2008 R2 instance, click the Repair Database button if it is enabled. Then, whether you want to store your MDS database in SQL Server 2008 R2 or SQL Server 2012, click the Upgrade Database button. The Upgrade Database Wizard displays the SQL Server instance and MDS database name, as well as the progress of the update. The upgrade process re-creates tables using the new schema and stored procedures.

> **Note** The upgrade process excludes business rules that you use to generate values for the code attribute. We explain the new automatic code generation in the "Entity Management" section later in this chapter. Furthermore, the upgrade process does not include model deployment packages. You must create new packages in your SQL Server 2012 installation.

When the new or upgraded database is created, you see the System Settings display on the Database Configuration page. You use these settings to control timeouts for the database or the web service, to name a few. If you upgraded your MDS installation, there are two new system settings that you can configure:

- **Show Add-in For Excel Text On Website Home Page** This setting controls whether users see a link to install the MDS Add-in on the MDS home page, as shown in Figure 8-1.

- **Add-in For Excel Install Path On Website Home Page** This setting defaults to the MDS Add-in download page on the Microsoft web site.

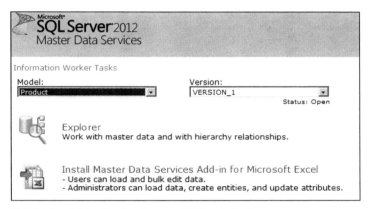

FIGURE 8-1 Add-in for Excel text on MDS website home page

Master Data Manager

Master Data Manager is the web application that data stewards use to manage master data and administrators use to manage model objects and configure security. For the most part, it works as it did in the previous version of MDS, although the Explorer and Integration Management functional areas now use Silverlight 5. As a result, you will find certain tasks are easier and faster to perform. In keeping with this goal of enabling easier and faster processes, you will find the current version of MDS also introduces a new staging process and slight changes to the security model.

Explorer

In the Explorer functional area, you add or delete members for an entity, update attribute values for members, arrange those members within a hierarchy, and optionally organize groups of members as collections. In SQL Server 2012, MDS improves the workflow for performing these tasks.

Entity Management

When you open an entity in the Explorer area, you see a new interface, as shown in Figure 8-2. The set of buttons now display with new icons and with descriptions that clarify their purpose. When you click the Add Member button, you type in all attribute values for the new member in the Details pane. To delete a member, select the member and then click the Delete button. You can also more easily edit attribute values for a member by selecting it in the grid and then typing a new value for the attribute in the Details pane.

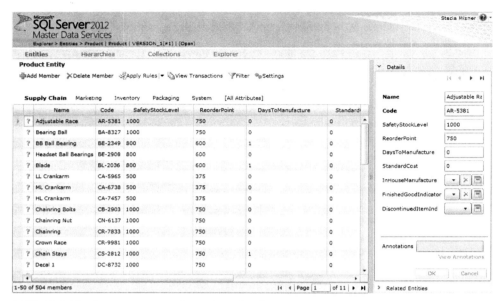

FIGURE 8-2 Member management for a selected entity

Rather than use a business rule to automatically create values for the Code attribute as you do in SQL Server 2008 R2, you can now configure the entity to automatically generate the code value. This automatic assignment of a value applies whether you are adding a member manually in Master Data Manager or importing data through the staging process. To do this, you must have permission to access the System Administration function area and open the entity. On the Entity Maintenance page, select the Create Code Values Automatically check box, as shown in Figure 8-3. You can optionally change the number in the Start With box. If you already have members added to the entity, MDS increments the maximum value by one when you add a new member.

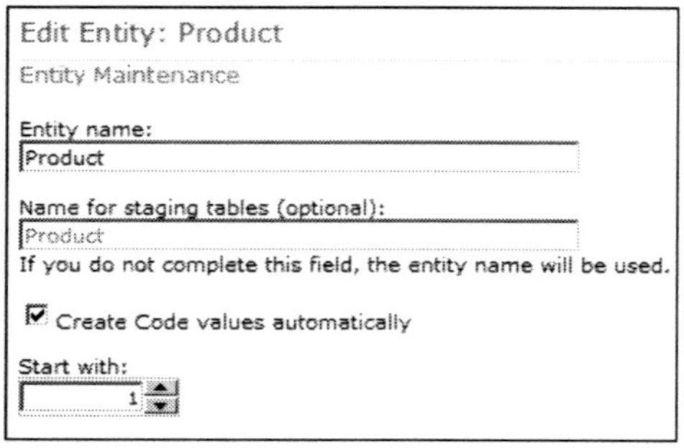

FIGURE 8-3 Check box to automatically generate code values

Note The automatic generation of a value occurs only when you leave the code value blank. You always have the option to override it with a different value when you add a new member.

Many-to-Many Mapping

Another improvement in the current version of MDS is the ability to use the Explorer functional area in Master Data Manager to view entities for which you have defined many-to-many mappings. To see how this works, consider a scenario in which you have products you want to decompose into separate parts and you can associate any single part with multiple products. You manage the relationships between products and parts in MDS by creating three entities: products, parts, and a mapping entity to define the relationship between products and parts, as shown in Figure 8-4. Notice that you need only a code value and attributes to store code values for the two related entities, but no name value.

[All Attributes]

	Name	Code	Product Code	Part Code
✓		BK-R93R-62-HB-R504	BK-R93R-62	HB-R504
✓		BK-R93R-62-SK-9283	BK-R93R-62	SK-9283
✓		BK-R93R-62-CH-0234	BK-R93R-62	CH-0234
✓		BK-R93R-62-FB-9873	BK-R93R-62	FB-9873
▸ ✓		BK-R93R-62-RB-9231	BK-R93R-62	RB-9231

FIGURE 8-4 Arrangement of members in a derived hierarchy

When you open the Product entity and select a member, you can open the Related Entities pane on the right side of the screen where a link displays, such as ProductParts (Attribute: Product Code). When you click this link, a new browser window opens to display the ProductParts entity window with a filter applied to show records related only to the selected product. From that screen, you can click the Go To The "<Name> Entity" To View Attribute Details button, as shown in Figure 8-5, to open yet another browser window that displays the entity member and its attribute values.

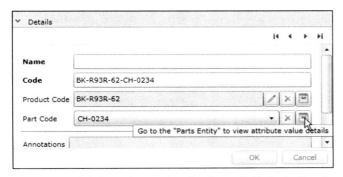

FIGURE 8-5 Click through to a related entity available in the Details pane

Hierarchy Management

The new interface in the Explorer functional area, shown in Figure 8-6, makes it easier for you to move members within a hierarchy when you want to change the parent for a member. A hierarchy pane displays a tree view of the hierarchy. There you select the check box for each member to move. Then you click the Copy button at the top of the hierarchy pane, select the check box of the member to which you want to move the previously selected members, and then click the Paste button. In a derived hierarchy, you must paste members to the same level only.

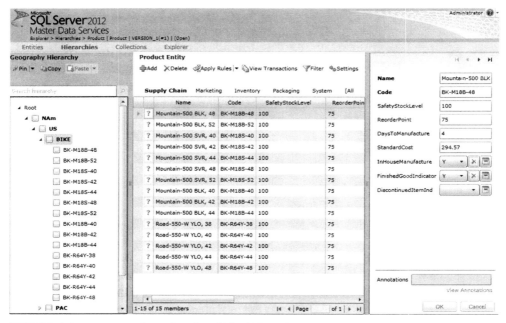

FIGURE 8-6 Arrangement of members in a derived hierarchy

Collection Management

You can organize a subset of entity members as a collection in MDS. A new feature is the ability to assign a weight to each collection member within the user interface, as shown in Figure 8-7. You use MDS only to store the weight for use by subscribing systems that use the weight to apportion values across the collection members. Accordingly, the subscription view includes the weight column.

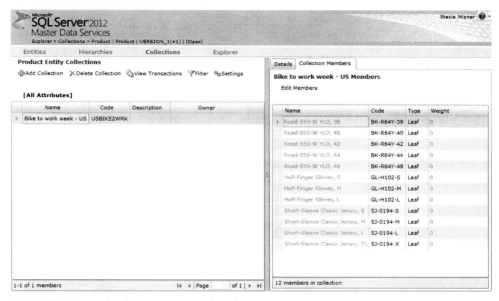

FIGURE 8-7 New collection-management interface

Integration Management

When you want to automate aspects of the master data management process, MDS now has a new, high-performance staging process. One benefit of this new staging process is the ability to load members and attribute values at one time, rather than separately in batches. To do this, you load data into the following tables as applicable, where *name* is the name of the staging table for the entity:

- **stg.*name*_Leaf**   Use this table to stage additions, updates, or deletions for leaf members and their attributes.

- **stg.*name*_Consolidated**   Use this table to stage additions, updates, or deletions for consolidated members and their attributes.

- **stg.*name*_Relationship**   Use this table to assign members in an explicit hierarchy.

There are two ways to start the staging process after you load data into the staging tables: by using the Integration Management functional area or executing stored procedures. In the Integration Management functional area, you select the model in the drop-down list and click the Start Batches button, which you can see in Figure 8-8. The data processes in batches, and you can watch the status change from Queued To Run to Running to Completed.

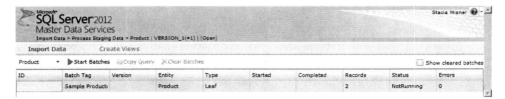

FIGURE 8-8 Staging a batch in the Integration Management functional area

If the staging process produces errors, you see the number of errors appear in the grid, but you cannot view them in the Integration Management functional area. Instead, you can click the Copy Query button to copy a SQL query that you can paste into a query window in SQL Server Management Studio. The query looks similar to this:

```
SELECT * from [stg].[viw_Product_MemberErrorDetails] WHERE Batch_ID = 1
```

This view includes an ErrorDescription column describing the reason for flagging the staged record as an error. It also includes AttributeName and AttributeValue columns to indicate which attribute and value caused the error.

If you use a stored procedure to execute the staging process, you use one of the following stored procedures, where *name* corresponds to the staging table:

- stg.udp_*name*_Leaf
- stg.udp_*name*_Consolidated
- stg.udp_*name*_Relationship

Each of these stored procedures takes the following parameters:

- **VersionName**   Provide the version name of the model, such as VERSION_1. The collation setting of the SQL Server database determines whether the value for this parameter is case sensitive.

- **LogFile**   Use a value of *1* to log transactions during staging or a value of *0* if you do not want to log transactions.

- **BatchTag**   Provide a string of 50 characters or less to identify the batch in the staging table. This tag displays in the batch grid in the Integration Management functional area.

For example, to load leaf members and log transactions for the batch, execute the following code in SQL Server Management Studio:

```
EXEC [stg].[udp_name_Leaf] @VersionName = N'VERSION_1', @LogFlag = 1, @BatchTag = N'batch1'
GO
```

Note Transaction logging during staging is optional. You can enable logging only if you use stored procedures for staging. Logging does not occur if you launch the staging process from the Integration Management functional area.

Important No validation occurs during the staging process. You must validate manually in the Version Management functional area or use the *mdm.udpValidateModel* stored procedure. Refer to *http://msdn.microsoft.com/en-us/library/hh231023(SQL.110).aspx* for more information about this stored procedure.

You can continue to use the staging tables and stored procedure introduced for the SQL Server 2008 R2 MDS staging process if you like. One reason that you might choose to do this is to manage collections, because the new staging process in SQL Server 2012 does not support collections. Therefore, you must use the previous staging process to create or delete collections, add members to or remove them from collections, or reactivate members and collections.

User and Group Permissions

Just as in the previous version of MDS, you assign permissions by functional area and by model object. When you assign Read-Only or Update permissions for a model to a user or group on the Models tab of the Manage User page, the permission also applies to lower level objects. For example, when you grant a user or group the Update permission to the Product model, as shown in Figure 8-9, the users can also add, change, or delete members for any entity in the model and can change any attribute value. You must explicitly change permissions on selected entities to Read-only when you want to give users the ability to view but not change entity members, and to Deny when you do not want them to see the entity members. You can further refine security by setting permissions on attribute objects (below the Leaf, Consolidate, or Collection nodes) to control which attribute values a user can see or change.

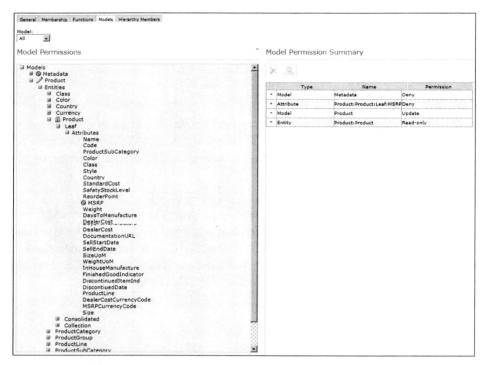

FIGURE 8-9 Model permissions object tree and summary

In SQL Server 2008 MDS, the model permissions object tree also includes nodes for derived hierarchies, explicit hierarchies, and attribute groups, but these nodes are no longer available in SQL Server 2012 MDS. Instead, derived hierarchies inherit permissions from the model and explicit hierarchies inherit permissions from the associated entity. In both cases, you can override these default permissions on the Hierarchy Members tab of the Manage User page to manage which entity members that users can see or change.

For attribute group permissions, you now use the Attribute Group Maintenance page in the System Administration functional area to assign permissions to users or groups, as shown in Figure 8-10. Users or groups appearing in the Assigned list have Update permissions only. You can no longer assign Read-Only permissions for attribute groups.

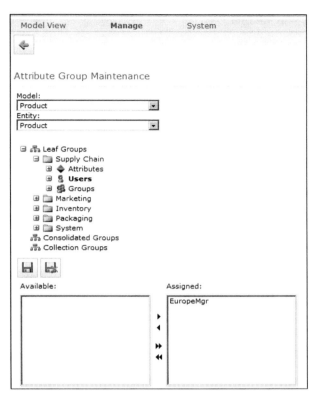

FIGURE 8-10 Users and Groups security for attribute groups

Model Deployment

A new high-performance, command-line tool is now available for deploying packages. If you use the Model Deployment Wizard in the web application, it deploys only the model structure. As an alternative, you can use the MDSModelDeploy tool to create and deploy a package with model objects only or a package with both model objects and data. You find this tool in the Program Files\Microsoft SQL Server\110\Master Data Services\Configuration folder.

> **Note** You cannot reuse packages you created using SQL Server 2008 MDS. You can deploy a SQL Server 2012 package only to a SQL Server 2012 MDS instance.

The executable for this tool uses the following syntax:

```
MDSModelDeploy <commands> [ <options> ]
```

You can use the following commands with this tool:

- *listservices*   View a list of all service instances.

- *listmodels*   View a list of all models.

- *listversions*   View a list of all versions for a specified model.

- *createpackage*   Create a package for a specified model.

- *deployclone*   Create a duplicate of a specified model, retaining names and identifiers. The model cannot exist in the target service instance.

- *deploynew*   Create a new model. MDS creates new identifiers for all model objects.

- *deployupdate*   Deploy a model, and update the model version. This option requires you to use a package with a model having the same names and identifiers as the target model.

- *help*   View usage, options, and examples of a command. For example, type the following command to learn how to use the *deploynew* command: **MDSModelDeploy help deploynew**.

To help you learn how to work with MDS, several sample packages containing models and data are available. To deploy the Product package to the MDS1 Web service instance, type the following command in the command prompt window:

```
MDSModelDeploy deploynew -package ..\Samples\Packages\product_en.pkg -model Product -service MDS1
```

Note To execute commands by using this utility, you must have permissions to access the System Administration functional area and you must open the command prompt window as an administrator.

During deployment, MDS first creates the model objects, and then creates the business rules and subscription views. MDS populates the model with master data as the final step. If any of these steps fail during deployment of a new or cloned model, MDS deletes the model. If you are updating a model, MDS retains the changes from the previous steps that completed successfully unless the failure occurs in the final step. In that case, MDS updates master data members where possible rather than failing the entire step and rolling back.

Note After you deploy a model, you must manually update user-defined metadata, file attributes, and user and group permissions.

MDS Add-in for Excel

The most extensive addition to MDS in SQL Server 2012 is the new user-interface option for enabling data stewards and administrators to manage master data inside Microsoft Excel. Data stewards can retrieve data and make changes using the familiar environment of Excel after installing the MDS Add-in for Excel. Administrators can also use this add-in to create new model objects, such as entities, and load data into MDS.

Installation of the MDS Add-in

By default, the home page of Master Data Manager includes a link to the download page for the MDS Add-in on the Microsoft web site. On the download page, you choose the language and version (32-bit or 64-bit) that matches your Excel installation. You open the MSI file that downloads to start the setup wizard, and then follow the prompts to accept the license agreement and confirm the installation. When the installation completes, you can open Excel to view the new Master Data tab in the ribbon, as shown in Figure 8-11.

FIGURE 8-11 Master Data tab in the Excel ribbon

Note The add-in works with either Excel 2007 or Excel 2010.

Master Data Management

The MDS add-in supports the primary tasks you need to perform for master data management. After connecting to MDS, you can load data from MDS into a worksheet to use for reference or to make additions or changes in bulk. You can also apply business rules and correct validation issues, check for duplicates using Data Quality Services integration, and then publish the modified data back to MDS.

Connections

Before you can load MDS data into a worksheet, you must create a connection to the MDS database. If you open a worksheet into which you previously loaded data, the MDS add-in automatically connects to MDS when you refresh the data or publish the data. To create a connection in the MDS Add-in for Excel, follow these steps:

1. On the Master Data tab of the ribbon, click the arrow under the Connect button, and click Manage Connections.

2. In the Manage Connections dialog box, click the Create A New Connection link.

3. In the Add New Connection dialog box, type a description for the connection. This description displays when you click the arrow under the Connect button.

4. In the MDS Server Address box, type the URL that you use to open the Master Data Manager web application, such as *http://myserver/mds*, and click the OK button. The connection displays in the Existing Connections section of the Manage Connections dialog box.

5. Click the Test button to test the connection, and then click the OK button to close the dialog box that confirms the connection or displays an error.

6. Click the Connect button.

7. In the Master Data Explorer pane, select a model and version from the respective drop-down lists, as shown here:

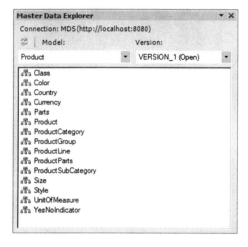

Data Retrieval

Before you load data from MDS into a worksheet, you can filter the data. Even if you do not filter the data, there are some limitations to the volume of data you can load. Periodically, you can update the data in the worksheet to retrieve the latest updates from MDS.

Filter data Rather than load all entity members from MDS into a spreadsheet, which can be a time-consuming task, you can select attributes and apply filters to minimize the amount of data you retrieve from MDS. You can choose to focus on selected attributes to reduce the number of columns to retrieve. Another option is to use filter criteria to eliminate members.

To filter and retrieve leaf data from MDS, follow these steps:

1. In the Master Data Explorer pane, select the entity you want to load into the spreadsheet.

2. On the Master Data tab of the ribbon, click the Filter button.

3. In the Filter dialog box, select the columns to load by selecting an attribute type, an explicit hierarchy (if you select the Consolidated attribute type), an attribute group, and individual attributes.

> **Tip** You can change the order of attributes by using the Up and Down arrows to the right of the attribute list to move each selected attribute.

4. Next, select the rows to load by clicking the Add button and then selecting an attribute, a filter operator, and filter criteria. You can repeat this step to continue adding filter criteria.

5. Click the Update Summary button to view the number of rows and columns resulting from your filter selections, as shown here:

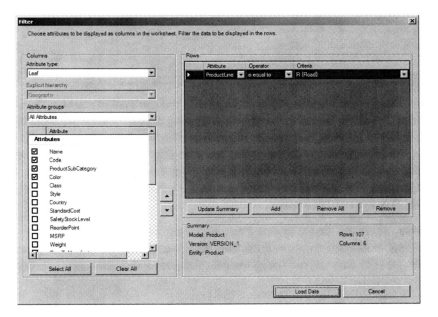

6. In the Filter dialog box, click the Load button. The data loads into the current spreadsheet, as shown here:

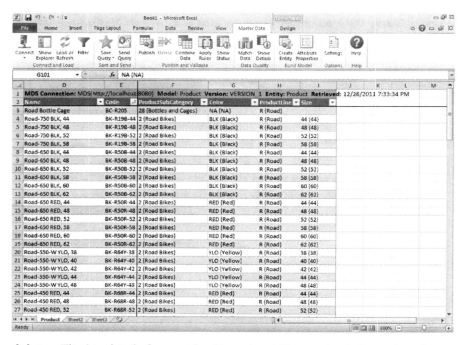

Load data Filtering data before you load is optional. You can load all members for an entity by clicking the Load Or Refresh button in the ribbon. A warning displays if there are more than 100,000 rows or more than 100 columns, but you can increase or decrease these values or disable the warning by clicking the Settings button on the ribbon and changing the properties on the Data page of the Settings dialog box. Regardless, if an entity is very large, the add-in automatically restricts the retrieval of data to the first one million members. Also, if a column is a domain-based attribute, the add-in retrieves only the first 1000 values.

Refresh data After you load MDS data into a worksheet, you can update the same worksheet by adding columns of data from sources other than MDS or columns containing formulas. When you want to refresh the MDS data without losing the data you added, click the Load Or Refresh button in the ribbon.

The refresh process modifies the contents of the worksheet. Deleted members disappear, and new members appear at the bottom of the table with green highlighting. Attribute values update to match the value stored in MDS, but the cell does not change color to identify a new value.

Warning If you add new members or change attribute values, you must publish these changes before refreshing the data. Otherwise, you lose your work. Cell comments on MDS data are deleted, and non-MDS data in rows below MDS data might be replaced if the refresh process adds new members to the worksheet.

Review transactions and annotations   You can review transactions for any member by right-clicking the member's row and selecting View Transactions in the context menu. To view an annotation or to add an annotation for a transaction, select the transaction row in the View Transactions dialog box, which is shown in Figure 8-12.

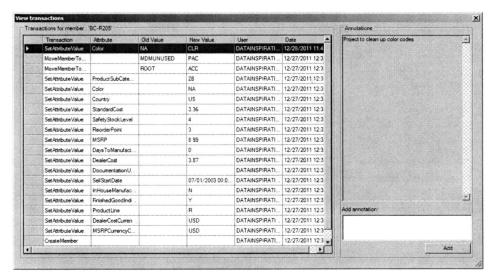

FIGURE 8-12 Transactions and annotations for a member

Data Publication

If you make changes to the MDS data in the worksheet, such as altering attribute values, adding new members, or deleting members, you can publish your changes to MDS to make it available to other users. Each change you make saves to MDS as a transaction, which you have the option to annotate to document the reason for the change. An exception is a deletion, which you cannot annotate although the deletion does generate a transaction.

When you click the Publish button, the Publish And Annotate dialog box displays (unless you disable it in Settings). You can provide a single annotation for all changes or separate annotations for each change, as shown in Figure 8-13. An annotation must be 500 characters or less.

> **Warning** Cell comments on MDS data are deleted during the publication process. Also, a change to the code value for a member does not save as a transaction and renders all previous transactions for that member inaccessible.

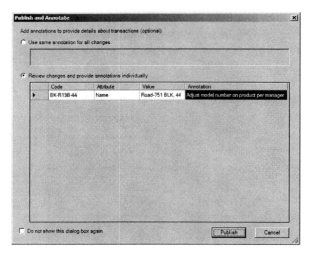

FIGURE 8-13 Addition of an annotation for a published data change

During the publication process, MDS validates your changes. First, MDS applies business rules to the data. Second, MDS confirms the validity of attribute values, including the length and data type. If a member passes validation, the MDS database updates with the change. Otherwise, the invalid data displays in the worksheet with red highlighting and the description of the error appears in the $InputStatus$ column. You can apply business rules prior to publishing your changes by clicking the Apply Rules button in the ribbon.

Model-Building Tasks

Use of the MDS Add-in for Excel is not limited to data stewards. If you are an administrator, you can also use the add-in to create entities and add attributes. However, you must first create a model by using Master Data Manager, and then you can continue adding entities to the model by using the add-in.

Entities and Attributes

Before you add an entity to MDS, you create data in a worksheet. The data must include a header row and at least one row of data. Each row should include at least a Name column. If you include a Code column, the column values must be unique for each row. You can add other columns to create attributes for the entity, but you do not need to provide values for them. If you do, you can use text, numeric, or data values, but you cannot use formulas or time values.

To create a new entity in MDS, follow these steps:

1. Select all cells in the header and data rows to load into the new entity.

2. Click the Create Entity button in the ribbon.

3. In the Create Entity dialog box, ensure the range includes only the data you want to load and do not clear the My Data Has Headers check box.

4. Select a model and version from the respective drop-down lists, and provide a name in the New Entity Name box.

5. In the Code drop-down list, select the column that contains unique values for entity members or select the Generate Code Automatically option.

6. In the Name drop-down list, select the column that contains member names, as shown next, and then click OK. The add-in creates the new entity in the MDS database and validates the data.

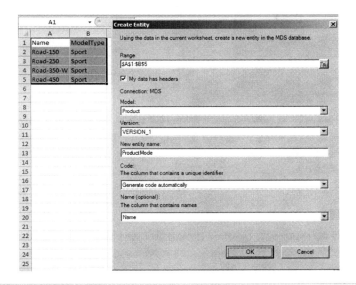

Note You might need to correct the data type or length of an attribute after creating the entity. To do this, click any cell in the attribute's column, and click the Attribute Properties button in the ribbon. You can make changes as necessary in the Attribute Properties dialog box. However, you cannot change the data type or length of the Name or Code column.

Domain-Based Attributes

If you want to restrict column values of an existing entity to a specific set of values, you can create a domain-based attribute from values in a worksheet or an existing entity. To create a domain-based attribute, follow these steps:

1. Load the entity into a worksheet, and click a cell in the column that you want to change to a domain-based attribute.

2. Click the Attribute Properties button in the ribbon.

3. In the Attribute Properties dialog box, select Constrained List (Domain-Based) in the Attribute Type drop-down list.

4. Select an option from the Populate The Attribute With Values From drop-down list. You can choose The Selected Column to create a new entity based on the values in the selected column, as shown next, or you can choose an entity to use values from that entity.

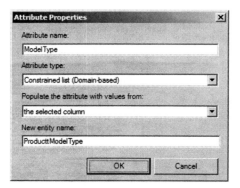

5. Click OK. The column now allows you to select from a list of values. You can change the available values in the list by loading the entity on which the attribute is based into a separate worksheet, making changes by adding new members or updating values, and then publishing the changes back to MDS.

Shortcut Query Files

You can easily load frequently accessed data by using a shortcut query file. This file contains information about the connection to the MDS database, the model and version containing the MDS data, the entity to load, filters to apply, and the column order. After loading MDS data into a worksheet, you create a shortcut query file by clicking the Save Query button in the ribbon and selecting Save As Query in the menu. When you want to use it later, you open an empty worksheet, click the Save Query button, and select the shortcut query file from the list that displays.

You can also use the shortcut query file as a way to share up-to-date MDS data with other users without emailing the worksheet. Instead, you can email the shortcut query file as long as you have Microsoft Outlook 2010 or later installed on your computer. First, load MDS data into a worksheet, and then click the Send Query button in the ribbon to create an email message with the shortcut query file as an attachment. As long as the recipient of the email message has the add-in installed, he can double-click the file to open it.

Data Quality Matching

Before you add new members to an entity using the add-in, you can prepare data in a worksheet and combine it with MDS data for comparison. Then you use Data Quality Services (DQS) to identify duplicates. The matching process adds detail columns to show matching scores you can use to decide which data to publish to MDS.

As we explained in Chapter 7, "Data Quality Services," you must enable DQS integration in the Master Data Services Configuration Manager and create a matching policy in a knowledge base. In addition, both the MDS database and the DQS_MAIN database must exist in the same SQL Server instance.

The first step in the data-quality matching process is to combine data from two worksheets into a single worksheet. The first worksheet must contain data you load from MDS. The second worksheet must contain data with a header row and one or more detail rows. To combine data, follow these steps:

1. On the first worksheet, click the Combine Data button in the ribbon.

2. In the Combine Data dialog box, click the icon next to the Range To Combine With MDS Data text box.

3. Click the second worksheet, and highlight the header and detail rows to combine with MDS data.

4. In the Combine Data dialog box, click the icon to the right of the Range To Combine With MDS Data box.

5. Navigate to the second worksheet, highlight the header row and detail rows, and then click the icon next to the range in the collapsed Combine Data dialog box.

6. In the expanded Combine Data dialog box, in the Corresponding Column drop-down list, select a column from the second worksheet that corresponds to the entity column that displays to its left, as shown here:

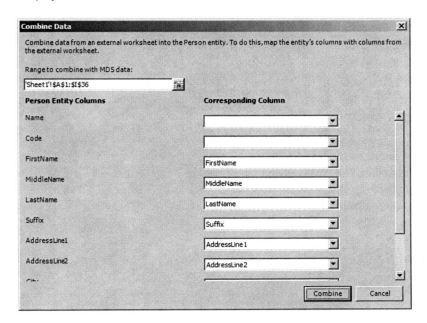

7. Click the Combine button. The rows from the second worksheet display in the first worksheet below the existing rows, and the SOURCE column displays whether the row data comes from MDS or from an external source, as shown here:

8. Click the Match Data button in the ribbon.

9. In the Match Data dialog box, select a knowledge base from the DQS Knowledge Base drop-down list, and map worksheet columns to each domain listed in the dialog box.

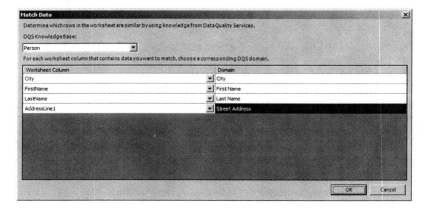

Note Rather than using a custom knowledge base as shown in the preceding screen shot, you can use the default knowledge base, DQS Data. In that case, you add a row to the dialog box for each column you want to use for matching and assign a weight value. The sum of weight values for all rows must equal 100.

10. Click OK, and then click the Show Details button in the ribbon to view columns containing matching details. The SCORE column indicates the similarity between the pivot record (indicated by Pivot in the PIVOT_MARK column) and the matching record. You can use this information to eliminate records from the worksheet before publishing your changes and additions to MDS.

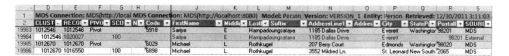

Miscellaneous Changes

Thus far in this chapter, our focus has been on the new features available in MDS. However, there are some more additions and changes to review. SQL Server 2012 offers some new features for SharePoint integration, and it retains some features from the SQL Server 2008 R2 version that are still available, but deprecated. There are also features that are discontinued. In this section, we review these feature changes and describe alternatives where applicable.

SharePoint Integration

There are two ways you can integrate MDS with SharePoint. First, when you add the Master Data Manager web site to a SharePoint page, you can add *&hosted=true* as a query parameter to reduce the amount of required display space. This query parameter removes the header, menu bar, and padding at the bottom of the page. Second, you can save shortcut query files to a SharePoint document library to provide lists of reference data to other users.

Metadata

The Metadata model continues to display in Master Data Manager, but it is deprecated. Microsoft recommends that you do not use it because it will be removed in a future release of SQL Server. You cannot create versions of the Metadata model, and users cannot view metadata in the Explorer functional area.

Bulk Updates and Export

Making changes to master data one record at a time can be a tedious process. In the previous version of MDS, you can update an attribute value for multiple members at the same time, but this capability is no longer available in SQL Server 2012. Instead, you can use the staging process to load the new values into the stg.*name*_Leaf table as we described earlier in the "Integration Management" section of this chapter. As an alternative, you can use the MDS add-in to load the entity into an Excel worksheet (described in the "Master Data Management" section of this chapter), update the attribute values in bulk using copy and paste, and then publish the results to MDS.

The purpose of storing master data in MDS is to have access to this data for other purposes. You use the Export To Excel button on the Member Information page when using the previous version of MDS, but this button is not available in SQL Server 2012. When you require MDS data in Excel, you use the MDS add-in to load entity members from MDS into a worksheet, as we described in the "Data Retrieval" section of this chapter.

Transactions

MDS uses transactions to log every change users make to master data. In the previous version, users review transactions in the Explorer functional area and optionally reverse their own transactions to restore a prior value. Now only administrators can revert transactions in the Version Management functional area.

MDS allows you to annotate transactions. In SQL Server 2008 R2, MDS stores annotations as transactions and allows you to delete them by reverting the transaction. However, annotations are now permanent in SQL Server 2012. Although you continue to associate an annotation with a transaction, MDS stores the annotation separately and does not allow you to delete it.

Windows PowerShell

In the previous version of MDS, you can use PowerShell cmdlets for administration of MDS. One cmdlet allows you to create the database, another cmdlet allows you to configure settings for MDS, and other cmdlets allow you to retrieve information about your MDS environment. No cmdlets are available in the current version of MDS.

CHAPTER 9

Analysis Services and PowerPivot

I n SQL Server 2005 and SQL Server 2008, there is only one mode of SQL Server Analysis Services (SSAS) available. Then in SQL Server 2008 R2, VertiPaq mode debuts as the engine for PowerPivot for SharePoint. These two server modes persist in SQL Server 2012 with some enhancements, and now you also have the option to deploy an Analysis Services instance in tabular mode. In addition, Microsoft SQL Server 2012 PowerPivot for Excel has several new features that extend the types of analysis it can support.

Analysis Services

Before you deploy an Analysis Services instance, you must decide what type of functionality you want to support and install the appropriate server mode. In this section, we compare the three server modes, explain the various Analysis Services templates from which to choose when starting a new Analysis Services project, and introduce the components of the new tabular mode. We also review several new options this release provides for managing your server. Last, we discuss the programmability enhancements in the current release.

Server Modes

In SQL Server 2012, an Analysis Services instance can run in one of the following server modes: multidimensional, tabular, or PowerPivot for SharePoint. Each server mode supports a different type of database by using different storage structures, memory architectures, and engines. Multidimensional mode uses the Analysis Services engine you find in SQL Server 2005 and later versions. Both tabular mode and PowerPivot for SharePoint mode use the VertiPaq engine introduced in SQL Server 2008 R2, which compresses data for storage in memory at runtime. However, tabular mode does not have a dependency on SharePoint like PowerPivot for SharePoint does.

Each server mode supports a different set of data sources, tools, languages, and security features. Table 9-1 provides a comparison of these features by server mode.

TABLE 9-1 Server-Mode Comparison of Various Sources, Tools, Languages, and Security Features

Feature	Multidimensional	Tabular	PowerPivot for SharePoint
Data Sources	Relational database	Relational database Analysis Services Reporting Services report Azure DataMarket dataset Data feed Excel file Text file	Relational database Analysis Services Reporting Services report Azure DataMarket dataset Data feed Excel file Text file
Development Tool	SQL Server Data Tools	SQL Server Data Tools	PowerPivot for Excel
Management Tool	SQL Server Management Studio	SQL Server Management Studio	SharePoint Central Administration PowerPivot Configuration Tool
Reporting and Analysis Tool	Report Builder Report Designer Excel PivotTable PerformancePoint dashboard	Report Builder Report Designer Excel PivotTable PerformancePoint dashboard Power View	Report Builder Report Designer Excel PivotTable PerformancePoint dashboard Power View
Application Programming Interface	AMO AMOMD.NET	AMO AMOMD.NET	No support
Query and Expression Language	MDX for calculations and queries DMX for data-mining queries	DAX for calculations and queries MDX for queries	DAX for calculations and queries MDX for queries
Security	Cell-level security Role-based permissions in SSAS	Row-level security Role-based permissions in SSAS	File-level security using SharePoint permissions

Another factor you must consider is the set of model design features that satisfy your users' business requirements for reporting and analysis. Table 9-2 shows the model design features that each server mode supports.

TABLE 9-2 Server-Mode Comparison of Design Features

Model Design Feature	Multidimensional	Tabular	PowerPivot for SharePoint
Actions	✔		
Aggregations	✔		
Calculated Measures	✔	✔	✔
Custom Assemblies	✔		
Custom Rollups	✔		
Distinct Count	✔	✔	✔
Drillthrough	✔		✔

Model Design Feature	Multidimensional	Tabular	PowerPivot for SharePoint
Hierarchies	✔	✔	✔
Key Performance Indicators	✔	✔	✔
Linked Objects	✔		✔ (Linked tables only)
Many-to-Many Relationships	✔		
Parent-Child Hierarchies	✔	✔	✔
Partitions	✔	✔	
Perspectives	✔	✔	✔
Semi-additive Measures	✔	✔	✔
Translations	✔		
Writeback	✔		

You assign the server mode during installation of Analysis Services. On the Setup Role page of SQL Server Setup, you select the SQL Server Feature Installation option for multidimensional or tabular mode, or you select the SQL Server PowerPivot For SharePoint option for the PowerPivot for SharePoint mode. If you select the SQL Server Feature Installation option, you will specify the server mode to install on the Analysis Services Configuration page. On that page, you must choose either the Multidimensional And Data Mining Mode option or the Tabular Mode option. After you complete the installation, you cannot change the server mode of an existing instance.

Note Multiple instances of Analysis Services can co-exist on the same server, each running a different server mode.

Analysis Services Projects

SQL Server Data Tools (SSDT) is the model development tool for multidimensional models, data-mining models, and tabular models. Just as you do with any business intelligence project, you open the File menu in SSDT, point to New, and then select Project to display the New Project dialog box. In the Installed Templates list in that dialog box, you can choose from several Analysis Services templates, as shown in Figure 9-1.

FIGURE 9-1 New Project dialog box displaying Analysis Services templates

There are five templates available for Analysis Services projects:

- **Analysis Services Multidimensional and Data Mining Project**   You use this template to develop the traditional type of project for Analysis Services, which is now known as the multidimensional model and is the only model that includes support for the Analysis Services data-mining features.

- **Import from Server (Multidimensional and Data Mining)**   You use this template when a multidimensional model exists on a server and you want to create a new project using the same model design.

- **Analysis Services Tabular Project**   You use this template to create the new tabular model. You can deploy this model to an Analysis Services instance running in tabular mode only.

- **Import from PowerPivot**   You use this template to import a model from a workbook deployed to a PowerPivot for SharePoint instance of Analysis Services. You can extend the model using features supported in tabular modeling and then deploy this model to an Analysis Services instance running in tabular mode only.

- **Import from Server (Tabular)**   You use this template when a tabular model exists on a server and you want to create a new project using the same model design.

Tabular Modeling

A tabular model is a new type of database structure that Analysis Services supports in SQL Server 2012. When you create a tabular project, SSDT adds a Model.bim file to the project and creates a workspace database on the Analysis Services instance that you specify. It then uses this workspace database as temporary storage for data while you develop the model by importing data and designing objects that organize, enhance, and secure the data.

> **Tip** You can use the tutorial at *http://msdn.microsoft.com/en-us/library /hh231691(SQL.110).aspx* to learn how to work with a tabular model project.

Workspace Database

As you work with a tabular model project in SSDT, a corresponding workspace database resides in memory. This workspace database stores the data you add to the project using the Table Import Wizard. Whenever you view data in the diagram view or the data view of the model designer, SSDT retrieves the data from the workspace database.

When you select the Model.bim file in Solution Explorer, you can use the Properties window to access the following workspace database properties:

- **Data Backup**   The default setting is Do Not Backup To Disk. You can change this to Backup To Disk to create a backup of the workspace database as an ABF file each time you save the Model.bim file. However, you cannot use the Backup To Disk option if you are using a remote Analysis Services instance to host the workspace database.

- **Workspace Database**   This property displays the name that Analysis Services assigns to the workspace database. You cannot change this value.

- **Workspace Retention**   Analysis Services uses this value to determine whether to keep the workspace database in memory when you close the project in SSDT. The default option, Unload From Memory, keeps the database on disk, but removes it from memory. For faster loading when you next open the project, you can choose the Keep In Memory option. The third option, Delete Workspace, deletes the workspace database from both memory and disk, which takes the longest time to reload because Analysis Services requires additional time to import data into the new workspace database. You can change the default for this setting if you open the Tools menu, select Options, and open the Data Modeling page in the Analysis Server settings.

- **Workspace Server**   This property specifies the server you use to host the workspace database. For best performance, you should use a local instance of Analysis Services.

> **Note** You must be an administrator for the Analysis Services instance hosting the workspace database.

Table Import Wizard

You use the Table Import Wizard to import data from one or more data sources. In addition to providing connection information, such as a server name and database name for a relational data source, you must also complete the Impersonation Information page of the Table Import Wizard. Analysis Services uses the credentials you specify on this page to import and process data. For credentials, you can provide a Windows login and password or you can designate the Analysis Services service account.

The next step in the Table Import Wizard is to specify how you want to retrieve the data. For example, if you are using a relational data source, you can select from a list of tables and views or provide a query. Regardless of the data source you use, you have the option to filter the data before importing it into the model. One option is to eliminate an entire column by clearing the check box in the column header. You can also eliminate rows by clicking the arrow to the right of the column name, and clearing one or more check boxes for a text value, as shown in Figure 9-2.

FIGURE 9-2 Selection of rows to include during import

As an alternative, you can create more specific filters by using the Text Filters or Numeric Filters options, as applicable to the column's data type. For example, you can create a filter to import only values equal to a specific value or values containing a designated string.

Note There is no limit to the number of rows you can import for a single table, although any column in the table can have no more than 2 billion distinct values. However, the query performance of the model is optimal when you reduce the number of rows as much as possible.

Tabular Model Designer

After you import data into the model, the model designer displays the data in the workspace as shown in Figure 9-3. If you decide that you need to rename columns, you can double-click on the column name and type a new name. For example, you might add a space between words to make the column name more user friendly. When you finish typing, press Enter to save the change.

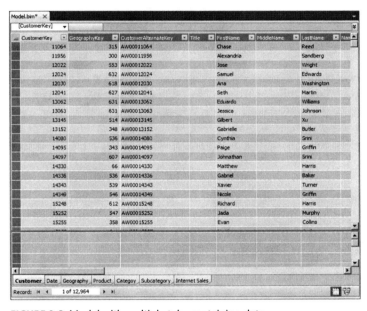

FIGURE 9-3 Model with multiple tabs containing data

When you import data from a relational data source, the import process detects the existing relationships and adds them to the model. To view the relationships, switch to Diagram View (shown in Figure 9-4), either by clicking the Diagram button in the bottom right corner of the workspace or by opening the Model menu, pointing to Model View, and selecting Diagram View. When you point to a line connecting two tables, the model designer highlights the related columns in each table.

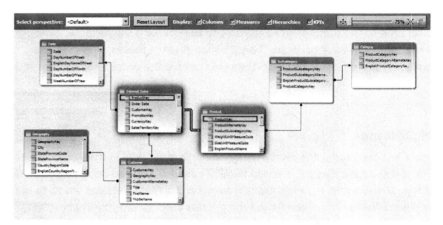

FIGURE 9-4 Model in diagram view highlighting columns in a relationship between two tables

Relationships

You can add new relationships by clicking a column in one table and dragging the cursor to the corresponding column in a second table. Because the model design automatically detects the primary table and the related lookup table, you do not need to select the tables in a specific order. If you prefer, you can open the Table menu and click Manage Relationships to view all relationships in one dialog box, as shown in Figure 9-5. You can use this dialog box to add a new relationship or to edit or delete an existing relationship.

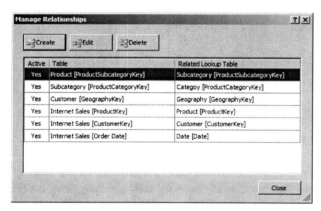

Active	Table	Related Lookup Table
Yes	Product [ProductSubcategoryKey]	Subcategory [ProductSubcategoryKey]
Yes	Subcategory [ProductCategoryKey]	Categoy [ProductCategoryKey]
Yes	Customer [GeographyKey]	Geography [GeographyKey]
Yes	Internet Sales [ProductKey]	Product [ProductKey]
Yes	Internet Sales [CustomerKey]	Customer [CustomerKey]
Yes	Internet Sales [Order Date]	Date [Date]

FIGURE 9-5 Manage Relationships dialog box displaying all relationships in the model

> **Note** You can create only one-to-one or one-to-many relationships.

You can also create multiple relationships between two tables, but only one relationship at a time is active. Calculations use the active relationship by default, unless you override this behavior by using the USERELATIONSHIP() function as we explain in the "DAX" section later in this chapter.

Calculated Columns

A calculated column is a column of data you derive by using a Data Analysis Expression (DAX) formula. For example, you can concatenate values from two columns into a single column, as shown in Figure 9-6. To create a calculated column, you must switch to Data View. You can either right-click an existing column and then select Insert Column, or you can click Add Column on the Column menu. In the formula bar, type a valid DAX formula, and press Enter. The model designer calculates and displays column values for each row in the table.

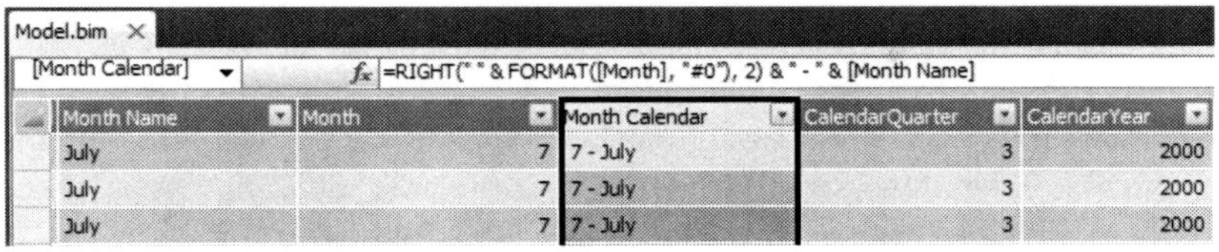

FIGURE 9-6 Calculated column values and the corresponding DAX formula

Measures

Whereas the tabular model evaluates a calculated column at the row level and stores the result in the tabular model, it evaluates a measure as an aggregate value within the context of rows, columns, filters, and slicers for a pivot table. To add a new measure, click any cell in the calculation area, which then displays as a grid below the table data. Then type a DAX formula in the formula bar, and press Enter to add a new measure, as shown in Figure 9-7. You can override the default measure name, such as Measure1, by replacing the name with a new value in the formula bar.

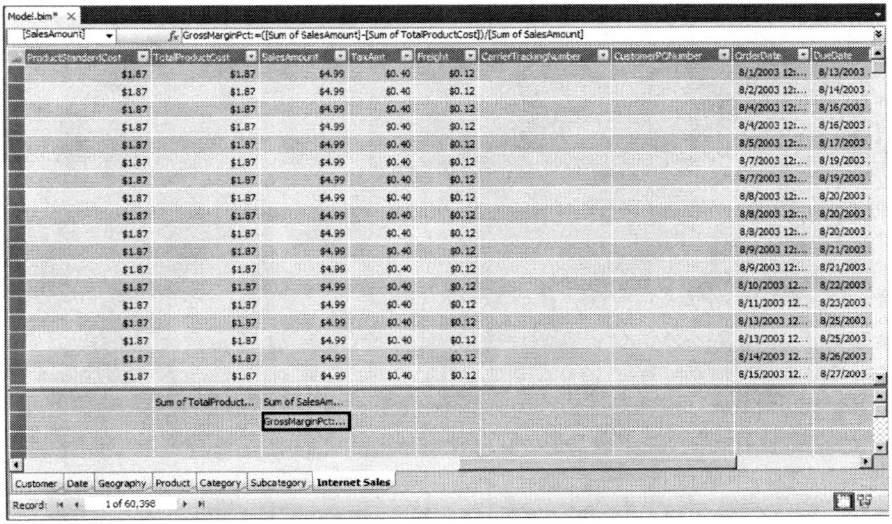

FIGURE 9-7 Calculation area displaying three measures

To create a measure that aggregates only row values, you click the column header and then click the AutoSum button in the toolbar. For example, if you select Count for the ProductKey column, the measure grid displays the new measure with the following formula: Count of ProductKey:=COUNTA([ProductKey]).

Key Performance Indicators

Key performance indicators (KPIs) are a special type of measure you can use to measure progress toward a goal. You start by creating a base measure in the calculation area of a table. Then you right-click the measure and select Create KPI to open the Key Performance Indicator (KPI) dialog box as shown in Figure 9-8. Next you define the measure or absolute value that represents the target value or goal of the KPI. The status thresholds are the boundaries for each level of progress toward the goal, and you can adjust them as needed. Analysis Services compares the base measure to the thresholds to determine which icon to use when displaying the KPI status.

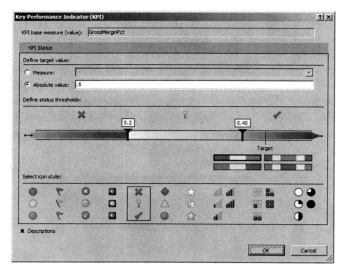

FIGURE 9-8 Key performance indicator definition

Hierarchies

A hierarchy is useful for analyzing data at different levels of detail using logical relationships that allow a user to navigate from one level to the next. In Diagram View, right-click on the column you want to set as the parent level and select Create Hierarchy, or click the Create Hierarchy button that appears when you hover the cursor over the column header. Type a name for the hierarchy, and drag columns to the new hierarchy, as shown in Figure 9-9. You can add only columns from the same table to the hierarchy. If necessary, create a calculated column that uses the RELATED() function in a DAX formula to reference a column from a related table in the hierarchy.

FIGURE 9-9 Hierarchy in the diagram view of a model

Perspectives

When you have many objects in a model, you can create a perspective to display a subset of the model objects so that users can more easily find the objects they need. Select Perspectives from the Model menu to view existing perspectives or to add a new perspective, as shown in Figure 9-10. When you define a perspective, you select tables, columns, measures, KPIs, and hierarchies to include.

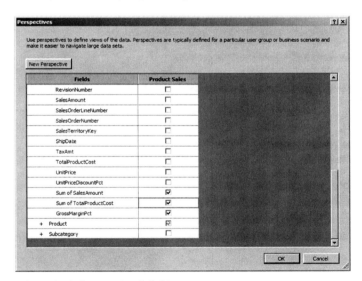

FIGURE 9-10 Perspective definition

Partitions

At a minimum, each table in a tabular model has one partition, but you can divide a table into multiple partitions when you want to manage the reprocessing of each partition separately. For example, you might want to reprocess a partition containing current data frequently but have no need to reprocess a partition containing historical data. To open the Partition Manager, which you use to create and configure partitions, open the Table menu and select Partitions. Click the Query Editor button to view the SQL statement and append a WHERE clause, as shown in Figure 9-11.

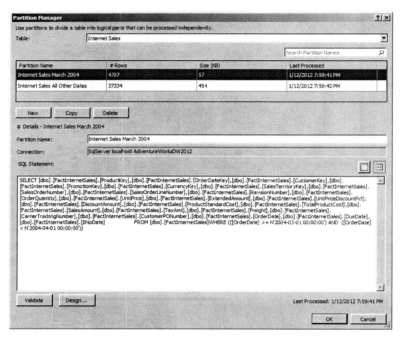

FIGURE 9-11 Addition of a WHERE clause to a SQL statement for partition

For example, if you want to create a partition for a month and year, such as March 2004, the WHERE clause looks like this:

```
WHERE
(([OrderDate] >= N'2004-03-01 00:00:00') AND
([OrderDate] < N'2004-04-01 00:00:00'))
```

After you create all the partitions, you open the table in Data View, open the Model menu, and point to Process. You then have the option to select Process Partitions to refresh the data in each partition selectively or select Process Table to refresh the data in all partitions. After you deploy the model to Analysis Services, you can use scripts to manage the processing of individual partitions.

Roles

The tabular model is secure by default. You must create Analysis Services database roles and assign Windows users or groups to a role to grant users access to the model. In addition, you add one of the following permissions to the role to authorize the actions that the role members can perform:

- **None**   A member cannot use the model in any way.

- **Read**   A member can query the data only.

- **Read And Process** A member can query the data and execute process operations. However, the member can neither view the model database in SQL Server Management Studio (SSMS) nor make changes to the database.

- **Process** A member can process the data only, but has no permissions to query the data or view the model database in SSMS.

- **Administrator** A member has full permissions to query the data, execute process operations, view the model database in SSMS, and make changes to the model.

To create a new role, click Roles on the Model menu to open the Role Manager dialog box. Type a name for the role, select the applicable permissions, and add members to the role. If a user belongs to roles having different permissions, Analysis Services combines the permissions and uses the least restrictive permissions wherever it finds a conflict. For example, if one role has None set as the permission and another role has Read permissions, members of the role will have Read permissions.

Note As an alternative, you can add roles in SSMS after deploying the model to Analysis Services.

To further refine security for members of roles with Read or Read And Process permissions, you can create row-level filters. Each row filter is a DAX expression that evaluates as TRUE or FALSE and defines the rows in a table that a user can see. For example, you can create a filter using the expression *=Category[EnglishProductCategoryName]="Bikes"* to allow a role to view data related to Bikes only. If you want to prevent a role from accessing any rows in a table, use the expression *=FALSE()*.

Note Row filters do not work when you deploy a tabular model in DirectQuery mode. We explain DirectQuery mode later in this chapter.

Analyze in Excel

Before you deploy the tabular model, you can test the user experience by using the Analyze In Excel feature. When you use the Analyze In Excel feature, SSDT opens Excel (which must be installed on the same computer), creates a data-source connection to the model workspace, and adds a pivot table to the worksheet. When you open this item on the Model menu, the Analyze In Excel dialog box displays and prompts you to select a user or role to provide the security context for the data-source connection. You must also choose a perspective, either the default perspective (which includes all model objects) or a custom perspective, as shown in Figure 9-12.

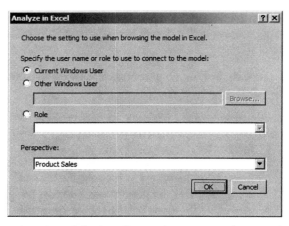

FIGURE 9-12 Selection of a security context and perspective to test model in Excel

Reporting Properties

If you plan to implement Power View (which we explain in Chapter 10, "Reporting Services"), you can access a set of reporting properties in the Properties window for each table and column. At a minimum, you can change the Hidden property for the currently selected table or column to control whether the user sees the object in the report field list. In addition, you can change reporting properties for a selected table or column to enhance the user experience during the development of Power View reports.

If you select a table in the model designer, you can change the following report properties:

- **Default Field Set**   Select the list of columns and measures that Power View adds to the report canvas when a user selects the current table in the report field list.

- **Default Image**   Identify the column containing images for each row in the table.

- **Default Label**   Specify the column containing the display name for each row.

- **Keep Unique Rows**   Indicate whether duplicate values display as unique values or as a single value.

- **Row Identifier**   Designate the column that contains values uniquely identifying each row in the table.

If you select a column in the model designer, you can change the following report properties:

- **Default Label**   Indicate whether the column contains a display name for each row. You can set this property to *True* for one column only in the table.

- **Image URL**   Indicate whether the column contains a URL to an image on the Web or on a SharePoint site. Power View uses this indicator to retrieve the file as an image rather than return the URL as a text.

- **Row Identifier** Indicate whether the column contains unique identifiers for each row. You can set this property to *True* for one column only in the table.

- **Table Detail Position** Set the sequence order of the current column relative to other columns in the default field set.

DirectQuery Mode

When the volume of data for your model is too large to fit into memory or when you want queries to return the most current data, you can enable DirectQuery mode for your tabular model. In DirectQuery mode, Analysis Services responds to client tool queries by retrieving data and aggregates directly from the source database rather than using data stored in the in-memory cache. Although using cache provides faster response times, the time required to refresh the cache continually with current data might be prohibitive when you have a large volume of data. To enable DirectQuery mode, select the Model.bim file in Solution Explorer and then open the Properties window to change the DirectQueryMode property from Off (the default) to On.

After you enable DirectQuery mode for your model, some design features are no longer available. Table 9-3 compares the availability of features in in-memory mode and DirectQuery mode.

TABLE 9-3 In-Memory Mode vs. DirectQuery Mode

Feature	In-Memory	DirectQuery
Data Sources	Relational database Analysis Services Reporting Services report Azure DataMarket dataset Data feed Excel file Text file	SQL Server 2005 or later
Calculations	Measures KPIs Calculated columns	Measures KPIs
DAX	Fully functional	Time intelligence functions invalid Some statistical functions evaluate differently
Security	Analysis Services roles	SQL Server permissions
Client tool support	SSMS Power View Excel	SSMS Power View

Note For a more in-depth explanation of the impact of switching the tabular model to DirectQuery mode, refer to *http://msdn.microsoft.com/en-us/library /hh230898(SQL.110).aspx*.

Deployment

Before you deploy a tabular model, you configure the target Analysis Services instance, running in tabular mode and provide a name for the model in the project properties, as shown in Figure 9-13. You must also select one of the following query modes, which you can change later in SSMS if necessary:

- **DirectQuery** Queries will use the relational data source only.

- **DirectQuery With In-Memory** Queries will use the relational data source unless the client uses a connection string that specifies otherwise.

- **In-Memory** Queries will use the in-memory cache only.

- **In-Memory With DirectQuery** Queries will use the cache unless the client uses a connection string that specifies otherwise.

> **Note** During development of a model in DirectQuery mode, you import a small amount of data to use as a sample. The workspace database runs in a hybrid mode that caches data during development. However, when you deploy the model, Analysis Services uses the Query Mode value you specify in the deployment properties.

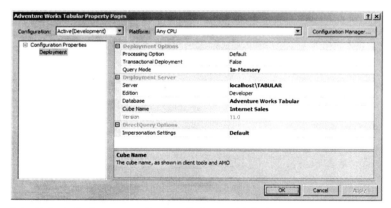

FIGURE 9-13 Project properties for tabular model deployment

After configuring the project properties, you deploy the model by using the Build menu or by right-clicking the project in Solution Explorer and selecting Deploy. Following deployment, you can use SSMS to can manage partitions, configure security, and perform backup and restore operations for the tabular model database. Users with the appropriate permissions can access the deployed tabular model as a data source for PowerPivot workbooks or for Power View reports.

Multidimensional Model Storage

The development process for a multidimensional model follows the same steps you use in SQL Server 2005 and later versions, with one exception. The MOLAP engine now uses a new type of storage for string data that is more scalable than it was in previous versions of Analysis Services. Specifically, the restriction to a 4-gigabyte maximum file size no longer exists, but you must configure a dimension to use the new storage mode.

To do this, open the dimension designer in SSDT and select the parent node of the dimension in the Attributes pane. In the Properties window, in the Advanced section, change the *StringStoreCompatibilityLevel* to *1100*. You can also apply this setting to the measure group for a distinct count measure that uses a string as the basis for the distinct count. When you execute a Process Full command, Analysis Services loads data into the new string store. As you add more data to the database, the string storage file continues to grow as large as necessary. However, although the file size limitation is gone, the file can contain only 4 billion unique strings or 4 billion records, whichever occurs first.

Server Management

SQL Server 2012 includes several features that can help you manage your server. In this release, you can more easily gather information for performance monitoring and diagnostic purposes by capturing events or querying Dynamic Management Views (DMVs). Also, you can configure server properties to support a Non-Uniform Memory Access (NUMA) architecture or more than 64 processors.

Event Tracing

You can now use the SQL Server Extended Events framework, which we introduced in Chapter 5, "Programmability and Beyond-Relational Enhancements," to capture any Analysis Services event as an alternative to creating traces by using SQL Server Profiler. For example, consider a scenario in which you are troubleshooting query performance on an Analysis Services instance running in multidimensional mode. You can execute an XML For Analysis (XMLA) create object script to enable tracing for specific events, such as Query Subcube, Get Data From Aggregation, Get Data From Cache, and Query End events. There are also some multidimensional events new to SQL Server 2012: Locks Acquired, Locks Released, Locks Waiting, Deadlock, and LockTimeOut. The event-tracing process stores the data it captures in a file and continues storing events until you disable event tracing by executing an XMLA delete object script.

There are also events available for you to monitor the other server modes: VertiPaq SE Query Begin, VertiPaq SE Query End, Direct Query Begin, and Direct Query End events. Furthermore, the Resource Usage event is also new and applicable to any server mode. You can use it to capture the size of reads and writes in kilobytes and the amount of CPU usage.

Note More information about event tracing is available at *http://msdn.microsoft.com /en-us/library/gg492139(SQL.110).aspx.*

XML for Analysis Schema Rowsets

New schema rowsets are available not only to explore metadata of a tabular model, but also to monitor the Analysis Services server. You can query the following schema rowsets by using Dynamic Management Views in SSMS for VertiPaq engine and tabular models:

- **DISCOVER_CALC_DEPENDENCY** Find dependencies between columns, measures, and formulas.

- **DISCOVER_CSDL_METADATA** Retrieve the Conceptual Schema Definition Language (CSDL) for a tabular model. (CSDL is explained in the upcoming "Programmability" section.)

- **DISCOVER_XEVENT_TRACE_DEFINITION** Monitor SQL Server Extended Events.

- **DISCOVER_TRACES** Use the new column, Type, to filter traces by category.

- **MDSCHEMA_HIERARCHIES** Use the new column, Structure_Type, to filter hierarchies by Natural, Unnatural, or Unknown.

Note You can learn more about the schema rowsets at *http://msdn.microsoft.com /en-us/library/ms126221(v=sql.110).aspx* and *http://msdn.microsoft.com/en-us/library /ms126062(v=sql.110).aspx.*

Architecture Improvements

You can deploy tabular and multidimensional Analysis Services instances on a server with a NUMA architecture and more than 64 processors. To do this, you must configure the instance properties to specify the group or groups of processors that the instance uses:

- **Thread pools** You can assign each process, IO process, query, parsing, and VertiPag thread pool to a separate processor group.

- **Affinity masks** You use the processor group affinity mask to indicate whether the Analysis Services instance should include or exclude a processor in a processor group from Analysis Services operations.

- **Memory allocation** You can specify memory ranges to assign to processor groups.

Programmability

The BI Semantic Model (BISM) schema in SQL Server 2012 is the successor to the Unified Dimensional Model (UDM) schema introduced in SQL Server 2005. BISM supports both an entity approach using tables and relationships and a multidimensional approach using hierarchies and aggregations. This release extends Analysis Management Objects (AMOs) and XMLA to support the management of BISM models.

Note For more information, refer to the "Tabular Models Developer Roadmap" at *http://technet.microsoft.com/en-us/library/gg492113(SQL.110).aspx.*

As an alternative to the SSMS graphical interface or to custom applications or scripts that you build with AMO or XMLA, you can now use Windows PowerShell. Using cmdlets for Analysis Services, you can navigate objects in a model or query a model. You can also perform administrative functions like restarting the service, configuring members for security roles, performing backup or restore operations, and processing cube dimensions or partitions.

Note You can learn more about using PowerShell with Analysis Services at *http://msdn.microsoft.com/en-us/library/hh213141(SQL.110).aspx.*

Another new programmability feature is the addition of Conceptual Schema Definition Language (CSDL) extensions to present the tabular model definition to a reporting client. Analysis Services sends the model's entity definitions in XML format in response to a request from a client. In turn, the client uses this information to show the user the fields, aggregations, and measures that are available for reporting and the available options for grouping, sorting, and formatting the data. The extensions added to CSDL to support tabular models include new elements for models, new attributes and extensions for entities, and properties for visualization and navigation.

Note A reference to the CSDL extensions is available at *http://msdn.microsoft.com/en-us /library/hh213142(SQL.110).aspx.*

PowerPivot for Excel

PowerPivot for Excel is a client application that incorporates SQL Server technology into Excel 2010 as an add-in product. The updated version of PowerPivot for Excel that is available as part of the SQL Server 2012 release includes several minor enhancements to improve usability that users will appreciate. Moreover, it includes several major new features to make the PowerPivot model consistent with the structure of the tabular model.

Installation and Upgrade

Installation of the PowerPivot for Excel add-in is straightforward, but it does have two prerequisites. You must first install Excel 2010, and then Visual Studio 2010 Tools for Office Runtime. If you were previously using SQL Server 2008 R2 PowerPivot for Excel, you must uninstall it because there is no upgrade option for the add-in. After completing these steps, you can install the SQL Server 2012 PowerPivot for Excel add-in.

> **Note** You can download Visual Studio 2010 Tools for Office Runtime at *http://www.microsoft.com/download/en/details.aspx?displaylang=en&id=20479* and download the PowerPivot for Excel add-in at *http://www.microsoft.com/download/en /details.aspx?id=28150*.

Usability

The usability enhancements in the new add-in make it easier to perform certain tasks during PowerPivot model development. The first noticeable change is in the addition of buttons to the Home tab of the ribbon in the PowerPivot window, shown in Figure 9-14. In the View group, at the far right of the ribbon, the Data View button and the Diagram View button allow you to toggle your view of the model, just as you can do when working with the tabular model in SSDT. There are also buttons to toggle the display of hidden columns and the calculation area.

FIGURE 9-14 Home tab on the ribbon in the PowerPivot window

Another new button on the Home tab is the Sort By Column button, which opens the dialog box shown in Figure 9-15. You can now control the sorting of data in one column by the related values in another column in the same table.

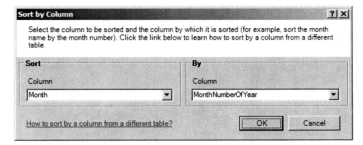

FIGURE 9-15 Sort By Column dialog box

The Design tab, shown in Figure 9-16, now includes the Freeze and Width buttons in the Columns group to help you manage the interface as you review the data in the PowerPivot model. These buttons are found on the Home tab in the previous release of the PowerPivot for Excel add-in.

FIGURE 9-16 Design tab on the ribbon in the PowerPivot window

Notice also the new Mark As Date Table button on the Design tab. Open the table containing dates, and click this button. A dialog box displays to prompt you for a column in the table that contains unique datetime values. Then you can create DAX expressions that use time intelligence functions and get correct results without performing all the steps necessary in the previous version of PowerPivot for Excel. You can select an advanced date filter as a row or column filter after you add a date column to a pivot table, as shown in Figure 9-17.

FIGURE 9-17 Advanced filters available for use with date fields

The Advanced tab of the ribbon does not display by default. You must click the File button in the top left corner above the ribbon and select the Switch To Advanced Mode command to display the new tab, shown in Figure 9-18. You use this tab to add or delete perspectives, toggle the display of implicit measures, add measures that use aggregate functions, and set reporting properties. With the exception of Show Implicit Measures, all these tasks are similar to the corresponding tasks in tabular model development. The Show Implicit Measures button toggles the display of measures that Power-Pivot for Excel creates automatically when you add a numeric column to a pivot table's values in the Excel workbook.

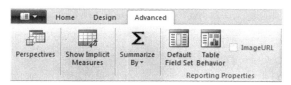

FIGURE 9-18 Advanced tab on the ribbon in the PowerPivot window

Not only can you add numeric columns as a pivot table value for aggregation, you can now also add numeric columns to rows or to columns as distinct values. For example, you can place the [Sales Amount] column both as a row and as a value to see the sum of sales for each amount, as shown in Figure 9-19.

	A	B
1	Row Labels ▾	Sum of SalesAmount
2	2.29	$7,307.39
3	3.99	$9,480.24
4	4.99	$44,046.73
5	7.95	$7,218.60
6	8.99	$40,185.30
7	9.99	$20,229.75

FIGURE 9-19 Use of numeric value on rows

In addition, you will find the following helpful enhancements in this release:

- In the PowerPivot window, you can configure the data type for a calculated column.

- In the PowerPivot window, you can right-click a column and select Hide From Client Tools to prevent the user from accessing the field. The column remains in the Data View in the PowerPivot window with a gray background, but you can toggle its visibility in the Data View by clicking the Show Hidden button on the Home tab of the ribbon.

- In the Excel window, the number format you specify for a measure persists.

- You can right-click a numeric value in the Excel window, and then select the Show Details command on the context menu to open a separate worksheet listing the individual rows that comprise the selected value. This feature does not work for calculated values other than simple aggregates such as sum or count.

- In the PowerPivot window, you can add a description to a table, a measure, a KPI label, a KPI value, a KPI status, or a KPI target. The description displays as a tooltip in the PowerPivot Field List in the Excel window.

- The PowerPivot Field List now displays hierarchies at the top of the field list for each table, and then displays all other fields in the table in alphabetical order.

Model Enhancements

If you have experience with PowerPivot prior to the release of SQL Server 2012 and then create your first tabular model in SSDT, you notice that many steps in the modeling process are similar. Now as you review the updated PowerPivot for Excel features, you should notice that the features of the tabular model that were different from the previous version of PowerPivot for Excel are no longer distinguishing features. Specifically, the following design features are now available in the PowerPivot model:

- Table relationships

- Hierarchies

- Perspectives

- Calculation area for designing measures and KPIs

In effect, you can create the same structure in SSDT as a tabular model or in Excel as a PowerPivot model. Although the modeling process is very similar, you can deploy a tabular model only to an Analysis Services tabular mode instance and a PowerPivot model only to a PowerPivot for Share-Point instance. That said, recall from the "Analysis Services Projects" section that you can import a PowerPivot model to create a tabular model project. However, there is no corresponding option to import a tabular model project into a PowerPivot model.

DAX

DAX is the expression language you use when creating calculated columns, measures, and KPIs for tabular models and PowerPivot models. The current release of SQL Server 2012 extends DAX to include many new statistical, information, logical, filter, and math functions, as shown in Table 9-4.

TABLE 9-4 New DAX Functions

Function Type	Function	Description
Statistical	ADDCOLUMNS()	Return a table with one or more calculated columns appended.
	CROSSJOIN()	Return a table containing the Cartesian product of rows in two or more tables.
	DISTINCTCOUNT()	Return a count of the distinct values in a column.
	GENERATE()	Return a table containing the Cartesian product of a table and a second table that is evaluated in the context of the first table. For example, if the first table contains countries, you can produce a second table that contains the top three products for each country and then produce a final table combining the results. If a row in the first table has no corresponding rows in the results of the second table, the row in the first table does not appear in the final result.
	GENERATEALL()	Return a table containing the Cartesian product of a table and a second table that is evaluated in the context of the first table, as with the *Generate()* function. However, if the row in the first table has no corresponding rows in the results of the second table, the row in the first table returns with null values for columns corresponding to the second table.
	RANK.EQ()	Return the rank of a specified value against a list of values.
	RANKX()	Return the rank of a value for each row in a specified table.
	ROW()	Return a single row containing one or more name/value column pairs where the value is the result of an expression that you specify as an argument for the function.
	STDEV.P()	Return the standard deviation for a column in a table where the table represents the entire population.
	STDEV.S()	Return the standard deviation for a column in a table where the table represents the sample population.
	STDEVX.P()	Return the standard deviation for an expression evaluated for each row in a table where the table represents the entire population.
	STDEVX.S()	Return the standard deviation for an expression evaluated for each row in a table where the table represents the sample population.

Function Type	Function	Description
	SUMMARIZE()	Return a table of aggregated values based on "group by" columns.
	TOPN()	Return a table containing the top N rows based on an "order by" expression.
	VAR.P()	Return the variance for a column in a table where the table represents the entire population.
	VAR.S()	Return the variance for a column in a table where the table represents the sample population.
	VARX.P()	Return the variance for an expression evaluated for each row in a table where the table represents the entire population.
	VARX.S()	Return the variance for an expression evaluated for each row in a table where the table represents the sample population.
Information	CONTAINS()	Return a Boolean value to indicate whether a table contains at least one row with specified name/value column pairs.
	LOOKUPVALUE()	Return the value in a column that matches criteria specified in name/value column pairs.
	PATH()	Return the identifiers for all ancestors of a specified identifier in a parent-child hierarchy.
	PATHCONTAINS()	Return a Boolean value to indicate whether an identifier exists in a specified path for a parent-child hierarchy.
	PATHITEM()	Return an ancestor identifier at the specified distance from the starting identifier in a parent-child hierarchy.
	PATHITEMREVERSE()	Return an ancestor identifier at the specified distance from the topmost identifier in a parent-child hierarchy.
	PATHLENGTH()	Return the count of identifiers in a path for a parent-child hierarchy, including the starting identifier.
Logical	SWITCH()	Evaluate an expression against a list of possible conditions, and return the value paired with the condition.
Filter	ALLSELECTED()	Evaluate an expression ignoring row and column filters while preserving all other filters.
	FILTERS()	Return the values that are currently filtering the specified column.
	HASONEFILTER()	Return a Boolean value to indicate whether a single filter applies to the specified column.
	HASONEVALUE()	Return a Boolean value to indicate whether the specified column returns a single distinct value.
	ISCROSSFILTERED()	Return a Boolean value to indicate whether a filter applies to the specified column or a column in the same table or a related table.
	ISFILTERED()	Return a Boolean value to indicate whether filters apply directly to the specified column.
	USERELATIONSHIP()	Override a default relationship with an alternate relationship by specifying the related columns in each table. For example, rather than use the relationship between the Date table and the OrderDate column in FactResellerSales, you can use the ShippingDate column instead.
Math	CURRENCY()	Return the expression as a currency data type.

Note You can learn more about these functions at *http://technet.microsoft.com/en-us /library/ee634822(SQL.110).aspx.*

PowerPivot for SharePoint

The key changes to PowerPivot for SharePoint in SQL Server 2012 provide you with a more straightforward installation and configuration process and a wider range of tools for managing the server environment. These changes should help you get your server up and running quickly and keep it running smoothly as usage increases over time.

Installation and Configuration

PowerPivot for SharePoint has many dependencies within the SharePoint Server 2010 farm that can be challenging to install and configure correctly. Before you install PowerPivot for SharePoint, you must install SharePoint Server 2010 and SharePoint Server 2010 Service Pack 1, although it is not necessary to run the SharePoint Configuration Wizard. You might find it easier to install the PowerPivot for SharePoint instance and then use the PowerPivot Configuration Tool to complete the configuration of both the SharePoint farm and PowerPivot for SharePoint as one process.

 Note For more details about the PowerPivot for SharePoint installation process, refer to *http://msdn.microsoft.com/en-us/library/ee210708(v=sql.110).aspx.* Instructions for using the PowerPivot Configuration Tool (or for using SharePoint Central Administration or PowerShell cmdlets instead) are available at *http://msdn.microsoft.com/en-us/library /ee210609(v=sql.110).aspx.*

 Note You can now perform all configuration tasks by using PowerShell script containing SharePoint PowerShell cmdlets and PowerPivot cmdlets. To learn more, see *http://msdn.microsoft.com/en-us/library/hh213341(SQL.110).aspx.*

Management

To keep PowerPivot for SharePoint running optimally, you must frequently monitor its use of resources and ensure that the server can continue to support its workload. The SQL Server 2012 release extends the management tools that you have at your disposal to manage disk-space usage, to identify potential problems with server health before users are adversely impacted, and to address ongoing data-refresh failures.

Disk Space Usage

When you deploy a workbook to PowerPivot for SharePoint, PowerPivot for SharePoint stores the workbook in a SharePoint content database. Then when a user later requests that workbook, PowerPivot for SharePoint caches it as a PowerPivot database on the server's disk at \Program Files \Microsoft SQL Server\MSAS11.PowerPivot\OLAP\Backup\Sandboxes\<*serviceApplicationName*> and then loads the workbook into memory. When no one accesses the workbook for the specified period of time, PowerPivot for SharePoint removes the workbook from memory, but it leaves the workbook on disk so that it reloads into memory faster if someone requests it.

PowerPivot for SharePoint continues caching workbooks until it consumes all available disk space unless you specify limits. The PowerPivot System Service runs a job on a periodic basis to remove workbooks from cache if they have not been used recently or if a new version of the workbook exists in the content database. In SQL Server 2012, you can configure the amount of total space that PowerPivot for SharePoint can use for caching and how much data to delete when the total space is used. You configure these settings at the server level by opening SharePoint Central Administration, navigating to Application Management, selecting Manage Services On Server, and selecting SQL Server Analysis Services. Here you can set the following two properties:

- **Maximum Disk Space For Cached Files** The default value of 0 instructs Analysis Services that it can use all available disk space, but you can provide a specific value in gigabytes to establish a maximum.

- **Set A Last Access Time (In Hours) To Aid In Cache Reduction** When the workbooks in cache exceed the maximum disk space, Analysis Services uses this setting to determine which workbooks to delete from cache. The default value is 4, in which case Analysis Services removes all workbooks that have been inactive for 4 hours or more.

As another option for managing the cache, you can go to Manage Service Applications (also in Application Management) and select Default PowerPivot Service Application. On the PowerPivot Management Dashboard page, click the Configure Service Application Settings link in the Actions section, and modify the following properties as necessary:

- **Keep Inactive Database In Memory (In Hours)** By default, Analysis Services keeps a workbook in memory for 48 hours following the last query. If a workbook is frequently accessed by users, Analysis Services never releases it from memory. You can decrease this value if necessary.

- **Keep Inactive Database In Cache (In Hours)** After Analysis Services releases a workbook from memory, the workbook persists in cache and consumes disk space for 120 hours, the default time span, unless you reduce this value.

Server Health Rules

The key to managing server health is by identifying potential threats before problems occur. In this release, you can customize server health rules to alert you to issues with resource consumption or server availability. The current status of these rules is visible in Central Administration when you open Monitoring and select Review Problems And Solutions.

To configure rules at the server level, go to Application Management, select Manage Services On Server, and then select the SQL Server Analysis Services link. Review the default values for the following health rules, and change the settings as necessary:

- **Insufficient CPU Resource Allocation**   Triggers a warning when the CPU utilization of msmdsrv.exe remains at or over a specified percentage during the data-collection interval. The default is 80 percent.

- **Insufficient CPU Resources On The System**   Triggers a warning when the CPU usage of the server remains at or above a specified percentage during the data collection interval. The default is 90 percent.

- **Insufficient Memory Threshold**   Triggers a memory warning when the available memory falls below the specified value as a percentage of memory allocated to Analysis Services. The default is 5 percent.

- **Maximum Number of Connections**   Triggers a warning when the number of connections exceeds the specified number. The default is 100, which is an arbitrary number unrelated to the capacity of your server and requires adjustment.

- **Insufficient Disk Space**   Triggers a warning when the percentage of available disk space on the drive on which the backup folder resides falls below the specified value. The default is 5 percent.

- **Data Collection Interval**   Defines the period of time during which calculations for server-level health rules apply. The default is 4 hours.

To configure rules at the service-application level, go to Application Management, select Manage Service Applications, and select Default PowerPivot Service Application. Next, select Configure Service Application Settings in the Actions list. You can then review and adjust the values for the following health rules:

- **Load To Connection Ratio**   Triggers a warning when the number of load events relative to the number of connection events exceeds the specified value. The default is 20 percent. When this number is too high, the server might be unloading databases too quickly from memory or from the cache.

- **Data Collection Interval**   Defines the period of time during which calculations for service application-level health rules apply. The default is 4 hours.

- **Check For Updates To PowerPivot Management Dashboard.xlsx**   Triggers a warning when the PowerPivot Management Dashboard.xlsx file fails to change during the specified number of days. The default is 5. Under normal conditions, the PowerPivot Management Dashboard.xlsx file refreshes daily.

Data Refresh Configuration

Because data-refresh operations consume server resources, you should allow data refresh to occur only for active workbooks and when the data refresh consistently completes successfully. You now have the option to configure the service application to deactivate the data-refresh schedule for a workbook if either of these conditions is no longer *true*. To configure the data-refresh options, go to Application Management, select Manage Service Applications, and select Default PowerPivot Service Application. Next, select Configure Service Application Settings in the Actions list and adjust the following settings as necessary:

- **Disable Data Refresh Due To Consecutive Failures**   If the data refresh fails a consecutive number of times, the PowerPivot service application deactivates the data-refresh schedule for a workbook. The default is 10, but you can set the value to 0 to prevent deactivation.

- **Disable Data Refresh For Inactive Workbooks**   If no one queries a workbook during the time required to execute the specified number of data-refresh cycles, the PowerPivot service application deactivates the workbook. The default is 10, but you can set the value to 0 if you prefer to keep the data-refresh operation active.

CHAPTER 10

Reporting Services

Each release of Reporting Services since its introduction in Microsoft SQL Server 2000 has expanded its feature base to improve your options for sharing reports, visualizing data, and empowering users with self-service options. SQL Server 2012 Reporting Services is no exception, although almost all the improvements affect only SharePoint integrated mode. The exception is the two new renderers available in both native mode and SharePoint integrated mode. Reporting Services in SharePoint integrated mode has a completely new architecture, which you now configure as a SharePoint shared service application. For expanded data visualization and self-service capabilities in SharePoint integrated mode, you can use the new ad reporting tool, Power View. Another self-service feature available only in SharePoint integrated mode is data alerts, which allows you to receive an email when report data meets conditions you specify. If you have yet to try SharePoint integrated mode, these features will surely entice you to begin!

New Renderers

Although rendering a report as a Microsoft Excel workbook has always been available in Reporting Services, the ability to render a report as a Microsoft Word document has been possible only since SQL Server 2008. Regardless, these renderers produce XLS and DOC file formats respectively, which allows compatibility with Excel 2003 and Word 2003. Users of Excel 2010 and Word 2010 can open these older file formats, of course, but they can now enjoy some additional benefits by using the new renderers.

Excel 2010 Renderer

By default, the Excel rendering option now produces an XLSX file in Open Office XML format, which you can open in either Excel 2007 or Excel 2010 if you have the client installed on your computer. The benefit of the new file type is the higher number of maximum rows and columns per worksheet that the later versions of Excel support—1,048,576 rows and 16,384 columns. You can also export reports with a wider range of colors as well, because the XLSX format supports 16 million colors in the 24-bit color spectrum. Last, the new renderer uses compression to produce a smaller file size for the exported report.

> **Tip** If you have only Excel 2003 installed, you can open this file type if you install the Microsoft Office Compatibility Pack for Word, Excel, and PowerPoint, which you can download at *http://office.microsoft.com/en-us/products/microsoft-office-compatibility-pack-for-word-excel-and-powerpoint-HA010168676.aspx*. As an alternate solution, you can enable the Excel 2003 renderer in the RsReportSErver.config and RsReportDesigner.config files by following the instructions at *http://msdn.microsoft.com/en-us/library/dd255234(SQL.110).aspx#AvailabilityExcel*.

Word 2010 Renderer

Although the ability to render a report as a DOCX file in Open Office XML format does not offer as many benefits as the new Excel renderer, the new Word render does use compression to generate a smaller file than the Word 2003 renderer. You can also create reports that use new features in Word 2007 or Word 2010.

> **Tip** Just as with the Excel renderer, you can use the new Word renderer when you have Word 2003 on your computer if you install the Microsoft Office Compatibility Pack for Word, Excel, and PowerPoint, available for download at *http://office.microsoft.com/en-us/products/microsoft-office-compatibility-pack-for-word-excel-and-powerpoint-HA010168676.aspx*. If you prefer, you can enable the Word 2003 renderer in the RsReportSErver.config and RsReportDesigner.config files by following the instructions at *http://msdn.microsoft.com/en-us/library/dd283105(SQL.110).aspx#AvailabilityWord*.

SharePoint Shared Service Architecture

In previous version of Reporting Services, installing and configuring both Reporting Services and SharePoint components required many steps and different tools to complete the task because SharePoint integrated mode was depending on features from two separate services. For the current release, the development team has completely redesigned the architecture for better performance, scalability, and administration. With the improved architecture, you also experience an easier configuration process.

Feature Support by SharePoint Edition

General Reporting Services features are supported in all editions of SharePoint. That is, all features that were available in previous versions of Reporting Services continue to be available in all editions. However, the new features in this release are available only in SharePoint Enterprise Edition. Table 10-1 shows the supported features by SharePoint edition.

TABLE 10-1 SharePoint Edition Feature Support

Reporting Services Feature	SharePoint Foundation 2010	SharePoint Server 2010 Standard Edition	SharePoint Server 2010 Enterprise Edition
General report viewing and subscriptions	✔	✔	✔
Data Alerts			✔
Power View			✔

Shared Service Architecture Benefits

With Reporting Services available as a shared service application, you can experience the following new benefits:

- Scale Reporting Services across web applications and across your SharePoint Server 2010 farms with fewer resources than possible in previous versions.

- Use claims-based authentication to control access to Reporting Services reports.

- Rely on SharePoint backup and recovery processes for Reporting Services content.

Service Application Configuration

After installing the Reporting Services components, you must create and then configure the service application. You no longer configure the Reporting Services settings by using the Reporting Services Configuration Manager. Instead, you use the graphical interface in SharePoint Central Administration or use SharePoint PowerShell cmdlets.

When you create the service application, you specify the application pool identity under which Reporting Services runs. Because the SharePoint Shared Service Application pool now hosts Reporting Services, you no longer see a Windows service for a SharePoint integrated-mode report server in the service management console. You also create three report server databases—one for storing server and catalog data; another for storing cached data sets, cached reports, and other temporary data; and a third one for data-alert management. The database names include a unique identifier for the service application, enabling you to create multiple service applications for Reporting Services in the same SharePoint farm.

As you might expect, most configuration settings for the Reporting Services correspond to settings you find in the Reporting Services Configuration Manager or the server properties you set in SQL Server Management Studio when working with a native-mode report server. However, before you can use subscriptions or data alerts, you must configure SQL Server Agent permissions correctly. One way to do this is to open SharePoint Central Administration, navigate to Application Management, access Manage Service Applications, click the link for the Reporting Services service application, and then open the Provision Subscriptions And Alerts page. On that page, you can provide the credentials if your SharePoint administrator credentials have db_owner permissions on the Reporting Services databases. If you prefer, you can download a Transact-SQL script from the same page, or run a PowerShell cmdlet to build the same Transact-SQL script, that you can later execute in SQL Server Management Studio.

Whether you use the interface or the script, the provisioning process creates the RSExec role if necessary, creates a login for the application pool identity, and assigns it to the RSExec role in each of the three report server databases. If any scheduled jobs, such as subscriptions or alerts, exist in the report server database, the script assigns the application pool identity as the owner of those jobs. In addition, the script assigns the login to the SQLAgentUserRole and grants it the necessary permissions for this login to interact with SQL Server Agent and to administer jobs.

> **Note** For detailed information about installing and configuring Reporting Services in SharePoint integrated mode, refer to *http://msdn.microsoft.com/en-us/library /cc281311(SQL.110).aspx.*

Power View

Power View is the latest self-service feature available in Reporting Services. It is a browser-based Silverlight application that requires Reporting Services to run in SharePoint integrated mode using SharePoint Server 2010 Enterprise Edition. It also requires a specific type of data source—either a tabular model that you deploy to an Analysis Services server or a PowerPivot workbook that you deploy to a SharePoint document library.

Rather than working in design mode and then previewing the report, as you do when using Report Designer or Report Builder, you work directly with the data in the presentation layout of Power View. You start with a tabular view of the data that you can change into various data visualizations. As you explore and examine the data, you can fine-tune and adjust the layout by modifying the sort order, adding more views to the report, highlighting values, and applying filters. When you finish, you can save the report in the new RDLX file format to a SharePoint document library or PowerPivot Gallery or export the report to Microsoft PowerPoint to make it available to others.

> **Note** To use Power View, you can install Reporting Services in SharePoint integrated mode using any of the following editions: Evaluation, Developer, Business Intelligence, or Enterprise. The browser you use depends on your computer's operating system. You can use Internet Explorer 8 and later when using a Windows operating system or Safari 5 when using a Mac operating system. Windows Vista and Windows Server 2008 both support Internet Explorer 7. Windows Vista, Windows 7, and Windows Server 2008 support Firefox 7.

Data Sources

Just as for any report you create using the Report Designer in SQL Server Data Tools or using Report Builder, you must have a data source available for use with your Power View report. You can use any of the following data source types:

- **PowerPivot workbook**   Select a PowerPivot workbook directly from the PowerPivot Gallery as a source for your Power View report.

- **Shared data source**   Create a Reporting Services Shared Data Source (RSDS) file with the Data Source Type property set to Microsoft BI Semantic Model For Power View. You then define a connection string that references a PowerPivot workbook (such as *http://SharePointServer/PowerPivot Gallery/myWorkbook.xlsx*) or an Analysis Services tabular model (such as *Data Source=MyAnalysisServer; Initial Catalog=MyTabularModel*). (We introduced tabular models in Chapter 9, "Analysis Services and PowerPivot.") You use this type of shared data source only for the creation of Power View reports.

> **Note** If your web application uses claims forms-based authentication, you must configure the shared data source to use stored credentials and specify a Windows login for the stored credentials. If the web application uses Windows classic or Windows claims authentication and your RSDS file references an Analysis Services outside the SharePoint farm, you must configure Kerberos authentication and use integrated security.

- **Business Intelligence Semantic Model (BISM) connection file**   Create a BISM file to connect to either a PowerPivot workbook or to an Analysis Services tabular model. You can use this file as a data source for both Power View reports and Excel workbooks.

> **Note** If your web application uses Windows classic or Windows claims authentication and your BISM file references an Analysis Services outside the SharePoint farm, you must configure Kerberos authentication and use integrated security.

BI Semantic Model Connection Files

Whether you want to connect to an Analysis Services tabular database or to a PowerPivot workbook deployed to a SharePoint server, you can use a BISM connection file as a data source for your Power View reports and even for Excel workbooks. To do this, you must first add the BI Semantic Model Connection content type to a document library in a PowerPivot site.

To create a BISM file for a PowerPivot workbook, you open the document library in which you want to store the file and for which you have Contribute permission. Click New Document on the Documents tab of the SharePoint ribbon, and select BI Semantic Model Connection on the menu. You then configure the properties of the connection according to the data source, as follows:

- **PowerPivot workbook**   Provide the name of the file, and set the Workbook URL Or Server Name property as the SharePoint URL for the workbook, such as *http://SharePointServer/PowerPivot Gallery/myWorkbook.xlsx.*

- **Analysis Services tabular database**   Provide the name of the file; set the Workbook URL Or Server Name property using the server name, the fully qualified domain name, the Internet Protocol (IP) address, or the server and instance name (such as MyAnalysisServer \MyInstance); and set the Database property using the name of the tabular model on the server.

You must grant users the Read permission on the file to enable them to open the file and use it as a data source. If the data source is a PowerPivot workbook, users must also have Read permission on the workbook. If the data source is a tabular model, the shared service requesting the tabular model data must have administrator permission on the tabular instance and users must be in a role with Read permission for the tabular model.

Power View Design Environment

You can open the Power View design environment for a new report in one of the following ways:

- **From a PowerPivot workbook**   Click the Create Power View Report icon in the upper-right corner of a PowerPivot workbook that displays in the PowerPivot Gallery, as shown in Figure 10-1.

- **From a data connection library**   Click the down arrow next to the BISM or RSDS file, and then click Create Power View Report.

FIGURE 10-1 Create Power View Report icon in PowerPivot Gallery

In the Power View design environment that displays when you first create a report, a blank view workspace appears in the center, as shown in Figure 10-2. As you develop the report, you add tables and data visualizations to the view workspace. The view size is a fixed height and width, just like the slide size in PowerPoint. If you need more space to display data, you can add more views to the report and then navigate between views by using the Views pane.

Above the view workspace is a ribbon that initially displays only the Home tab. As you add fields to the report, the Design and Layout tabs appear. The contents of each tab on the ribbon change dynamically to show only the buttons and menus applicable to the currently selected item.

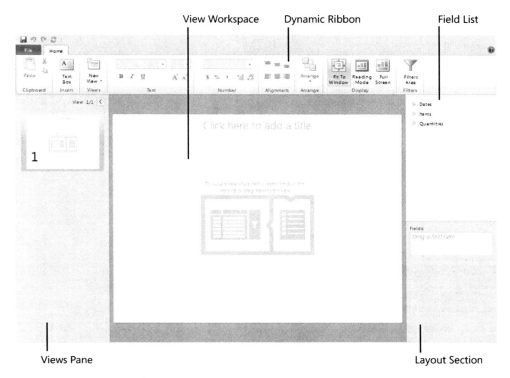

FIGURE 10-2 Power View design environment

The field list from the tabular model appears in the upper-right corner. When you open the design environment for a new report, you see only the table names of the model. You can expand a table name to see the fields it contains, as shown in Figure 10-3. Individual fields, such as Category, display in the field list without an icon. You also see row label fields with a gray-and-white icon, such as Drawing. The row label fields identify a column configured with report properties in the model, as we explain in Chapter 9. Calculated columns, such as Attendees, display with a sigma icon, and measures, such as Quantity Served YTD, appear with a calculator icon.

You select the check box next to a field to include that field in your report, or you can drag the field into the report. You can also double-click a table name in the field list to add the default field set, as defined in the model, to the current view.

Tip The examples in this chapter use the sample files available for download at *http://www.microsoft.com/download/en/details.aspx?id=26718* and *http://www.microsoft.com/download/en/details.aspx?id=26719*. You can use these files with the tutorial at *http://social.technet.microsoft.com/wiki/contents/articles/6175.aspx* for a hands-on experience with Power View.

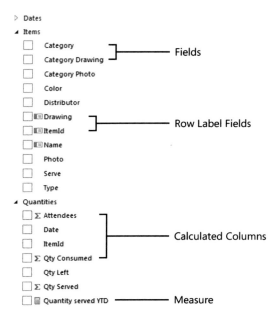

FIGURE 10-3 Tabular model field list

You click a field to add it to the view as a single column table, as shown in Figure 10-4. You must select the table before you select additional fields, or else selection of the new field starts a new table. As you add fields, Power View formats the field according to data type.

FIGURE 10-4 Single-column table

> **Tip** Power View retrieves only the data it can display in the current view and retrieves additional rows as the user scrolls to see more data. That way, Power View can optimize performance even when the source table contains millions of rows.

The field you select appears below the field list in the layout section. The contents of the layout section change according to the current visualization. You can use the layout section to rearrange the sequence of fields or to change the behavior of a field, such as changing which aggregation function to use or whether to display rows with no data.

After you add fields to a table, you can move it and resize it as needed. To move an item in the view, point to its border and, when the cursor changes to a hand, drag it to the desired location. To resize it, point again to the border, and when the double-headed arrow appears, drag the border to make the item smaller or larger.

To share a report when you complete the design, you save it by using the File menu. You can save the file only if you have the Add Items permission on the destination folder or the Edit Items permission to overwrite an existing file. When you save a file, if you keep the default option set to Save Preview Images With Report, the views of your report display in the PowerPivot gallery. You should disable this option if the information in your report is confidential. The report saves as an RDLX file, which is not compatible with the other Reporting Services design environments.

Data Visualization

A table is only one way to explore data in Power View. After you add several fields to a table, you can then convert it to a matrix, a chart, or a card. If you convert it to a scatter chart, you can add a play axis to visualize changes in the data over multiple time periods. You can also create multiples of the same chart to break down its data by different categorizations.

Charts

When you add a measure to a table, the Design tab includes icons for chart visualizations, such as column, bar, line, or scatter charts. After you select the icon for a chart type, the chart replaces the table. You can then resize the visualization to improve legibility, as shown in Figure 10-5. You can continue to add more fields to a visualization or remove fields by using the respective check boxes in the field list. On the Layout tab of the ribbon, you can use buttons to add a chart title, position the legend when your chart contains multiple series, or enable data labels.

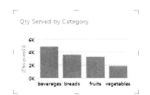

FIGURE 10-5 Column chart

Tip You can use an existing visualization as the starting point for a new visualization by selecting it and then using the Copy and Paste buttons on the Home tab of the ribbon. You can paste the visualization to the same view or to a new view. However, you cannot use shortcut keys to perform the copy and paste.

Arrangement

You can overlap and inset items, as shown in Figure 10-6. You use the Arrange buttons on the Home tab of the ribbon to bring an item forward or send it back. When you want to view an item in isolation, you can click the button in its upper-right corner to fill the entire view with the selected visualization.

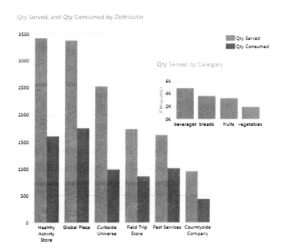

FIGURE 10-6 Overlapping visualizations

Cards and Tiles

Another type of visualization you can use is *cards*, which is a scrollable list of grouped fields arranged in a card format, as shown in Figure 10-7. Notice that the default label and default image fields are more prominent than the other fields. The size of the card changes dynamically as you add or remove fields until you resize using the handles, after which the size remains fixed. You can double-click the sizing handle on the border of the card container to revert to auto-sizing.

FIGURE 10-7 Card visualization

You can change the sequence of fields by rearranging them in the layout section. You can also move a field to the Tile By area to add a container above the cards that displays one tile for each value in the selected field, as shown in Figure 10-8. When you select a tile, Power View filters the collection of cards to display those having the same value as the selected tile.

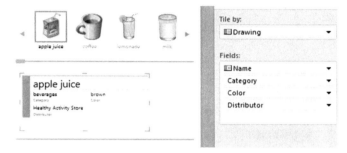

FIGURE 10-8 Tiles

The default layout of the tiles is tab-strip mode. You can toggle between tab-strip mode and cover-flow mode by using the respective button in the Tile Visualizations group on the Design tab of the ribbon. In cover-flow mode, the label or image appears below the container and the current selection appears in the center of the strip and slightly larger than the other tile items.

Tip You can also convert a table or matrix directly to a tile container by using the Tiles button on the Design tab of the ribbon. Depending on the model design, Power View displays the value of the first field in the table, the first row group value, or the default field set. All other fields that were in the table or matrix display as a table inside the tile container.

Play Axis

When your table or chart contains two measures, you can convert it to a scatter chart to show one measure on the horizontal axis and the second measure on the vertical axis. Another option is to use a third measure to represent size in a bubble chart that you define in the layout section, as shown in Figure 10-9. With either chart type, you can also add a field to the Color section for grouping purposes. Yet one more option is to add a field from a date table to the Play Axis area of the layout section.

FIGURE 10-9 Layout section for a bubble chart

With a play axis in place, you can click the play button to display the visualization in sequence for each time period that appears on the play axis or you can use the slider on the play axis to select a specific time period to display. A watermark appears in the background of the visualization to indicate the current time period. When you click a bubble or point in the chart, you filter the visualization to focus on the selection and see the path that the selection follows over time, as shown in Figure 10-10. You can also point to a bubble in the path to see its values display as a tooltip.

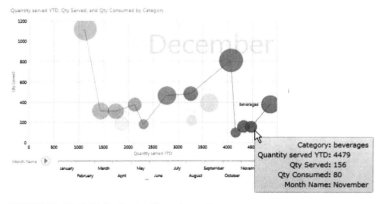

FIGURE 10-10 Bubble chart with a play axis

Multiples

Another way to view data is to break a chart into multiple copies of the same chart. You place the field for which you want to create separate charts in the Vertical Multiples or Horizontal Multiples area of the layout section. Then you use the Grid button on the Layout tab of the ribbon to select the number of tiles across and down that you want to include, such as three tiles across and two tiles down, as shown in Figure 10-11. If the visualization contains more tiles than the grid can show, a scroll bar appears to allow you to access the other tiles. Power View aligns the horizontal and vertical axes in the charts to facilitate comparisons between charts.

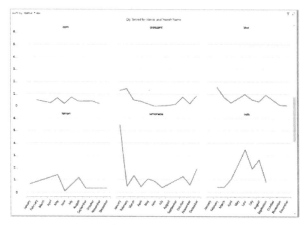

FIGURE 10-11 Vertical multiples of a line chart

Sort Order

Above some types of visualizations, the sort field and direction display. To change the sort field, click on it to view a list of available fields, as shown in Figure 10-12. You can also click the abbreviated direction label to reverse the sort. That is, click Asc to change an ascending sort to a descending sort which then displays as Desc in the sort label.

FIGURE 10-12 Sort field selection

Multiple Views

You might find it easier to explore your data when you arrange visualizations as separate views. All views in your report must use the same tabular model as their source, but otherwise each view can contain separate visualizations. Furthermore, the filters you define for a view, as we explain later in this chapter, apply only to that view. Use the New View button on the Home tab of the toolbar to create a new blank view or to duplicate the currently selected view, as shown in Figure 10-13.

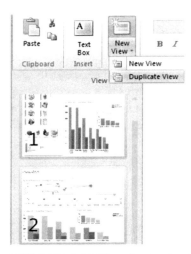

FIGURE 10-13 Addition of a view to a Power View report

Highlighted Values

To help you better see relationships, you can select a value in your chart, such as a column or a legend item. Power View then highlights related values in the chart. You can even select a value in one chart, such as Breads, to highlight values in other charts in the same view that are related to Breads, as shown in Figure 10-14. You clear the highlighting by clicking in the chart area without clicking another bar.

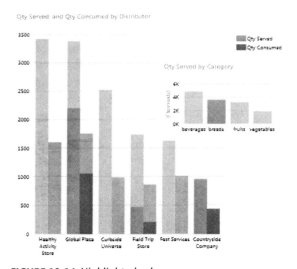

FIGURE 10-14 Highlighted values

Filters

Power View provides you with several ways to filter the data in your report. You can use a slicer or tile container to a view to incorporate the filter selection into the body of the report. As an alternative, you can add a view filter or a visualization filter to the Filter Area of the design environment for greater flexibility in the value selections for your filters.

Slicer

When you create a single-column table in a view, you can click the Slicer button on the Design tab of the ribbon to use the values in the table as a filter. When you select one or more labels in a slicer, Power View not only filters all visualizations in the view, but also other slicers in the view, as shown in Figure 10-15. You can restore the unfiltered view by clicking the Clear Filter icon in the upper-right corner of the slicer.

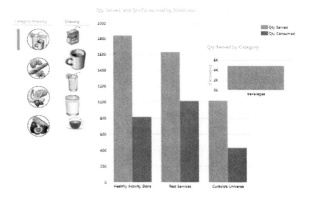

FIGURE 10-15 Slicers in a view

Tile Container

If you add a visualization inside a tile container, as shown in Figure 10-16, the tile selection filters both the cards as well as the visualizations. However, the filtering behavior is limited only to the tile selection. Other visualizations or slicers in the same view remain unchanged.

FIGURE 10-16 Tile container to filter a visualization

When you add a visualization to a tile container, Power View does not synchronize the horizontal and vertical axes for the visualizations as it does with multiples. In other words, when you select one tile, the range of values for the vertical axis might be greater than the range of values on the same axis for a different tile. You can use the buttons in the Synchronize group of the Layout tab to synchronize axes, series, or bubbles across the tiles to more easily compare the values in the chart from one tile to another.

View Filter

A view filter allows you to define filter criteria for the current view without requiring you to include it in the body of the report like a slicer. Each view in your report can have its own set of filters. If you duplicate a view containing filters, the new view contains a copy of the first view's filters. That is, changing filter values for one view has no effect on another view, even if the filters are identical.

You define a view filter in the Filters area of the view workspace, which by default is not visible when you create a new report. To toggle the visibility of this part of the workspace, click the Filters Area button on the Home tab of the ribbon. After making the Filters area visible, you can collapse it when you need to increase the size of your view by clicking the left arrow that appears at the top of the Filters area.

To add a new filter in the default basic mode, drag a field to the Filters area and then select a value. If the field contains string or date data types, you select one or more values by using a check box. If the field contains a numeric data type, you use a slider to set the range of values. You can see an example of filters for fields with numeric and string data types in Figure 10-17.

FIGURE 10-17 Filter selection of numeric and string data types in basic filter mode

To use more flexible filter criteria, you can switch to advanced filter mode by clicking the first icon in the toolbar that appears to the right of the field name in the Filters area. The data type of the field determines the conditions you can configure. For a filter with a string data type, you can create conditions to filter on partial words using operators such as Contains, Starts With, and so on. With a numeric data type, you can use an operator such as Less Than or Greater Than Or Equal To, among others. If you create a filter based on a date data type, you can use a calendar control in combination with operators such as Is Before or Is On Or After, and others, as shown in Figure 10-18. You can also create compound conditions by using AND and OR operators.

FIGURE 10-18 Filter selection of date data types in advanced filter mode

Visualization Filter

You can also use the Filters area to configure the filter for a selected visualization. First, you must click the Filter button in the top-right corner of the visualization, and then fields in the visualization display in the Filters area, as shown in Figure 10-19. When you change values for fields in a visualization's filter, Power View updates only that visualization. All other visualizations in the same view are unaffected by the filter. Just as you can with a view filter, you can configure values for a visualization filter in basic filter mode or advanced filter mode.

FIGURE 10-19 Visualization filter

Display Modes

After you develop the views and filters for your report, you will likely spend more time navigating between views and interacting with the visualizations than editing your report. To provide alternatives for your viewing experience, Power View offers the following three display modes, which you enable by using the respective button in the Display group of the Home tab of the ribbon:

- **Fit To Window** The view shrinks or expands to fill the available space in the window. When you use this mode, you have access to the ribbon, field list, Filters area, and Views pane. You can switch easily between editing and viewing activities.

- **Reading Mode** In this mode, Power View keeps your browser's tabs and buttons visible, but it hides the ribbon and the field list, which prevents you from editing your report. You can navigate between views using the arrow keys on your keyboard, the multiview button in the lower right corner of the screen that allows you to access thumbnails of the views, or the arrow buttons in the lower right corner of the screen. Above the view, you can click the Edit Report button to switch to Fit To Window mode or click the other button to switch to Full Screen mode.

- **Full Screen Mode**   Using Full Screen mode is similar to using the slideshow view in PowerPoint. Power View uses your entire screen to display the current view. This mode is similar to Reading mode and provides the same navigation options, but instead it hides your browser and uses the entire screen.

You can print the current view when you use Fit To Window or Reading mode only. To print, open the File menu and click Print. The view always prints in landscape orientation and prints only the data you currently see on your screen. In addition, the Filters area prints only if you expand it first. If you have a play axis on a scatter or bubble chart, the printed view includes only the current frame. Likewise, if you select a tile in a tile container before printing, you see only the selected tile in the printed view.

PowerPoint Export

A very useful Power View feature is the ability to export your report to PowerPoint. On the File menu, click Export To PowerPoint and save the PPTX file. Each view becomes a separate slide in the PowerPoint file. When you edit each slide, you see only a static image of the view. However, as long as you have the correct permissions and an active connection to your report on the SharePoint server when you display a slide in Reading View or Slideshow modes, you can click the Click To Interact link in the lower-right corner of the slide to load the view from Power View and enable interactivity. You can change filter values in the Filters area, in slicers, and in tile containers, and you can highlight values. However, you cannot create new filters or new data visualizations from PowerPoint. Also, if you navigate to a different slide and then return to the Power View slide, you must use the Click To Interact link to reload the view for interactivity.

Data Alerts

Rather than create a subscription to email a report on a periodic basis, regardless of the data values that it contains, you can create a data alert to email a notification only when specific conditions in the data are true at a scheduled time. This new self-service feature is available only with Reporting Services running in SharePoint integrated mode and works as soon as you have provisioned subscriptions and alerts, as we described earlier in the "Service Application Configuration" section of this chapter. However, it works only with reports you create by using Report Designer or Report Builder. You cannot create data alerts for Power View reports.

Data Alert Designer

You can create one or more data alerts for any report you can access, as long as the data store uses a data source with stored credentials or no credentials. The report must also include at least one data region. In addition, the report must successfully return data at the time you create the new alert. If these prerequisites are met, then after you open the report for viewing, you can select New Data Alert from the Actions menu in the report toolbar. The Data Alert Designer, as shown in Figure 10-20, displays.

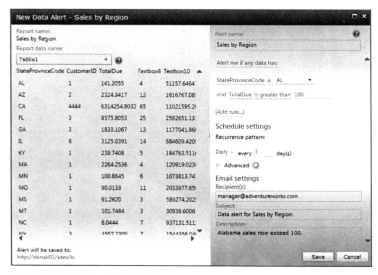

FIGURE 10-20 Data Alert Designer

> **Tip** You must have the SharePoint Create Alert permission to create an alert for any report for which you have permission to view.

You use the Data Alert Designer to define rules for one or more data regions in the report that control whether Reporting Services sends an alert. You also specify the recurring schedule for the process that evaluates the rules and configure the email settings for Reporting Services to use when generating the email notifications. When you save the resulting alert definition, Reporting Services saves it in the alerting database and schedules a corresponding SQL Server Agent job, as shown in Figure 10-21.

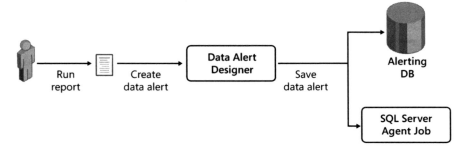

FIGURE 10-21 Data alert creation process

In the Data Alert Designer, you select a data region in the report to view a preview of the first 100 rows of data for reference as you develop the rules for that data region, which is also known as a *data feed*. You can create a simple rule that sends a data alert if the data feed contains data when the SQL

Server Agent job runs. More commonly, you create one or more rules that compare a field value to value that you enter or to a value in another field. The Data Alert Designer combines multiple rules for the same data feed by using a logical AND operator only. You cannot change it to an OR operator. Instead, you must create a separate data alert with the additional condition.

In the Schedule Settings section of the Data Alert Designer, you can configure the daily, weekly, hourly, or minute intervals at which to run the SQL Server Agent job for the data alert. In the Advanced settings, shown in Figure 10-22, you can set the date and time at which you want to start the job, and optionally set an end date. You also have the option to send the alert only when the alert results change.

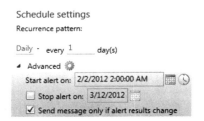

FIGURE 10-22 Data alert advanced schedule settings

Last, you must provide email settings for the data alert by specifying at least one email address as a recipient for the data alert. If you want to send the data alert to multiple recipients, separate each email address with a semicolon. You can also include a subject and a description for the data alert, both of which are static strings.

Alerting Service

The Reporting Services alerting service manages the process of refreshing the data feed and applying the rules in the data alert definition, as shown in Figure 10-23. Regardless of the results, the alerting service adds an alerting instance to the alerting database to record the outcome of the evaluation. If any rows in the data feed satisfy the conditions of the rules during processing, the alerting services generate an email containing the alert results.

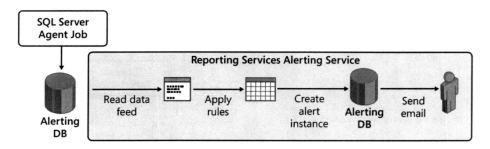

FIGURE 10-23 Alerting service processing of data alerts

The email for a successful data alert includes the user name of the person who created the alert, the description of the alert from the alert definition, and the rows from the data feed that generated the alert, as shown in Figure 10-24. It also includes a link to the report, a description of the alert rules, and the report parameters used when reading the data feed. The message is sent from the account you specify in the email settings of the Reporting Services shared services application.

FIGURE 10-24 Email message containing a successful data alert

Note If an error occurs during alert processing, the alerting service saves the alerting instance to the alerting database and sends an alert message describing the error to the recipients.

Data Alert Manager

You use the Data Alert Manager to lists all data alerts you create for a report, as shown in Figure 10-25. To open the Data Alert Manager, open the document library containing your report, click the down arrow to the right of the report name, and select Manage Data Alerts. You can see the alerts listed for the current report, but you can use the drop-down list at the top of the page to change the view to a list of data alerts for all reports or a different report.

FIGURE 10-25 Data Alert Manager

The Data Alert Manager shows you the number of alerts sent by data alert, the last time it was run, the last time it was modified, and the status of its last execution. If you right-click a data alert on this page, you can edit the data alert, delete it, or run the alert on demand. No one else can view, edit, or run the data alerts you create, although the site administrator can view and delete your data alerts.

If you are a site administrator, you can use the Manage Data Alerts link on the Site Settings page to open the Data Alert Manager. Here you can select a user from a drop-down list to view all data alerts created by the user for all reports. You can also filter the data alerts by report. As a site administrator, you cannot edit these data alerts, but you can delete them if necessary.

Alerting Configuration

Data does not accumulate indefinitely in the alerting database. The report server configuration file contains several settings you can change to override the default intervals for cleaning up data in the alerting database or to disable alerting. There is no graphical interface available for making changes to these settings. Instead, you must manually edit the RsReportServer.config file to change the settings shown in Table 10-2.

TABLE 10-2 Alerting Configuration Settings in RsReportServer.config

Alerting Setting	Description	Default Value
AlertingCleanupCyclingMinutes	Interval for starting the cleanup cycle of alerting	20
AlertingExecutionLogCleanupMinutes	Number of minutes to retain data in the alerting execution log	10080
AlertingDataCleanupMinutes	Number of minutes to retain temporary alerting data	360
AlertingMaxDataRetentionDays	Number of days to retain alert execution metadata, alert instances, and execution results	180
IsAlertingService	Enable or disable the alerting service with *True* or *False* values, respectively	True

The SharePoint configuration database contains settings that control how many times the alerting service retries execution of an alert and the delay between retries. The default for *MaxRetries* is *3* and for *SecondsBeforeRetry* is *900*. You can change these settings by using PowerShell cmdlets. These settings apply to all alert retries, but you can configure different retry settings for each of the following events:

- **FireAlert** On-demand execution of an alert launched by a user
- **FireSchedule** Scheduled execution of an alert launched by a SQL Server Agent job
- **CreateSchedule** Process to save a schedule defined in a new or modified data alert
- **UpdateSchedule** Modification of a schedule in a data alert
- **DeleteSchedule** Deletion of a data alert
- **GenerateAlert** Alerting-service processing of data feeds, rules, and alert instances
- **DeliverAlert** Preparation and delivery of email message for a data alert

Index

Symbols

32-bit editions of SQL Server 2012, 17
64-bit editions of SQL Server 2012, 17
64-bit processors, 17
    debugging on, 99
[catalog].[executions] table, 137

A

absolute environment references, 133–135
Active Directory security modules, 71
Active Operations dialog box, 130
active secondaries, 32–34
Administrator account, 176
Administrator permissions, 211
administrators
    data alert management, 250
    Database Engine access, 72
    entity management, 192
    master data management in Excel, 187–196
    tasks of, 135–139
ADO.NET connection manager, 112–113
ad reporting tool, 229
Advanced Encryption Standard (AES), 71
affinity masks, 216
aggregate functions, 220
alerting service, 248–249. *See also* data alerts
All Executions report, 138
allocation_failure event, 90
All Operations report, 138
Allow All Connections connection mode, 33
Allow Only Read-Intent Connections connection mode, 33
All Validations report, 138
ALTER ANY SERVER ROLE, permissions on, 72
ALTER ANY USER, 70
ALTER SERVER AUDIT, WHERE clause, 63

ALTER USER DEFAULT_SCHEMA option, 59
AlwaysOn, 4–6, 21–23
AlwaysOn Availability Groups, 4–5, 23–32
    availability group listeners, 28–29
    availability replica roles, 26
    configuring, 29–31
    connection modes, 27
    data synchronization modes, 27
    deployment examples, 30–31
    deployment strategy, 23–24
    failover modes, 27
    monitoring with Dashboard, 31–32
    multiple availability group support, 25
    multiple secondaries support, 25
    prerequisites, 29–30
    shared and nonshared storage support, 24
AlwaysOn Failover Cluster Instances, 5, 34–36
Analysis Management Objects (AMOs), 217
Analysis Services, 199–217
    cached files settings, 225
    cache reduction settings, 225
    credentials for data import, 204
    database roles, 210–211
    DirectQuery mode, 213
    event tracing, 215
    in-memory vs. DirectQuery mode, 213
    model designer, 205–206
    model design feature support, 200–202
    multidimensional models, 215
    multiple instances, 201
    with NUMA architecture, 216
    PowerShell cmdlets for, 217
    Process Full command, 215
    processors, number of, 216
    programmability, 217
    projects, 201–202
    query modes, 214
    schema rowsets, 216

data visualization (*continued*)
    sort order, 241
    tile containers, 243–244
    tiles, 239
    view filters, 244–245
    visualization filters, 245
data warehouses
    queries, improving, 6
    query speeds, 44–45
    sliding-window scenarios, 7
date filters, 219–220, 244–245
DAX (Data Analysis Expression)
    new functions, 222–224
    row-level filters, 211
dbo schema, 58
debugger for Transact-SQL, 7
debugging on 64-bit processors, 99
Default Field Set property, 212
Default Image property, 212
Default Label property, 212
default schema
    creation script, 59
    for groups, 58–59
    for SQL Server users, 58
delegation of permissions, 139
DeleteSchedule event, 250
delimiters, parsing, 152
DeliverAlert event, 250
dependencies
    database, 9
    finding, 216
    login, 67
Deploy Database To SQL Azure wizard, 9
deployment models, 116–122
    switching, 118
deployment, package, 120
Description parameter property, 123
Designing and Tuning for Performance Your SSIS
    Packages in the Enterprise link, 96–97
destinations, 103–105
Developer edition of SQL Server 2012, 15
Digital Trowel, 167
directory name, enabling, 79
DirectQuery mode, 213–215
DirectQuery With In-Memory mode, 214
disaster recovery, 21–40
disconnected components, 108
discovery. *See* knowledge discovery
DMV (Dynamic Management View), 8
documents, finding, 85

DOCX files, 230
domain-based attributes, 193–194
domain management, 143–154
    DQS Data knowledge base, 144–145
    exiting, 154
    knowledge base creation, 145–154
    monitoring, 167
domain rules, 150–151
    disabling, 151
    running, 155
domains
    composite, 151–152
    creating, 146
    data types, 146
    importing, 146
    linked, 153–154
    mapping to source data, 158, 161–162, 164
    properties, 146–147
    term-based relations, 149
domain values
    cross-domain rules, 152
    domain rules, 150–151
    formatting, 146
    leading values, 148–149, 173
    managing, 156–157
    setting, 147
    spelling checks, 146
    synonyms, 148–149, 163, 173
    type settings, 147–148
downtime, reducing, 40
dqs_administrator role, 142
DQS Cleansing transformation, 107
DQS Cleansing Transformation log, 170
DQS Data knowledge base, 144–145, 196
DQS (Data Quality Services), 107, 141–173
    administration, 143, 166–170
    architecture, 141–143
    configuration, 167–170
    connection manager, 171
    Data Quality Client, 142–143. *See also* Data
        Quality Client
    data quality projects, 161–166
    Data Quality Server, 141–142. *See also* Data
        Quality Server
    Domain Management area, 143–154
    Excel, importing data from, 147
    integration with SQL Server features, 170–173
    knowledge base management, 143–161
    Knowledge Discovery area, 154–157
    log settings, 169–170

T

U

About the Authors

ROSS MISTRY is a best-selling author, public speaker, technology evangelist, community champion, principal enterprise architect at Microsoft, and former SQL Server MVP.

Ross has been a trusted advisor and consultant for many C-level executives and has been responsible for successfully creating technology roadmaps, including the design and implementation of complex technology solutions for some of the largest companies in the world. He has taken on the lead architect role for many Fortune 500 organizations, including Network Appliance, McAfee, The Sharper Image, CIBC, Wells Fargo, and Intel. He specializes in data platform, business productivity, unified communications, core infrastructure, and private cloud.

Ross is an active participant in the technology community—specifically the Silicon Valley community. He co-manages the SQL Server Twitter account and frequently speaks at technology conferences around the world such as SQL Pass Community Summit, SQL Connections, and SQL Bits. He is a series author and has written many whitepapers and articles for Microsoft, SQL Server Magazine, and Techtarget.com. Ross' latest books include *Windows Server 2008 R2 Unleashed* (Sams, 2010), and the forthcoming *SQL Server 2012 Management and Administration (2nd Edition)* (Sams, 2012).

You can follow him on Twitter at @RossMistry or contact him at *http://www.rossmistry.com*.

STACIA MISNER is a consultant, educator, mentor, and author specializing in Business Intelligence solutions since 1999. During that time, she has authored or co-authored multiple books about BI. Stacia provides consulting and custom education services through Data Inspirations and speaks frequently at conferences serving the SQL Server community. She writes about her experiences with BI at *blog.datainspirations.com*, and tweets as @StaciaMisner.

What do you think of this book?

We want to hear from you!
To participate in a brief online survey, please visit:

microsoft.com/learning/booksurvey

Tell us how well this book meets your needs—what works effectively, and what we can do better. Your feedback will help us continually improve our books and learning resources for you.

Thank you in advance for your input!

CPSIA information can be obtained at www.ICGtesting.com
Printed in the USA
BVOW022226170512

290478BV00002B/3/P